SWAN SEASON

Caroline Fabre

ARROW

First published in Arrow 1993

1 3 5 7 9 10 8 6 4 2

Copyright © Caroline Fabre 1992

First published in the United Kingdom in 1992 by
Century
Random House, 20 Vauxhall Bridge Road, London SW1V 2SA

Random House Australia (Pty) Limited
20 Alfred Street, Milsons Point, Sydney,
New South Wales 2061, Australia

Random House New Zealand Limited
18 Poland Road, Glenfield
Auckland 10, New Zealand

Random House South Africa (Pty) Limited
PO Box 337, Bergvlei, South Africa

Random House UK Limited Reg. No. 954009

A CIP catalogue record for this book
is available from the British Library

ISBN 0 09 923351 7

Printed and bound in Great Britain by
Bookmarque Ltd, Croydon, Surrey

For Robert Fabre, with love . . .

My thanks go to the following people: Philippe Fabre for his unswerving faith; John Pawsey, my agent, who made a dream come true; Lizy Buchan, my editor, and to Madeleine and Robert Going, my parents and best pals.

Unwearied still, lover by lover,
They paddle in the cold
Companionable streams or climb the air;
Their hearts have not grown old;
Passion or conquest, wander where they will,
Attend upon them still.

from *The Wild Swans at Coole*, W.B. Yeats.

Whooper Swans breed in the northern countries. Most of the Icelandic birds migrate before the winter to the mild climate and widespread lakes and wetlands of Ireland, a journey across the North Atlantic of seven or eight hundred miles. The arrival of the Whoopers in the autumn, and their departure in the spring, is part of the changing seasons.

As far as the hazards of nomadic life permit, the Whooper Swan stays faithful to its partner.

PROLOGUE

Ireland, the winter of 1985

I am living in hiding with Jean, in this remote and lonely spot on the south east coast of Ireland, in a broken-down railway cottage overlooking the sea. The cottage was once a waiting room, an intermediate stop for the odd passenger train bound for Rosslaire, but the railway line was later moved further inland, away from the eroding coastline. Now the rails are rusting away, the struts are broken, and weeds grow wildly along the deserted line, while the lane that leads to the cottage is overgrown with bracken and brushwood. In summer the gorse is aflame and linnets sing amongst the privet bushes, but now the only sounds are the wind rattling against the broken tiles, or the distant thunder of a passing train.

Nobody would think of looking for us here, for it is way off the beaten track, yet my nights are spent in wakefulness, straining fearfully for every noise, whilst during the day I am forever glancing over my shoulder. Some days I walk along the deserted beach, hunched against the cold east wind, or stand by the window, gazing out to where the grey sea merges with the grey sky, and try to come to terms with what has happened.

Winter is a bleak time here. The days are short and wet, the dark evenings close in early. White sea mist rolls up from the channel like fallen clouds, sometimes enveloping the whole coastline so that nothing is visible for hours. Days can go by without sight of a passing boat, but at night I often see the fishing trawlers going out to lay their nets, seagulls shrieking around them.

At first, I would wake with a sense of disorientation, and look out of the window expecting to see the lake stretching below, white sailing boats skimming the waves. I would stare at the bare horizon bewildered, searching for a glimpse of the Alps but finding nothing – just an expanse of sea, a bleak view that brought a vague sense of relief coupled with an aching loss. Not for Switzerland, with its icy beauty, but for what might have been.

3

There can be no going back now, however. The past has finally caught up with me, as it has a habit of doing, and there is too much stacked against me. By running away, as I have, I can only have strengthened Michel's case. Yet I had no choice.

Only moving to the opposite window, to look across the salt marshes towards the Wicklow mountains, do I become oriented, brought back to reality. Then the fear is at its worst.

The fear is not only for the present, but for what lies ahead. To a single woman with a child, trying to make ends meet, the future looks bleak. Sometimes, watching the pale evening sun slide down behind the mountains, I feel that my chances of ever being self-sufficient and content again are remote. Statistics claim that women in my category are the loneliest people in the world. The money will run out sooner or later, and then what? Until now Great Aunt Geraldine has been helping out. It was she who led me to the railway cottage, when I realised I could not stay at Heronlough House. That house, where Mother grew up and which she left under such mysterious circumstances, has come up in past conversations, and a week ago the Gardai came by again . . .

I have been thinking more and more about Mother recently, since I now follow the paths she once trod, and have come to learn more of the extraordinary circumstances that shaped her life. Aunt Geraldine has told me parts of the story, which started years ago, with a family feud that resulted in Mother leaving Ireland, and is still going on. Something tells me there was more to it than that, however – some other factor that caused her to flee like she did. But Aunt G has warned me not to delve too deep. Yet it seems that by coming here I have already been drawn into it, and there are still so many unanswered questions.

Over the last few days, there have been a couple of incidents that make me believe somebody is on our trail. This forces me out of the cottage, down the lane to the main road which leads to the village, with Jean trotting along behind me, his short legs tiring within minutes. In the village fears of a different nature take over – a curious glance from a passer-by, the sight of a Garda strolling along, a car slowing down beside us.

The only way to keep the fears at bay, I've discovered, is to write about what happened. In reconstructing the events that led to this end, and in bringing Michel back, albeit temporarily, there is a

4

sense of relief and continuity. Some writers claim it is easier to write about the event once removed from the time and place in which it occurred; that from a distance there is clarity in remembrance. In my case, there is also the desire to forget.

For to give an accurate, unbiased account, everything must be included, even the most bitter moments. The accident; that dreadful evening the police raided a Mayfair apartment; how tragedy struck one cold November night. All the things that were to have such enormous repercussions later on.

I also write in the hope that, one day, this story will be published and Michel will read it. Perhaps then he might understand better my fears, my jealousy, and above all my sense of inadequacy.

This is how I escape from the present, sitting at the window writing while Jean sleeps, pausing every so often to scan the horizon and seeing Lake Geneva as I saw it then, framed by the Alps, before going further back in time to the Isle of Wight, with the ferry boat crossing the Solent on its way to Portsmouth.

Perhaps by reliving it, I too will understand better; will pinpoint where it started to go wrong. Why everything suddenly went spiralling out of control until the marriage broke down, and how an emotional battle that might have been won almost became a legal war, with losses all round.

PART ONE

Chapter One

The Isle of Wight, 1979

My father drowned at sea, in an accident that made the headlines of all the newspapers. He and Mother lived on the Isle of Wight then, between Fishbourne Point and East Cowes, in a tall stone-grey house overlooking the Solent. Father owned a boatyard in Cowes and spent his days there, restoring old boats. Sailing was his life, wooden boats his great obsession. As a young naval officer he had bought himself a yacht, a William Fife built in the 1920s, which he had carefully maintained over the years and referred to as 'a rare beauty', longing for the day he could sail away in her. If he'd had his way he would probably have sold up everything to finance his dream and spent the rest of his days at sea.

We were not islanders by birth, but 'blow-ins' according to our local acquaintances. We 'blew in' from Portsmouth, a year after Father retired from the Navy, by which time he had already bought the boatyard and was managing it from across the water. It was hard for my sister and me to make the transition: I had reached an age when it was difficult to begin again with new friends – cliques of teenagers were already formed, their circles closed to outsiders – while most girls of Charlotte's age had left for colleges and universities. For Mother it must have been the hardest of all, though, forcing her even further into the sailing scene, what with the endless regattas and great events such as Cowes Week, when she wouldn't see Father for days. Father seemed to have found his haven, but the three of us drifted disconsolately behind him like a gaggle of reluctant geese until Charlotte and I took off for London, where it didn't much matter whether you belonged or not.

I was glad to get away from that damp house, those musty rooms and stained ceilings. It had the fusty atmosphere of a winter boarding house, with its lingering cooking smells and the sea view after which it was unimaginatively named. Father would stand by the window day and night, telescope poised, naming each passing vessel out loud.

'There goes a tanker, bound for the Fawley Refinery, I'll bet,' he'd declare, or 'an old coaster heading for the River Medina . . .'

It was a triumphant moment to witness the passage of a large yacht in full sail. 'Look at the cut of her,' he'd exclaim, beckoning us to the window, while he grumbled constantly at the sight of the car ferry going back and forth from Portsmouth, referring to it disgustedly as 'that blasted boat'.

Father never really left the Navy in spirit. He lived a great deal in the past; focused on the war, reliving those last adventures over and over again. There were many great moments, but his favourite was a rescue operation that had taken place in the North Sea, when his convoy protection ship had rescued part of a fleet from attack by German U-Boats. It had been a difficult manoeuvre – the light fading, the waves high, and the current against them – and it had been taking far too long. Father, without much thought for what he was doing, had dived into the icy sea and thrown the nets across to the stricken ship. Had he stopped to think about it, he once admitted, he might never have jumped. 'Father's Finest Hour', for which he was awarded his DSC; those heroic moments which nothing else ever quite matched. That was the way he was. Thoughtless, impulsive, even reckless at times, but far braver than he would ever admit.

Soon after he married Mother, he set off with her in the 'rare beauty' (which he christened Running Tide, from John Masefield's poem Sea Fever) across the Atlantic and through the Panama Canal to Australia. He had planned a honeymoon voyage, but for Mother it must have seemed more like a nightmare. As they drew close to the Barrier Reef the weather suddenly changed, and they found themselves sailing headlong into a freak storm that threatened to propel the boat onto the reef. But instead of attempting to turn back, instead of heeding the forecasts, Father decided to plough on through dangerous, uncharted waters – a reckless move that almost cost both their lives. He was experienced enough to know that, without the backup of an equally able seaman, the risk was incalculable, and perfectly aware that Mother was the worst person to rely on in a crisis. It seemed he was searching for another glorious moment.

The mast broke somewhere off Orpheus Island. Father hoisted a jury rig and sent out a May Day, but by then *Running Tide* had been driven onto the sharp coral bed of the Barrier Reef.

This time, though, luck was on his side. A rescue boat from Townesville reached them, just as *Running Tide* was about to keel over. Father was standing on a coral ledge up to his neck in shark-infested water, examining the damage done to his beloved boat, while Mother was still clinging stiffly to the tiller as if she had been instructed by Father to do so.

Father claimed he knew he wasn't going to die that time. Had it not been for *Running Tide*, things might have turned out differently, he said, but she had been a long way from breaking up. The accident if anything reinforced his great faith in wooden boats. The advent of the plastic boat, or GRP, in the late fifties was for him worse than a catastrophe; it was the bitter end. Plastic boats, he swore, would be the death of him.

He tried with limited success to steer Charlotte and me into his nautical world. I loved the pleasure trips we made together, taking turns with Father at the helm, but disliked the regattas which were so much a part of it, while Charlotte never really took to sailing at all. When we first moved across to the island, he would drag us to the Maritime Museum at Bembridge, to look at models of ships and numerous photographs of the lifeboat in action. Charlotte, who was four years older than me, didn't bother to hide her indifference, whereas I would try to think of an appropriate question, while longing for the tour to be over and for the walk that accompanied these expeditions, when we would go down to the harbour to see the pilot boat, or if the weather was good up to Culver Cliff, where herring gulls nested and campion grew. I often thought how much better off Father would have been with two outgoing sons, of whom at least one might have shared his interest. As it was, he was surrounded by none too daring women.

In the short time we spent on the island, a lot of things happened within the family. There was the fight between Charlotte and I, which I named the 'double betrayal'. There was Mother's illness, no more than a cloudy suspicion at the time; Father's financial problems with the boatyard; and other troublespots looming on the horizon. But all these were overshadowed by a darker memory, of the night Toddy Freeman disappeared, perhaps because it was the first in a series of disasters that suddenly descended upon us.

Tod, as he was better known, was Father's closest friend. They had gone through Dartmouth together, served in HMS Lion together, and kept in close contact over the years, before both ended up retiring to the Isle of Wight and living virtually next door to one another. Tod had partly financed the boatyard, so they had become business partners as well. He owned an old wooden sloop, half the size of *Running Tide*, which he'd christened *Merryman*. He often went out alone for hours at a time, but always returned before nightfall. Father had recently done some work on *Merryman*, who had been listing slightly, he said, so that Tod wanted her realigned.

The day after the work was completed, Tod left the harbour at eight o'clock in the morning, and never returned. All through the evening and into the night helicopters circled, throwing long beams of light onto the inky sea. Father paced the harbour, distraught. He couldn't, *wouldn't* believe that anything bad had happened. He returned to the house every hour, and sat by the window peering out into the darkness. They called off the search at midnight, by which time everyone except Father had given up hope. The next morning the search was resumed, but at that stage it was only a formality.

They never found Toddy Freeman, or *Merryman*, and after some months he was listed as missing at sea. But Father stubbornly refused to believe he was dead. He claimed old Tod had simply done what both of them had always wanted to do – just packed up and sailed away. And jolly good luck to him, too!

But all the same, he only partially recovered his spirits again. Whether he believed that the work he'd done on *Merryman* had had some part in it, or else Tod's absence was enough to knock the stuffing out of him, it was hard to tell. He began to spend more and more time at sea, going out in the worst conditions, pushing *Running Tide* to ever greater limits. A kind of recklessness came over him, and when the mast broke again and the boat was laid up in dry dock, he accepted offers to race on other yachts, disappearing for days at a time. He no longer discriminated over what kind of boat or with whom he sailed. He raced on monohulls and multihulls, fibreglass and custom-built yachts, returning from each trip restless and disgruntled, claiming there was no beauty in boat building any more. At home, he spent more time at the window squinting through his telescope, focusing on every yacht in sight.

Mother wrung her hands in despair as the weeks passed and he kept up this lonely vigil. 'If only he'd accept Tod's dead and gone,' she said, over and over again. But I understood what Father was going through. It seemed to me an even worse fate than death, to be missing in that vast expanse of sea.

Poor Mother was going through her own private hell at that stage, what with Charlotte putting on weight at an alarming rate and blaming everyone else for it, and her own recent dizzy spells, which spoke of some deeper health problem.

Mother was a wishy-washy woman, with bright, suspicious eyes and a deep fear of the world outside her back door – the world without Father. When she had to travel without him, for instance – driving us to school, or later to the airport, when we started boarding – she became quite frantic, hurrying us along blindly without thinking where she was going. The system terrified her; instructions and signs bypassed her; her head would turn in every direction, like a hen searching for food. Sometimes she'd completely lose her bearings, and freeze into immobility as the crowds surged by. 'Where are we, Emily? I couldn't make head or tail of what that girl was saying . . . Let me gather my scattered wits . . .' And I would stand miserably beside her, wishing fervently that Father were with us, to guide us through the obstacles that loomed for her and her alone. In the terror of the moment, she'd lose our boarding passes or tickets, ending up rummaging in the depths of her handbag, her head buried, oblivious to those who tried to rally round her. Without Father, she seemed to go to pieces.

Later, when she started succumbing to dizzy spells in public and had to be revived with smelling salts, it became clear that she could no longer accompany us anywhere – we had to accompany her. Within her organised domain, however, she was an articulate, bookish woman, with the great love of literature and verse I shared – burying herself in the classics to escape from the outside world, perhaps.

She worshipped Father with the dedication of one whose life revolves solely around another. She had grown up on the south

13

east coast of Ireland, the youngest daughter of a large Huguenot family who had settled there around the time of the Battle of the Boyne. The family, who were too English to integrate fully with the Irish, and too Irish (especially on foreign soil) to call themselves English, considered themselves Anglo-Irish. It was therefore quite acceptable to marry an Englishman and cross the water – better that than to marry a Catholic on home ground. So Mother's marriage to a British naval officer was considered in a friendly light. It was the fact that she renounced her Irish ties in the process that was a mystery.

When I was fourteen years old, the mystery was partly solved when Mother, Charlotte and I (Father was away at sea at the time) caught the ferry across to Ireland one summer, to attend the funeral of our Irish granny whom I'd never met. We stayed at Heronlough House, where Great Aunt Geraldine now lived, a crumbling Georgian mansion with pale pink-washed walls and fanlight windows.

Formerly a shooting lodge, the house was built overlooking a lough where wild swans and herons nested, and had a spectacular view across the sea to Wicklow Head. There was about it an air of gentle decay – the brass knockers no longer shone, and part of the stonework had crumbled away – yet it retained some of its grandeur, as a lot of those old Irish country houses do, defying the long winters and the rain, which comes frequently to that part of the world. Behind the house, the terns had found a sanctuary in the salt marshes and bogland that stretched inland towards the small village of Rathegan.

Inside, it was the antithesis of our own charmless home. Aunt Geraldine was a talented artist, and the house was filled with scenes she had painted; 'Wild Swans on the Lough', depicting the graceful Whooper swan who migrated from Iceland in the winter; 'The Sugar Loaf', the mountain that stood to the east of Heronlough, with its dusty sprinkling of rocks; and my favourite, 'The Railway Cottage', an isolated cottage standing behind a railway line, with the shadowy outline of a woman inside. Her paintings seemed to encapsulate the south of Ireland, with all its wild atmospheric beauty.

There were two crooked rooms where the servants had once slept tucked away under the eaves, while the other bedrooms were

14

large and stately, with intricate plaster-worked ceilings and adjoining dressing rooms. My room had a spectacular view through the fanlight over the lough to the headland. There was a portrait of Mother hanging on the wall which Aunt G had never completed because, she admitted once, it evoked too many memories. Looking closely at that unfinished work, at Mother staring bleakly out of a white background, it seemed as if her eyes were brighter than ever, filled with unshed tears.

The drawing room was a hotch potch of Victorian and Georgian furniture and Oriental knick-knacks from Singapore and China – souvenirs collected by the Flavells over the years that had been part of Mother's life once, but held no interest for her now. I saw then how little she had carried forward from her childhood. Whereas once she had eaten her meals in a cluttered kitchen with a flagstone floor, an Aga, and portraits of Georgian Dublin on the walls, now she cooked on an electric stove and wore an apron sporting a Union Jack.

The purpose of that visit was not even a sentimental one, a desire to show us where she had grown up. She went to attend the funeral of the mother she had not seen nor spoken to in over twenty years, to tie up the will and settle her deeds on the house.

There was some signing done in front of a pale-faced lawyer, and long intense conversations between Mother and Aunt G in the kitchen, while Bridget the housekeeper produced endless pots of black tea and barmbrack, most of which Charlotte and I ate.

Mother remained tight-lipped over the death of her mother, speaking in a hushed voice that hinted at past misdeeds, unforgotten and unforgiven. Listening to the two women, I thought that even though they were part of the same family, the differences between them were enormous. Mother spoke with barely a trace of an Irish accent now. She sat rigidly upright in her chair, her mouth pursed against the smoke from Aunt Geraldine's cigarette and the general air of chaos around her. The kitchen was a far cry from the gleaming, orderly place she kept at home. Brass pots and pans, tarnished from the years, cluttered one dresser, while willow patterned plates and cups were propped higgledy-piggledy against the other. On the kitchen table, the debris of the last meal remained. Aunt Geraldine's philosophy was 'better a house unkept than a life unlived', while Mother's whole life seemed to be structured around keeping the house in order and coping with Father's daily needs.

They talked, among other things, of the family feud that had been going on for decades between the Flavells and the Murphys from the village. According to Aunt G it had all begun over a land eviction order more than a hundred years ago, and never been resolved. 'A squabble over a potato patch,' she called it, but there was obviously more to it than that. The Flavells had later closed a footpath that accessed Murphy land, and made it part of the long driveway to Heronlough. Across the fields behind Heronlough was Murphy's chicken farm. Some days, when the wind was blowing from a certain direction, the smell of manure wafted across the lawns of Heronlough and into the house. Aunt G said it was bad enough that the Murphys had monopolised the village, without having to put up with the pong from their farm as well.

In those days, the main street of Rathegan consisted of two pubs, a grocer's store with petrol pumps outside it, a newsagent and a bookmaker, while in the centre of the village was the Catholic church. The Murphys owned the larger pub and the bookie's, and one of the brothers worked the petrol pumps. They were now trying to take over the other pub, whose present owner was losing trade to Murphy's Lounge Bar. Aunt Geraldine called them a 'desperate lot', claiming that the new generation were even worse. 'They'll be taking over from poor old Paddy Whelan before we know it,' she said crossly. (Paddy Whelan owned the grocer's and the two petrol pumps outside it.) As for the youth, they were 'malodorous malingerers', she said, and warned us to keep out of their way.

I had seen two of the Murphy boys in the village on a couple of occasions, and was more struck by their appearance than their behaviour. They both had those wild gypsy looks, with black curly hair and pale blue eyes. Aunt G claimed they were a throwback from the days when the Spanish Armada was wrecked off the west coast of Ireland and the surviving crew integrated with the locals, resulting in this angry race. They certainly behaved a bit like hot-blooded Mediterraneans, stalking the village at night and hissing at any woman who passed by.

I was aware that Mother was particularly affected by this conversation. She fiddled nervously with her teacup, and her lips were so set it seemed her mouth might cave in. Then she jerked to life and, fixing her bright eyes on her aunt, said, 'Any news on Thomas since. . . ?'

There was a silence, then Aunt Geraldine said, 'Ah Peg, why are you bringing it up now, of all times? Please . . . Let it rest, for all our sakes.'

Although she spoke harshly, she leant across the table and covered Mother's hand affectionately with her own.

'I only asked if there was any news,' replied Mother stiffly, pulling her hand away. Her face had taken on a cornered expression.

Aunt Geraldine sighed. 'I never go into Rathegan these days, if I can help it,' she emphasised, 'so not much news travels my way. I haven't heard a thing since he took himself off across the water . . . As for the rest of them, "blood will out" as they say. They're a dreadful lot, just like their father.'

'What did they do?' I asked. Family intrigues had always fascinated me.

Aunt G glanced sharply at Mother, then said evasively, 'There have been problems between our families for donkey's years – way before my time, even . . .' That was when she told me about the squabble over the potato patch. 'Murphy's a rough diamond,' she concluded, 'and the less said about the rest of them, the better.' And yet she seemed to have more to say. 'I found one of them trespassing on my land only the other day – cut right across that field yonder to the beach. A dreadful gombeen man, so he was. I sent Jimmy after him' – Jimmy was Aunt G's gardener, driver and odd job man – 'but we never caught him – seemed to disappear into thin air.'

Aunt G lit another cigarette and tried to change the subject. 'I saw Sheelagh de Courcy Evans at the Grand in Wicklow the other day – you remember Sheelagh, Peg?'

Mother appeared to be no longer listening; she had that whitewashed, fearful look about her that was sometimes triggered by a domestic crisis. But I was longing to hear more about the wicked Murphys.

'What's a gombeen man?' I inquired.

Great Aunt Geraldine turned to me and said, 'Depending on interpretation – a chancer, or somebody who has a finger in every pie and rides roughshod over others to advance himself.' She paused, glancing meaningfully at Mother again, and I was about to ask her to expand when Charlotte barged in demanding tea and biscuits, and the conversation moved on.

Mother, Charlotte and I walked through the village later that day, when the sea was white with horses and a grey drizzly fog blew in from the Irish sea. The summer had not yet arrived, it seemed, although it was almost July. We stopped at the newsagents first, where Mother bought the *Irish Times* and Charlotte and I stocked up on Smith's crisps and red lemonade, then passed the dingy entrance of Murphy's Lounge Bar, where a wooden board advertising Guinness swung on a rusty nail. Mother made a great to-do of crossing the street, which seemed a bit unnecessary, I thought, since the Murphys didn't appear to put up a very formidable front.

As we were leaving the village two boys, around my own age, suddenly appeared out of the fog like dark phantoms, glancing at us curiously as they passed. While Mother hurried us on through the driving wet wind, her body straining forwards as if pursued by some ghostly memory of her own.

I looked around once, and saw they had stopped and were staring after us. One of them had a beautiful, chiselled face, framed by a tangle of black curls. He smiled oddly, and lifted his hand in greeting, causing me to turn away in confusion and Mother to snap, 'Do hurry up, Emily, or we'll be soaked to the skin!'

Mother finally told us, on the way back to Heronlough, that Tom Murphy was the reason she had left Ireland. He was, as Aunt Geraldine had said, 'a rough diamond, and a chancer, with the gift of the gab and a great talent with music,' but there was a darker side. After beating around the bush for a while, and falling back on the comfortable clichés she always used (she had been led a song and dance, up the garden path, taken in by a rogue), she finally admitted that he had broken her heart.

Charlotte and I listened, fascinated by the thought of Mother in the midst of a romantic dilemma. Yet looking at her now, in her yellow sou'wester, her face creased against the gusts of rain, I could still imagine how she must once have looked. Striking, almost, with her blue eyes, her small neat features and hour-glass figure.

'Don't you girls go falling into that kind of trap,' she said grimly. We had reached the long driveway of Heronlough by now, and were walking beneath the dripping elms and beech trees towards the house.

'What kind of trap?' asked Charlotte immediately. Her mind was obviously travelling along another route, of unwanted babies and shotgun weddings.

But Mother was talking about a different trap, the sort of impasse that comes from falling in love with a man with whom there can be no future. She continued speaking, but as if she were talking to herself now.

'We were completely different, that was the problem,' she was saying. 'Different background, different religion, different values . . .'

'You and the rough diamond?' I asked, keen to clarify the story.

'I was extremely foolish,' she continued. 'I thought it would all work out in spite of everything. I underestimated the power of the family. You can't change history; people stay the way they are, and that's a fact of life.'

'Why didn't you just run away together?' asked Charlotte, who for once didn't have the bored look on her face that normally accompanied one of Mother's stories.

We were approaching the humpback bridge that crossed the swamp, where tall rushes grew, and rustled in the breeze.

'Because,' replied Mother bitterly, 'he couldn't stand up to his family after all . . .' She shrugged her shoulders, as though she had never quite come to terms with it herself, and added: 'Just as well, really; it would never have worked. There was no common ground, we hardly spoke the same language – the only way he could communicate was through his music . . . But by the time I realised all that, it was too late.' She sighed, muttering, 'Many a road to victory ends in defeat.' That was Mother all right, I thought irritably. So easily defeated. She pursed her mouth (to indicate that was the end of it, only I knew that there was more she had stopped herself from saying).

'I've always had a preference for foreign men,' said Charlotte provocatively. 'Opposites tend to attract because of their differences.' Charlotte was going through her anti-establishment phase then, always taking the contrary view. The battle with

19

her weight had already begun, and was taking its toll on all of us.

'Prefer them if you want,' said Mother shortly, 'but don't marry one. Marry somebody from your own background, of the same ilk . . . That's my advice, for what it's worth. You can take it or leave it, of course.'

'But you didn't,' Charlotte argued.

'In the literal sense, no,' Mother replied. 'A stretch of water divides Ireland from England, but the differences between your Father and me are few. We're from similar backgrounds.'

'But,' Charlotte persisted, determined to find a flaw in Mother's logic, 'you're not the same nationality.'

I understood what Mother had been trying to say. She had been talking of differences that had their roots buried in elements deeper than nationality – class, religion, and way of life. She was trying to say that coming from the type of background that she had, she would naturally find more in common with a man like Father than 'the rough diamond'. A sentiment Charlotte would have immediately rejected as snobbery.

The conversation ended as we reached the house. It would be years before I learnt more of Mother's extraordinary story and the war between the Flavells and Murphys.

Chapter Two

Aunt G told us many a tale of shame and scandal amongst the Flavells as she sat behind her easel under the rowan tree, sketching the lough. There was her eccentric aunt 'Mad Maud', who legend said was found in the tall rushes that grew in the swamps beside Heronlough and adopted by the family; there was Loony Liam, a cousin 'afflicted of God', who went off with the tinkers; and Josephine Flavell, who eloped with the local bus driver. Past sins that had become legends, embellished over the years, and now seemed detached from reality. A lot of water under the bridge. But she did not talk of Mother and 'the rough diamond' in this way, and by not being acknowledged, it remained oddly alive – still waters continuing to run deep.

The rest of that trip has faded from my memory, apart from one event, which I remember as clearly as yesterday.

The sea mist finally blew over, and the sun shone over the damp lawns of Heronlough. One morning, woken by the sound of the swans honking on the lough, I gazed out of the fanlight window and saw a small punt grazing the pontoon below. A dark-haired boy was standing in the shallows, searching for something in the water. It was one of the Murphys, I knew instinctively.

It was still early, the dawn just breaking, casting silvery grey light over the sea. He must have reckoned on nobody being up at this time, I thought. I pulled on my clothes and crept out of the room, along the landing and down the stairs. Aunt G's ancient retriever Sambo wagged his tail as I passed by, but didn't bark. I opened the front door and, leaving it on the latch, walked across the dewy grass to the lough, leaving my footprints on the lawn.

The boy looked up and grinned as I approached. He was the one with the chiselled face. I drew closer, as if impelled by the pull of a magnet, then stopped, embarrassed suddenly.

'Grand day,' he called. 'Come to scare me away then, have you?'

His voice was loud and rebellious, with a country lilt. I recognised the accent as local.

'No,' I replied, mesmerised by him, 'but you'd better be careful nobody sees you . . .' My voice trailed off awkwardly.

'I'm looking for bait,' he told me. 'No law against that.'

I smelt the whiff of manure from the chicken farm on the breeze, and said, 'You're one of the Murphys, aren't you?'

'No law against that, either,' he replied. He stared into the muddy water with great concentration, then crouched down and scooped up a handful of mud, letting the water sift through his fingers. Gently, he picked a wriggling worm from the layer of silt that remained, and dropped it into a rusty tin.

'This is private property,' I said, at a loss.

'Is that so?' he replied without interest.

'Yes.' I cleared my throat, aware I had sounded prissy and schoolmarmish.

He straightened up and stared at me. 'I seen you in the village, with your Mam and a fat girl, only the other day. I didn't realise you were one of them.'

He pronounced 'th' as 'd', so 'them' sounded like 'dem'.

'What do you mean?' I asked, disconcerted.

He climbed onto the pontoon, pulling at the rope of the punt so it bumped against the strut.

'A West Brit; a polishtin,' he said, stepping carefully into the boat.

'A what?' I stared at him, bewildered. 'Wait a minute,' I said as he untied the rope and pushed himself off from the jetty. 'What do you mean by that?'

But he just grinned and lifted his hand in farewell, as he had that time in the village, without replying.

Aunt G tried to explain it to me later that afternoon. She was sitting in her favourite spot under the rowan tree, sketching a line of pine trees that served as a windbreak in front of the house.

When I told her of the morning's encounter she looked annoyed, as if I were the one at fault for having gone down to the lough and spoken to him.

'That would be one of the older Murphy boys,' she said, her eyes flicking from the trees back to the easel. She sighed, adding, 'There are a pair of mute swans down there – I do hope he didn't disturb them.'

'I don't think so,' I said, for he hadn't seemed the type of boy who went about destroying nature.

She shook her head crossly. 'Jimmy calls it Murphy's Law – if they can use the lough to look for bait, then they will. We can't do much about it.'

I frowned. 'What did he mean by calling me a polishtin?' I asked curiously.

A ghost of a smile crossed Aunt G's face.

'It's extraordinary how these sayings last,' she said, reminiscently. 'When I was a girl I had a dear friend called Jacintha Fahy, who lived in the village, and used to sneak away to meet me down by the bridge over the swamp. We'd play "pooh sticks" for hours . . . we were bosom friends. And then one day, she stopped coming. I bumped into her in the village, some weeks later, and she told me that her mother had forbidden her to play with the "polishtins". The woman had said protestants, of course, but somehow the term stuck, and we became known as polishtins . . .' She paused, then said with irony, 'A symbolic connotation of something that's easy to kick around, I suppose. Only in reality it's quite the opposite!'

I stared away across the lough to where I had seen the Murphy boy that morning, unable fully to comprehend this. Until then I had never thought much about religion and its varieties. But in parts of Ireland it was still like a badge, separating the rich from the poor, the gentry from the gombeen man. I thought of the Murphy boy, remembering how he had stared at me in that half teasing, challenging way, as if he couldn't care less about people like the Flavells, with their grand old houses and their land – or the fact that he was trespassing upon it.

By the end of that week, Mother had handed over her deeds to Heronlough House to her Aunt, thus severing her last ties with Ireland.

Aunt Geraldine came over to visit us from time to time, but we never went back to Ireland again. Father wouldn't have chosen to holiday there, unless it was to sail around it, and he claimed the sea was too rough. Now he followed the yachting trail down to Cannes or St Tropez, preferring the warmer winds of the Mediterranean.

Mother's dizzy spells worsened, and she took to lying on her bed

23

after lunch. She still raced with Father from time to time, though; hating it, convinced each trip would be her last. Then one morning, before the start of a two-day regatta, she suddenly keeled over at the breakfast table, landing face down in her cornflakes in a parody of a slapstick comedy, as if she'd had one too many. That was her first heart attack.

Soon after she came out of hospital, Father took her to London to see a specialist, who diagnosed high blood pressure and a weak heart. He prescribed complete rest, and forbade any more braving the high seas. So Mother had finally become exempt from Father's ambitious projects. A sort of sagging relief came over her, and she slunk around like a wounded animal for a while, burying herself in novels, before turning her new energy into the house. Now she cleaned, swept and polished from dawn till dusk. Pained by a speck of dust, or the disorder Charlotte and I created, Mother's frantic hoovering became an obsession.

Charlotte claimed that Father had crushed her spirit, turned her into the dithering creature she was, but I saw it differently. It was plain to me, recognising my own traits in another, that she simply lacked the courage of her convictions. Only much later, when I learnt more about her past and found myself in an equally desperate situation, did I realise that circumstance can make or break a person, and Mother's spirit had been broken long before she'd met Father. But she was a good mother, in her undemonstrative way. Kind, but detached; concerned, but inept; willing to listen but incapable of really helping.

Mother made her biggest mistake on Charlotte, by trying to turn her into the sort of daughter Father would have liked her to be – an organised, energetic person, a keen sportswoman with a jolly nature and community spirit, like those women who hung around the sailing club, puffed up with life jackets, with cropped salty hair and permanent squints. When Father finally realised Charlotte was never going to take an interest in sailing, he suggested she join the WRNS. He loved the idea of a disciplined career and uniforms. This was surely the way to reform the sloppy, lethargic person she was becoming.

Charlotte had started out the prettier of the two of us, with her thick glossy hair of a particular ash blonde and pale blue eyes. We had both inherited Mother's full figure, large breasted and narrow

24

waisted; the type of build which with inertia, as in Charlotte's case, can turn to fat. I was a darker version of her, with finer brown hair (*chatin*, Michel would call it, although it was closer to a field mouse). My eyes were a brownish-green – the colour, Father said, of the sea. Not the warm turquoise of the Caribbean, but the deep, turbid green of the English channel.

I would have loved an older brother, with courage and determination, whom I could have looked up to. Charlotte and I had never got along together. There was the usual bickering that goes on between sisters, but more than that – a kind of unspoken resentment lay between us, as if by coming along four years later I had pushed her out of the limelight. Aunt G, who was constantly fighting with one of her sisters, used to say 'You can choose your friends, but you're stuck with your family.' And I was 'stuck' with Charlotte.

One day, in the intuitive and tactless way of a child, I accused Charlotte of having a jealous nature. She resented the fact that I seemed to get on better with Mother than she did, and had started calling me 'Mummy's girl'. This was not altogether true; Mother and I shared a deep interest in books, nothing more.

My jibe must have cut deeper than any of the others I had thrown at her, because she went completely wild. It was as though, by getting to the root of the problem between us, I had betrayed her. She was never the same towards me afterwards.

As she battled with her weight, I was planning to become a writer. I read some of the novels that Mother read (she loved the romantics, especially the Brontë sisters, after whom we had been named) and others of my own choosing, escaping into a fictitious world that made my own life seem very dull. Father had brought us up on books like *Swallows and Amazons*, *Moonfleet* and *Three Men in a Boat*, while he buried himself in biographies such as *The Eye of the Wind*. But now I discovered other lives, the lives led by beautiful, tormented women of Charlotte's age.

In my eyes, Charlotte grew even dimmer. What hope had she of ever attracting romance? I thought, as I watched her lounging in front of the TV one hot afternoon with one of her fat friends. They were eating crisps and drinking cans of cola, screeching with laughter over boys whom they considered way beneath them. Charlotte reminded me of a picture of a large sperm whale

Father had shown me once – an animal, he professed, whose message is faint but travels far, reaching only those of its own kind. Was that the best Charlotte could hope for, another sperm whale?

It was around that time I started keeping a diary, filling it religiously in the quiet of my bedroom. But gradually, as one uneventful day followed another, it began to lose its appeal. Nothing happened between the dull routine of school and the holidays; nothing worth writing about, anyway.

That was when I created Kimberly. Kimberly was a product of my imagination, a stock character of fiction, based on the kind of contemporary woman who fascinated me. She was very beautiful and led a glamorous life, surrounded by handsome suitors, who were all dark and swarthy – French or Italian mostly, or from even further afield; Argentina, Australia, whichever country fascinated me at the time. She had wardrobes filled with elegant clothes, and drawers containing love tokens from all her beaus – sapphires and emeralds, some rare and priceless pieces. She was very dramatic and demanding, a social butterfly, flitting from one man to the next, lavished upon by each of them. I recorded intimate details of her life with her latest lover, Marco, an Italian count – where they went, what she wore, and the lovestruck dialogue that passed between them. In Marco, I created the ideal man; brilliant, handsome and accomplished, the perfect partner who did not exist. They were married, with great pomp and splendour. Then I decided Kimberly didn't deserve all this, and began to guide their marriage up hill and down dale, through peaks and troughs, then steadily onto the rocks.

Reading back over the script one warm summer afternoon, as the starter guns announcing another race boomed in the distance, I was suddenly disappointed at how false it seemed. It was comic-strip dialogue. I re-read the love scene in front of me with a sinking heart.

'Kimberly's heart beat wildly in her chest . . . She trembled as Marco took her in his arms and crushed her to him . . . Faint with longing, their lips met . . .'

I threw down the diary in disgust. I could see Kimberly's blonde head exuding speech bubbles. I picked up my pen and started rewriting the scene, becoming Kimberly's narrative voice.

'My heart was beating wildly in my chest . . . I thought my legs might give way beneath me, as I fell into Marco's arms . . .'

I put down the pen with satisfaction. It seemed to me that Kimberly had finally come alive.

Charlotte was still furious with me over my comment about her jealousy. She was going through a tough time, what with Mother nagging her over her untidy room, Father for her sloppy ways: on top of that she had put on half a stone, after another failed diet. She came flying out of the bathroom one evening, her hair in wet strings around her shoulders, a towel wrapped like a toga around her: it bit into her skin, so the fat swelled above it. She had somehow got hold of my diary, and was halfway through a passionate scene between Kimberly and Marco, when they had just begun courting. She burst into my room before I could stop her and lunged onto the bed, legs raised, and started to read out loud, punctuating the story with bouts of laughter.

In a fury I tried to snatch it from her, but she held on, ripping the page in her agitation to finish it. Then she stuck out her foot and kicked me off the bed.

'Good God!' she exclaimed, reaching the end. 'What have you been reading to churn out stuff like this? Kimberly and Marco! I've never read anything so trite in my life. It's straight out of *True Love Romances*!'

'Oh, shut your big mouth,' I snapped, hot with humiliation and anger.

'You've copied it from a magazine; go on, admit it,' she jibed. 'It's certainly bad enough!'

'I haven't copied it from anything,' I replied furiously.

' "Marco's eyes were like chips of ice," ' she quoted with a shriek. 'Where *do* you get your analogies from?'

'I hate you,' I said.

'Plagiarism,' she announced, quoting Mother. 'You haven't an original idea in your head.'

'Get out of my room!' I shouted, trembling with anger. I wasn't sure what she meant by plagiarism; I suspected it had something to do with having the plague. 'You're a fat slob,' I yelled. 'You'll never be anything but a jealous bitch.'

She glared at me with such loathing that I shivered. 'And what do you think you'll be?' she inquired coldly. 'A writer?' She threw the diary across the room with a snort. 'You haven't a hope in hell!'

With that, she heaved herself off the bed and swaggered out of the room, gathering her towel around her as she went. I caught sight of her naked backside as she walked. It swelled with a double motion, although it hadn't reached half the proportions it would one day reach. 'Fat bottom,' I muttered under my breath. Our relationship had reached an all-time low.

In the days that followed, she took to quoting bits and pieces of the dialogue between Kimberly and Marco in front of Mother. When Mother asked her what she was talking about, she said smugly, 'Emily's got a new hobby. She's writing romances!'

Mother put down the novel she was reading. 'Oh yes?' she said with interest. 'What sort of romances?'

'Stories of forbidden love,' Charlotte announced dramatically, adding: 'between Marco, the swarthy Italian count with eyes like chips of ice, and Kimberly the glamour puss! I think she's planning on marrying a foreigner in spite of your advice . . . "Get out of my life, Kimberly, said Marco, his mouth a bitter twisted line . . ." ' (She was quoting the part when they'd first started having marital problems.)

'Shut up, Charlotte,' I snapped, puce with embarrassment. 'You're such a bitch . . . just because you can't lose weight,' I added, landing once again on a sore point.

'Emily, your language,' said Mother severely. 'Charlotte, I don't think it's very nice of you to tease her like that. I suppose you read it without her permission?'

'She shouldn't have left it lying around,' replied Charlotte. 'She obviously wanted her great work to be discovered!'

I considered it the double betrayal.

Later, Mother said, 'Try not to take it to heart, Emily. She doesn't mean to be so unkind. I do wish you wouldn't harp on about her weight though – it's obviously troubling her. "Tread softly" with Charlotte,' she quoted, ' "for you tread on her dreams".'

'Charlotte doesn't have any dreams,' I replied sulkily.

'Everybody has dreams, Emily. Some of us just never realise them, that's all.' I had no doubt she considered herself one of them.

Father must have heard about it all from Mother, because he said if I wanted to be a writer that was fine, as long as I wrote 'decent stuff'. None of this women's nonsense – swarthy 'Eyties' luring butterfly women away to foreign parts with their fast cars and their 'boodle'. All that was codswallop, he said.

But not long afterwards, he bought me a small manual typewriter, proudly presenting it as 'the tool of my trade'. Then he delivered his final lecture on the subject. 'Write abut life, Emily,' he urged, 'about the biggest adventure in the world . . .' His voice faded away on a dreamy note. He meant the sea, of course.

Chapter Three

Charlotte went off to technical college in Exeter for two years, to learn about the catering business. Perhaps Father felt the sight of all that food would put her off eating so much. And sure enough, her weight did seem to stabilise, and her face lose some of its pudginess. After she'd received her diploma, she announced she wanted to travel before settling down to a steady job, although she seemed to have no clear idea of where she wanted to go. London to start with, then maybe Paris to learn the finer art of cuisine. Father scraped together the money, giving into her nebulous plans as to the unpredictable change of the wind, and she took herself off to London to become one of those lonely bedsit people, before moving on to Paris to work in a restaurant off the Bois de Boulogne.

After I'd completed a course in journalism, I followed her as far as London, to begin work as a freelance writer. I moved into a flat off the Finchley Road, sharing with a girl called Amanda Ellis Smith who was the proverbial social butterfly – the type of woman whose life was fraught with dramas, in which I would become fatally enmeshed. Father once said that the higher up the mast you climbed, the less stable it became, and urged me to steer clear of social climbers, but I only remembered his advice when it was too late.

I was working for a new magazine called *Healthy Lifestyle* the summer of the accident (and had other freelance work that was keeping me busy), and seeing a journalist called Elliot Watts. He wrote political articles for the newspaper, although undoubtedly his appeal lay more in his way with words than in his beliefs. But life was just beginning for me, it seemed. We were reaching the end of the decade, the first woman prime minister was in office, and I was going to write a novel.

Mother telephoned like clockwork every Monday night at seven o'clock, with the weekly news. That Monday, she informed me her blood pressure was up again, what with one thing and another.

The one thing was Charlotte, who had suddenly descended for the week with another girl in tow, and eaten her out of house and home: the other was Father, who she said was in a feverish state. The Admiral's Cup had been on, and she was worn out from all the cooking and entertaining that accompanied it. Father had been pacing the house like a caged bear before each race, desperate to be out at sea. Yet the competition seemed to bring him no joy any more. He claimed the boat he was racing on this year was a 'bloody bathtub'. The boatyard was in financial difficulties too, but Father's time was now limited with the regattas.

I didn't take all this in, since it was a weekly scenario, even when Mother said, 'I'm worried about him, Emily; he's been very itchy-scratchy lately. He thought he saw *Merryman* on the horizon the other day. He still believes Toddy Freeman is alive and kicking . . .'

She moved on then to the house, which she said was in a chaotic state thanks to Charlotte and her friend, to which I replied, 'I don't understand why you don't arrange for some weekly help. It shouldn't cost that much.' But this fell on deaf ears. Mother would never 'pass the buck'; she would doggedly follow the exhausting programme she had set herself, even if it killed her.

It was a conversation like many other conversations, and yet when I put down the receiver I felt vaguely uneasy. I decided then I would go and see her the following weekend, in spite of my deadlines. The work would just have to wait.

I never went in the end, though, and Father drowned a week later. On August 29th, along with fourteen others, in the catastrophic Fastnet Race.

Mother learnt about it on the six o'clock news, and semi-collapsed from shock. She was almost incoherent by the time she telephoned me. I called her every hour on the hour, all through that dreadful night, but somehow we both knew before it was finally confirmed.

It was some time before I could bring myself to read the following report, written by one of the survivors.

'Monday, 22.00. In the increasing storm, all batteries failed . . . Yacht's electrics all failing, but decided to press on for Fastnet all the same . . .'

I thought of the last time Father had tried to beat a storm, years ago, on the Barrier Reef.

'Tuesday, 06.00. Huge wave (approx 35ft) swamped the boat. 2 crew whose harnesses failed swept overboard. Both visible, but in spite of every effort, crew unable to turn boat around to pick them up . . .'

It wasn't clear how the third man had fallen. Was he knocked overboard by the same wave, or did he, in a mad moment, make a desperate rescue leap, as he had once before, into the treacherous waves of the North Sea – a final glorious moment, but this time with no reprieve?

'. . . all lost,' continued the report. 'Morale on board very low.'

Afterwards, the boat was so damaged that the rest of the crew had to be lifted off by helicopter, while the battered remains were towed away by a Royal Naval Rescue boat. The yacht was an Ohlson 35, made of fibreglass – the kind of boat Father had always claimed would be the death of him.

Mother had her second heart attack the day after the accident. They took her to the main hospital on the island, and by the time I reached her she was in a critical state. She opened her eyes and I watched them swivel fearfully around the room before focusing on me, the whites gleaming like a frightened African.

'Charlotte,' she whispered – then, realising it was me, 'Emily dear, thank goodness you came . . .'

I walked over and sat on the edge of the bed; took her limp hand in mine.

'It was exactly how he would have chosen to go,' she said painfully. 'He wasn't happy, Emily; he'd become obsessed with Toddy's disappearance . . .'

My chest constricted so that I could barely speak. 'Mother, please get well,' I whispered. 'You're all I have left.'

It seems odd, thinking back, that neither of us mentioned Charlotte, that Mother didn't urge me to try and mend the rift between us. Perhaps she didn't want to waste her dying breath on such a futile cause. Instead she said, 'Now listen to me, there's Aunt Geraldine . . . She was like a mother to me . . . If anything should happen . . .' She paused, as if overcome by terror at the thought of her impending death. '. . . If you ever need somebody to turn to,' she continued with difficulty, 'go to Heronlough.'

A nurse appeared and hovered around, straightening Mother's

blanket and taking her pulse. 'Your mother's tired now,' she whispered. 'She needs to rest.'

I moved to go, but Mother clung onto my hand with all her remaining strength and said, 'There were so many things I wanted to tell you . . . but I promised your father . . .' She seemed to be struggling with her breathing now, and her face had turned an alarming shade of purple.

'You'd better rest first,' I said, fearfully. 'I'll stay here until you wake up.'

'Emily, your father made me promise . . .' she repeated, and I saw the familiar signs of a terrible dilemma in her eyes.

Tears splashed down my cheeks and my heart started pumping frantically, as if it, too, were in distress. 'Was it something to do with Tom Murphy?' I asked her.

'Tom. . . ?' she repeated. She looked confused now. A tear ran down her discoloured cheek, and she said faintly, 'I had no choice, they were all against me . . . The whole family, except Aunt G . . .' Then she closed her eyes.

'Shhh,' said the nurse, looking alarmed. 'You must leave now,' she ordered. 'She's becoming distressed.'

I got up and loosened Mother's grip on my wrist. 'I'll come back when you've slept a bit,' I promised, in a shaky voice, but it seemed to me that she was already asleep.

I paced the corridor with a leaden tread for what seemed like hours before I spotted Charlotte, lumbering towards me as if she had all the time in the world. She greeted me awkwardly, pecking me on both cheeks as the French do, and asked 'How is she?'

'Bad,' I replied. Her face had settled into fat folds, and there was an unpleasant smell of warm flesh about her, in spite of the coolness she portrayed.

'How bad?'

'Very. Her heart can't take it.'

'Just as well I got here, then,' she replied, as if it all depended on her. But I noticed a flicker of alarm cross her face.

'I think she wanted to talk to us,' I said numbly.

'What about?'

'I'm not sure . . . She's sleeping now.'

'Well, no doubt we'll find out,' said Charlotte, sinking down on a chair with a deep sigh.

But we never did find out. Mother didn't recover consciousness again. She died from heart failure an hour later.

A memorial service was held for both of them in Portsmouth, in the town where Father had spent most of his life. Most of the mourners were local people and islanders, and some of the Flavells came over from Ireland. Mother's remaining sister and her husband; two elderly female cousins, Lilly and Louise, whom I hadn't heard of before; and, of course, Great Aunt Geraldine. Others more distantly connected to the Flavells also came to pay their last respects, but Aunt G was the only ray of comfort over that dreadful time.

She moved purposefully through the shadowy figures milling around and came over, taking my hand in an iron grip. She wore a rough tweed suit that was far too warm for the day, lisle stockings, and brown leather walking shoes. Her grey hair was swept up in a bun on the top of her head, but wisps of it had escaped and blew around her face. She smelt of lavender water and cigarettes, and I noticed her hands had stiffened from all those damp winters at Heronlough.

'There'll always be a home for yourself and your sister across the water, if ever you need one,' she said breathlessly, 'as long as I'm still in the land of the living. Don't you forget that.'

'Thanks, Aunt G,' I muttered numbly.

'God, 'tis a dreadful business,' she said, gazing over my head, towards the sea, 'people dying who have never died before.'

I smiled weakly, in spite of everything. Aunt G always managed to make me smile.

At last it was all over, and Charlotte and I were saying goodbye to one another.

'Come over to Paris and visit me, some time,' she said vaguely, in the way people make such offers only to fill a silence, while I replied in the same empty tones that she must do likewise if ever she was in London. Then I watched her lumber away, thinking with a dull ache that she was all that remained of the family now.

Like Toddy Freeman, I was adrift on the ocean, lost in a sea of people who were strangers to me. Aunt G was the only one who connected me to the past, but even she couldn't ease the sense of loss and grief that raged inside.

Chapter Four

London, 1980

Soon after Mother and Father had gone, what I called 'the dark period' began.

I returned to London the evening after the memorial service, reaching Swiss Cottage as it was growing dark. Thick black clouds hung over the city, and the air was stuffy and strangely still, as if all hell were about to break loose. I walked towards the Finchley Road, then turned right into College Crescent, past some closed shops, until I reached the flat.

Inside, everything was equally dark and silent. Amanda had apparently spent the week away, for it was exactly as I had left it before setting off for the Isle of Wight. The remains of our last evening meal were still in the sink, while the rubbish had spilled over from the dustbin onto the floor. There was a sharp smell of rotting vegetables. I quickly closed the kitchen door and went into the living room, where glasses smeared with lipstick and dirty ashtrays were still strewn about. But the worst mess was over by the window, where I had recently moved my desk so I could gaze out over the Finchley Road. The surface was covered in pages of unfinished work, and crinkled balls of rejected papers lay scattered at its feet.

A wave of fury came over me, in spite of the fact that part of the mess was mine. It brought the loss of Mother sharply to mind. It seemed to me that all her efforts to instil a sense of order in my life had been futile and wasted. She would have hated this scene in front of me. We had, in the beginning, made an effort to clear up once a week, but defeated by the lack of space, and the fact that everything became untidy again within minutes, had soon given up. Now it seemed I had become like Charlotte, making a pointless point by taking the opposite route to Mother's obsessive tidiness.

In my bedroom I was greeted by more chaos – piles of dirty

clothes lying on the floor, books strewn about, more paper spilling out of the wastepaper basket. I lay on the bed suddenly overcome by exhaustion and fury – directing most of it against Amanda, who under the circumstances, I felt, could have tidied up. No doubt all her efforts were being put into her latest love affair. Another affair, I thought wearily, which like all the others would probably come to nothing.

Since I had met Amanda, she had been pursuing love with the kind of desperation that left no time for anything else, especially mundane things like cleaning up. Her targets were usually foreign, always wealthy, and more often than not slightly depraved. In the time I'd known her, she had pursued a Greek shipping magnate, fallen in love with a South American oil broker, and become caught up in a nasty situation with an Arab who wanted to take her back to Saudi Arabia. She worked for an up-market secretarial agency in South Moulton Street, although I don't think they hired her for her typing and shorthand skills, which were virtually non-existent. Their clientele were mainly Arabs, and Amanda was hired to answer their phones, book their flights, organise their schedules and drive the wives and entourages to Harrods. Every so often the phone would ring and a woman called Mrs Poppelwell announced herself in clipped tones. 'I hev a job for Amanda. People called Hussein.' And in her voice was the faintest trace of disgust, as if to say, 'Well we all have to earn a living one way or another.' Amanda would be up at the crack of dawn the following day, wearing a shiny blouse and tight pencil skirt, her feet jammed into high-heeled shoes, applying layer upon layer of make-up for her new job. She missed being beautiful by several degrees: she was too tall, even without the high heels, her features too large, and in some peculiar way her head seemed too big for her body. She had a hard, calculating face, bleached blonde hair, and a contrived habit of swooping it back at a chosen moment, and her time was spent investing in an illusory future of romance, marriage and money. She laid the groundwork with the bleach, the mascara and the hair swooping, and accepted invitations to dinner, to swinging parties and to bed in the hope that *this* occasion would finally be her salvation.

But each new-born hope died a swift death. Jesus, Jermain or Faahid usually had a wife hovering in the background, who would suddenly materialise when the relationship had run its course and demand to be driven to Harrods by a furious Amanda. Her lovers only wanted a diversion. They shone with distant promise before evaporating like a mirage, leaving Amanda hopelessly distraught – until the next time.

Her latest goal was a young Lebanese property developer called Shariffi. He was dark and spooky, with long pin-thin legs and a shifty smile. His eyes were covered in a yellow film that spoke of bad living, and he seemed to have a permanent cold. He held wild and wonderful parties in his Mayfair apartment where, according to Amanda, anything and everything happened. Sometimes I feared for Amanda. But at the same time, I found it all rather fascinating. My own life was far removed from wild parties and dark exotic men. She was the Kimberly of my former imaginings. 'You could write my life story, Emily,' she'd say theatrically from time to time. It had taken only a short time, however, to realise that she hadn't one. Her life was made up of a series of repeated incidents, all ending on the same bitter note. Marco the fictitious Count, as I had always suspected, did not exist.

I lay in the dark listening to the storm break, suddenly wishing for the diversion of Amanda's company despite my fury against her. But she didn't return until around two o'clock in the morning, by which time the storm was dying down and I still hadn't slept. I called out to her as she passed, and she came into my room, her hair glistening with raindrops.

'Emily, you're back,' she exclaimed. 'I didn't expect you until tomorrow. How are you? Was is dreadful?'

'To say the least,' I replied dully.

'How do you feel?' she asked, plonking herself down on the edge of the bed.

'Drained . . . like a dead weight.'

She placed a beautifully manicured hand over mine in a gesture of heavy sympathy, and sighed. Tragedies of this nature were beyond her scope. She tried to deal with it in the only way she knew. 'There's a party on Saturday night,' she said finally. 'Now, I don't want any excuses. Shariffi's got a very handsome friend,' she added enticingly. 'I'll arrange for us all to have a drink together before the party. Go and buy yourself something decent to wear – we'll go shopping one lunch time, if you like. I could do with a new outfit myself, come to think of it . . .'

On and on she went on this track, while my thoughts drifted away. These were Amanda's solutions to the troughs – new outfits, smart restaurants; another opportunity to enter that charmed life.

'I'm just not up to it,' I told her. 'It's the last thing I feel like at the moment. To be honest, all I want to do is sleep.' I was overcome by a sense of hopelessness. Falling asleep was only a temporary escape. I would still have to wake up again, and face the shock of remembering. Fresh tears burned behind my eyes, and my voice broke. 'I don't even want to go on living.'

She patted my hand consolingly, as if she were quite used to sudden declarations of this nature, and whispered, 'Hold on a minute, I'll get you something to help you sleep.' She tottered out of the room, and was back in moments with a bottle of white pills. 'Take one now, and one later if you need to. They're not strong, but they'll knock you out and send you cruising into the land of Nod. When you wake you'll feel better, believe me.' She handed me one with a glass of water, but I put it beside my bed, saying I would take it later. I seldom took pills of any kind, but then I'd never needed anything stronger than an aspirin before now.

'God, what a week,' she sighed, making me wonder for a moment if she was talking about my problems or her own. 'Did you get something to eat earlier, by the way? I left one of those frozen meals in the fridge for you.'

'I could hardly get into the kitchen,' I replied irritably.

'Don't worry, I'll get up early and clean up,' she announced.

'Amanda, it's two o'clock in the morning. That means you'll have to get up before you go to bed!'

But for her, the night was still young. She glanced at her diamond-studded watch, and settled herself more comfortably on the bed. She seemed alert and restless, as if sleep were the last thing on her mind. I wondered vaguely if she had taken some sort of stimulant at Shariffi's that would keep her going until morning. 'What's happening with Elliot, by the way?' she asked suddenly. 'Why isn't he here, whispering sweet nothings in your ear?'

'It's over with Elliot,' I told her, thinking that 'sweet nothings' was all they ever were. His words meant nothing to me now; I knew I would find no consolation there. Nor was Amanda's company making me feel better, I thought, wondering how to get rid of her.

'Wait until you meet Jeddi – Shariffi's friend,' she was saying dreamily. 'He's unattached and gorgeous – drives a red Lamborghini and . . .'

'Amanda, I think I could fall asleep now,' I cut in, sinking down beneath the sheets.

To my relief, she said, 'I'll go then,' and got up gracefully, tiptoeing out of the room.

But sleep did not come. I lay there for another hour, then in desperation swallowed one of the white pills.

Amanda's description had not been far off – it knocked me out, then sent me cruising through rough waters. I dreamt I was adrift in a wooden rowing boat that was slowly sinking. As I sank into the cold sea, I knew with an extraordinary clarity that I was drowning, but had neither the energy nor the will to fight. Then suddenly Father was trying to save me. He was able to speak, although we were both under the waves, and he was saying 'Keep calm, Emily, if you keep calm, nothing will happen. It's panic that kills . . .' and the next moment he was guiding me upwards towards the surface. But as I rose, he started sinking. I reached out to try and pull him back, but his white hair was moving further and further out of my reach. Then I started to scream. I knew I had to wake up, but the pill I had swallowed earlier was preventing me from surfacing, and I couldn't open my eyes.

At last I came round, to find Amanda sitting on the edge of the bed as if she had never left, except that now her hair was blown back in the shape of two horns, and her skin was oily from layers of newly applied foundation. She handed me a chipped mug full of pale tea, and waited while I struggled to sit up.

'God, what the hell did you give me last night?' I said thickly, still fighting off the ebbing waves of sleep.

'It was only mild,' she replied evasively. 'I often take them when I can't sleep.'

'That was no sleeping pill. It was more like an hallucinatory drug!'

'You slept, didn't you?' she said aggrievedly.

'I think I'd prefer to have lain awake all night,' I said, shuddering at the memory of the glassy look in Father's eyes. 'I had the most horrific nightmare.'

'Here, drink your tea,' she said.

After she'd left for work, I lay there drowsily, wondering how I was going to get through the day that stretched ahead. She telephoned during the morning and informed me that it was all organised for Saturday night. Shariffi and his handsome friend would come to the flat for a drink then take us on to the party.

If only I'd just said no and stuck to it, I was to berate myself afterwards. I didn't want to get caught up in Amanda's reckless life which, hectic as it was, seemed even more lonely than my own.

During that week, I returned to the Isle of Wight and, with the help of one of Father's friends, put the house on the market. The boatyard was sold too, and there were a number of offers for *Running Tide* – she went immediately. It all seemed horribly unreal, as if it were happening to somebody else. Numb and exhausted, I went back to London and tried to work. Over those bleak days, sustained by black coffee and cigarettes, I discovered that an excess of red wine would put me to sleep at night. But it also brought disquieting dreams, in which Mother and Father were still alive. I'd wake up with a start, only to sink into that dark hole again.

On the day of the famous sortie, I awoke feeling muzzy and disoriented, and informed Amanda that I didn't feel up to going.

'Oh, Emily, it's all arranged now,' she exclaimed. 'You *must* come. I'd be so disappointed.' Something in her manner hinted that I was letting her down badly. I wondered rather unkindly if her duties as Shariffi's mistress included providing his friends with partners, too. I knew Amanda well enough to know that love turned her ruthless.

She produced a polythene bag from a boutique in High Street Kensington that we both loved, saying, 'I even got you this, knowing you'd never go out and look for something yourself.'

Inside was a midnight blue crushed velvet dress with a plunging neckline. She was given to sudden bouts of generosity such as this, but they were seldom entirely altruistic.

My heart sank, but I managed to smile. 'Thanks,' I said defeatedly, 'but you shouldn't have.'

The dress fitted, in a contrived, revealing sort of way (Amanda said it showed off my enviable cleavage). I thanked her dutifully and, in spite of a presentiment that it was not a good idea, reluctantly agreed to go.

She left early that morning to spend the day with Shariffi, while I forced myself to sit at my desk and catch up on the backlog of work that had piled up over the last week. Among other things, I had to finish an article for *Healthy Lifestyle* on sea water as a beauty therapy. Thalassotherapy was coming into vogue, cosmetic companies making soap from seaweed and talking about its health-giving properties, and Sam Brooks, my editor, had suggested I visit some salt-water baths in Victoria and find out about any new treatments they were using in the salons.

The electric typewriter wasn't working. Irritated, I went into the kitchen to make myself a cup of coffee, only to realise the electricity had been cut off. It had been Amanda's turn to pay the bill. Cursing her, I fumbled around in the door of the fridge and found a carton of orange juice, poured some of it into a glass, and topped it up with vodka. I drank it down in one go and poured another. Then, feeling marginally better, I took out the little manual typewriter Father had given me and typed the heading: THE SEA – A LIFE SUPPORT SYSTEM.

Instantly I had a vivid picture of Father standing in front of me, back ramrod-straight, fiddling with the white tip of his moustache. He was so different from the glassy, drowning man I had seen in my dream that I felt a vague uplifting of spirits.

'Write about the biggest adventure of all, Emily,' he was saying, and suddenly my chest ached, and I bent over the machine and wept in an agony of tears for Father, larger than life, and for the great void he had left behind; for Mother, who had never managed to escape the past in spite of her efforts; and for myself, who now had to live without them.

I opened the window and stared out over the Finchley Road, watching the endless stream of traffic, the shoppers, mothers with pushchairs and men heading for the pubs, and wondered where all these people were going and why. Whatever they were doing seemed pointless; buying food that would soon be eaten, objects that would become worn out, gifts later discarded.

And I, writing articles soon to be forgotten? To what end? I thought.

Dazedly, I moved closer to the window and watched, as if in a dream, my body float through the air and land with a thud on the pavement. I imagined the passers-by, stopping and gathering in a silent circle around me . . . My breath was coming in short gasps as I stood swaying in front of the open window; the street below wavered in and out of focus.

And then the phone rang, and I jumped back in alarm.

I slammed the window shut, and moved swiftly towards it. It was Amanda.

'Just checking,' she said gaily. 'Everything OK?'

'Fine,' I said, aware my body was shaking uncontrollably, in spasm.

'Are you sure?'

'Quite sure.' My voice seemed to be wavering too.

'You sound a bit strange.' To my relief she moved on. 'I was ringing to say I'll be home early, to help tidy up and change. Shariffi and Jeddi will come around eight.'

For a moment I couldn't think what she was talking about. Then I remembered the party. 'We'd better meet them somewhere else,' I said. 'The electricity's been cut off.'

'Damn, it's my fault, I've been meaning to pay the bill for ages, but it went right out of my mind. I'm sorry, Em – look, you could come and spend the afternoon here?'

'No, it's all right,' I said hastily. 'I'm working on the manual typewriter.'

'Well look at it this way,' she said with a giggle. 'It'll be all the more romantic!'

Jeddi was, as Amanda had promised, handsome, cultivated and charming. At least that was the initial impression. He greeted me with a slight bow, presenting a single red rose. But the gesture itself turned me cold. The events of the last few days had left me feeling oddly detached, as if I weren't taking part in the evening at all, but watching it from afar. I sat there in a daze as candles were lit, champagne opened and glasses produced, the shadows from the flickering light adding to the general haziness.

Shariffi and Jeddi wore dark suits, white silk scarves, and slip-on shoes that shone like mirrors. They reeked of conflicting after-shaves, and sat like bookends on either end of the sofa with Amanda wedged between them. Shariffi glared around the room through hooded eyes, as if searching for a hidden diversion in some dark corner – a naked dancer, perhaps, to appear and perform for him.

Amanda was in her element. She laughed and flirted, tossing her stiff hair, captivating the two men within minutes. Her dress was tight and as shiny as an oil slick, and a rope of black pearls, a gift from a past lover, was wound around her slender neck. Her heels were so high and spindly I feared they might snap off.

'Em's the clever one,' she announced (using a nickname she had recently devised, and which I hated). She spoke in the high, girlish voice she reserved for occasions such as these, insinuating that she was therefore the pretty one. And, in her overt way, she was the focal point in the room – the type of woman whose beauty is questionable, but whose drawing power is undeniable.

We drank a couple of bottles of champagne, but somehow the evening remained flat. Amanda put on some music in a futile attempt to bridge the silences, making it even more difficult to converse.

I felt that, by agreeing to come, I had wantonly accepted some unwritten contract, while knowing all the time I wasn't going to fulfil the terms. The champagne, the rose, the escort, the party – my presentiment that something bad was going to happen had been replaced by a dull sense of inevitability. It was only a matter of time before the seducing began.

They talked between themselves for a while, about some Arab who wanted to buy a famous department store in London, and about Shariffi's less ambitious but nonetheless grandiose plan to purchase a shopping precinct outside London, on the A4. Amanda's expression of contrived interest implied this was all part and parcel of the high life she lived, but I could tell she was finding it as dull as I was.

As the evening wore on, Shariffi wound up like a spring. He tapped his skinny leg to a rhythm of its own and shifted on the sofa as though eager to be off. Jeddi's interest in me had started to pall, apart from the occasional glance at my chest, but he too seemed poised for action, like a wild animal ready to pounce.

Amanda, bored by the conversation, suggested it was time we leave, so we got up and trooped out into the late summer evening to where an ugly white sportscar with black spoilers was parked, and set off towards Park Lane. Amanda and I were ushered into the cramped back seat, while Shariffi behind the wheel sat so low down he almost disappeared. And then we were off, revving up with a roar, white scarves flying in the breeze as we fish-tailed our way through the congested evening traffic. Their dark hair gleamed in oily waves and they embarked on a guttural exchange, apparently forgetting our presence, as they drove.

Amanda, furious at being relegated to the back, went into a sulk, and I too sat mute and cramped, numbed by the champagne and the circumstances. But in spite of my befuddled stated, I had a plan of escape. I would put in an appearance, as I had promised, then make an excuse and take a taxi home.

We pulled up outside a tall, Regency-style building and went into a marble foyer, past a dripping stone fountain, up in a caged lift to a large, dimly lit apartment, where it seemed the party was already in full swing. Framed Dalis covered one wall (the one with the face pinned down had been blown up to gigantic proportions), and I recognised a couple of Esher's famous labyrinths on the opposite wall. Rock music blared from two giant speakers, and in the centre of the room a jumble of swaying bodies moved to their own rhythm. Some danced crazily, performing an odd ritual of their own, others swayed on the spot like reeds in the wind; there seemed to be no direct communication between each couple. There were champagne corks popping everywhere, and the feel of mounting tension in the air, as if everything was heading towards some strange climax.

Somebody handed us champagne, and we were drawn into the mêlée by a twisting, gyrating Shariffi, who seemed to have been waiting all night for this moment. Forgetting all about us, he melted into the crowd of dancers, removed his belt and, using it as a whip, slashed a circle of space around him, so the dancers moved back. Now his eyes had taken on a crazed look, and he danced to his own tune. Amanda bobbed along beside him for a while, then went and sat dejectedly on a black leather couch close to the door, while I made my way through the alcove into the adjoining room – partly out of curiosity, but also to get away from the thumping music, which was beginning to pound in my head.

Here, groups of people sat around talking in low, intense voices, and I watched a dark-faced man lift a tiny spoon to his nose, sniff deeply, then hand it to the girl beside him, who touched it with the tip of her tongue. After some moments I heard Jeddi's voice behind me. 'Why don't you sit down and partake?' He placed his hand on the small of my back and urged me forwards.

'I'd rather not,' I said coldly, moving away. He was starting to give me the creeps.

'What are you doing in the "powder room" then?' he inquired with irony.

'Just visiting,' I replied, backing away.

'You know that curiosity killed the cat,' he said, causing a shiver to go through me.

I sensed his eyes travelling up and down the length of my body as I retreated, then saw him sit down beside a girl with matchstick arms and legs.

Back in the main room, the people still danced. Rich beyond dreams, they sought an even higher plane, free at last from the restrictions of life in their own war-torn country.

Jeddi came out of the 'powder room' some time later, with the matchstick girl; I watched them go towards what must have been the bedrooms, and had a vivid picture of two naked bodies clanking together in the dark. So this is how it all ends, I thought – the climax of the evening. Time to leave.

I went across the room to where Amanda was sitting on the sofa, smoking what looked like a joint. The music was so loud my throat ached when I spoke. 'Amanda, let's get out of here,' I shouted.

'But it's still early,' she replied distantly. Her eyes were fixed on Shariffi, who was winding down now, as the music slowed, sweat pouring down his face.

'Well I'm going,' I told her. 'It's too loud and hectic, and I'm starting to get a headache. I'll get a taxi.'

But as I spoke, Shariffi came up behind me and wound a skinny arm around my waist.

'You're not leaving yet, I hope,' he said seductively. 'The party has only just begun.'

It was the first time he had addressed me all evening. He spun me around and stared into my eyes. 'What's the problem? You seem nervous . . . Emily.' He touched the side of my face with a bony finger, making me flinch. 'I have something that will take the tension away.'

'No thanks,' I said, edging out of his grasp. 'I'm not too keen on your remedies!' But before I could escape, he had pulled me down beside him on the leather sofa, next to Amanda. He took a scrunched-up ball of silver foil from his pocket and carefully unwrapped it. I watched him stick two cigarette papers together then carefully mix some of the contents of the foil with tobacco, before rolling it into what looked like a giant cigarette.

'Here,' he said, when it was lit, 'it'll give you pleasant dreams.'

I had had it before, of course. At college it was often floating around, and later with Elliot, who claimed it helped him write great words of wisdom. But it had never affected me like the drug Shariffi handed me that night.

Through a haze, I was aware of some sort of commotion at the door. Everything happened so fast after that. Shariffi bolted up, and somebody shouted 'Turn the music down!' causing people to stop dancing and turn in silent horror towards the door. I looked too; saw the blue uniforms, and froze.

One non-uniformed man stood slightly apart from the rest, pointing towards the alcove. The man who had turned the music down spun around like a top, and yelled through into the adjoining room 'Cops!' causing a sudden silence. Shariffi made a strange guttural noise in the back of his throat, as if he were choking, before attempting to dart away towards the bedrooms. But the plain-clothes officer yelled, 'Nobody move! Arrest the whole lot of 'em!'

In the ensuing chaos, I remember only three things clearly. A policeman sprinting through to the other room; the young sergeant standing over me, his eyes trained on the ball of silver paper that now lay in my lap; and Shariffi's eyes glittering as he turned away.

Amanda had started sobbing hysterically. 'Tell them we had nothing to do with it,' she implored Shariffi, 'tell them, for Christ's sake!'

The young policeman had found the smoking joint on the floor close to the sofa, where I had thrown it, and was sniffing at it suspiciously.

'She has nothing to do with all this,' Amanda shrieked, as the policeman led me away. 'Tell him, Shariffi, tell him . . .'

The wrenching sound of her sobs made the policeman hesitate.

He turned around, still holding my arm, and we all waited in silence for Shariffi to say something. But it was the policeman who spoke.

'May I remind you that anything you say may be taken down and used in evidence?'

'Tell him, Shariffi,' Amanda begged, 'for God's sake.'

Shariffi's eyes were wide and staring. There was a feverish, jaundiced look about him, standing there jiggling his foot like a tap dancer. He glanced from Amanda to the policeman and back again, and I saw a sudden spark of hatred in his black eyes. It burnt for only a brief instant, then he turned away without a word.

The police rounded up the group from the 'powder room' and herded them into a van, while Amanda and I were hustled into a Black Maria and driven to Savile Row station. It was all very dramatic, but unreal. Anaesthetised by other recent horrors, the seriousness of our situation didn't hit me then, nor for some time afterwards.

After a nightmarish weekend in jail – for nothing could be done until Monday – Amanda and I were released on bail. Marijuana being a soft drug, it was considered a misdemeanour. Had we been caught partaking in the 'powder room', we would have been given a prison sentence.

Shariffi was sentenced and later extradited. Jeddi followed, having been caught on top of the matchstick girl, several grams of cocaine hidden in his discarded trousers.

While I walked away, with a criminal record.

Of course it could have been a lot worse. We had a three-month suspended sentence, which we knew we would never serve, but there was the humiliating business of probation ahead, as well as the uncomfortable knowledge that we would remain on police files for the rest of our lives.

Only later, much later, when I was in the midst of the worst battle of my life, would I realise the full implications of all this. And become, like Mother, a victim of the past.

Chapter Five

Amanda moved out soon afterwards. Our relationship was never the same again. She remained contrite for about a week, then bounced back with her usual resilience, but I had lost patience with her by then, and blamed her for what had happened. She had finally destroyed my last illusions about butterfly women.

Mrs Poppelwell still telephoned looking for her, turning a blind eye on recent events, and I gave her Amanda's new number, but she continued to ring in an absent-minded sort of way. Some time later I saw Amanda in Harrods, arm in arm with a stocky little man with hairy hands and a gold tooth. They were so engrossed in one another that she didn't notice me.

I found a new flatmate, a girl called Clare Meadows, who worked for a bank and was very tidy and hard-working. She paid the bills on time, did her share of the cleaning, and we got on well in a polite sort of way, but from time to time I missed Amanda. Through good times and bad, she had always been a source of entertainment.

The visits to the probation officer ended, but the dark period continued, a dull and lonely time when sometimes, sitting at my desk staring out over the Finchley Road, I wondered again whether life was worth living. We were approaching the end of the year. Mother and Father had been gone for three months, yet it still felt like yesterday.

As the weather grew colder, I began work on my novel – a doomed love story, loosely based on Mother's life. But even as I wrote, her memory was already slipping away. Like a dying snail, she had left only a thin trace behind her – a pile of novels, a couple of photo albums dating back to the early days on the Isle of Wight, and an unfinished portrait that hung in the bedroom at Heronlough.

I wrote to Aunt G at the end of November, asking if she had kept any photographs of Mother as a girl. I also asked about the love affair; hoping, perhaps, that by learning more I could keep her memory alive.

Only in the final paragraph, like an afterthought, did I mention the drama with Amanda and my 'run in' with the law. I might have had difficulty explaining this to Mother and Father, had they been alive. I could imagine Mother's reaction – that bewildered expression which crossed her face when something bad had happened. She would have sat down defeatedly, hunched against the weight of it, and wondered where she had gone wrong. Whereas Aunt G was more likely to blame the Fates for having landed me in the wrong place at the wrong time. And in this case, I was proved right. But although her reply was consoling with regard to my own bad fortune, it was disappointing vis-à-vis Mother's. Once again she evaded the issue.

Her handwriting was almost illegible, as if she had guided her pen painfully across the page before veering off the edge, the effort having proved too much for her. I couldn't make out some of the words on the right hand side of the thin sheet of paper.

'My dear Emily,' she began, 'what a run of bad luck you've had! Those dreadful . . .' I stared at the next word; it looked like 'Turks' (Aunt G had a habit of calling any foreigner of dusky origin a Turk). '. . . sound a desperate lot – you poor girl.'

The next part was illegible, then I read, 'I worry about you, Emily dear, all alone in that large unfriendly city. I wish you'd come and spend some time at Heronlough. It would do you the world of good to get away from that nasty smog . . .' (Aunt G's memories of London were still shrouded in smog.) I skipped the next bit – a further illegible comment about London – and read on.

'The garden is looking windswept and bedraggled, what with all the rain we've been having. There has been flooding all over the country in the last few days and the lough is higher than I have ever known it.

'. . . as far as your poor mother is concerned, I can only tell you that the business with Murphy was a chapter of her life she wanted more than anything to forget. It left a very bad atmosphere indeed, hence her decision to leave Ireland and the past behind. I have always respected her wishes, knowing better than anyone, perhaps, what a wrench it was for her to leave the country she loved.'

I stared at the next paragraph, trying to decipher the few scrawled words. '. . . in spite of everything, she left a part of herself behind . . .'

'Come and spend Christmas with me at Heronlough,' she continued. 'I have written to Charlotte suggesting the same, and am still awaiting a reply. I know it's a busy time for her with the restaurant. Christmas can be lonely. Yours, Geraldine.'

I decided I would take the week off, catch the train to Holyhead and from there the ferry across to Dunlaoghaire, as Mother, Charlotte and I had done almost ten years earlier.

Slowly, painfully, over the days leading up to Christmas, I started writing Mother's story, a love affair between two people from different worlds, based on my own conjectures of how it must have been. Tom Murphy, the dashing hero, romantic and happy-go-lucky, had lured Mother away from the fold with his talent and his charm. I imagined Mother, hypnotised and helpless against the magnetic pull of him, yet terrorised by the consequences; the two families, already at war, up in arms against it. There had been only the one route open to them, as far as I could tell – to run away and get married. I could imagine the frantic plans they must have made, which had come to nothing. The families had proved too strong for them. I called the novel *The Love Trap*, and imagined I was portraying a fairly universal picture of forbidden love. But only when my own life had veered off course, drawing me closer to the truth, did I realise how close I had been, yet how far away.

Aunt G sent Jimmy to meet me off the boat at Dunlaoghaire and drive me to Heronlough. He had aged considerably since I'd last seen him; the remains of his hair hung in thin wisps over his forehead, and he had lost most of his teeth.

''Tis grand to see you, Miss Emily,' he greeted me heartily. 'Sorry to hear of your troubles.'

He talked non-stop as he drove, embarking on his own troubles – a dreadful story of his cousin Aggie, who had also recently passed away.

''Twas a terrible thing, Miss Emily,' he said, his lips collapsing into the cavern of his mouth as he spoke. 'She took to her bed on the Friday, just like that, and they brought her into the hospital on the Satherday . . .' He paused and made the sign of the cross, losing control of the Daimler for a second and narrowly avoiding a milk float, then continued on a dramatic note. 'On the Sunday –

the Lord's day,' he emphasised, 'before I'd even got to Mass, they put her down like a common dog, so they did. A common dog.'

I was momentarily lost for words. 'That's awful, Jimmy,' I said at last, shocked, yet trying hard not to smile at the image of poor Aggie being injected with a fatal dose. 'I'm so sorry!'

'A common dog,' he kept repeating at intervals, as we crawled along the wet winding roads towards Heronlough.

'How is Aunt G?' I ventured, in an effort to get him off the subject. 'Is she getting out and about much?'

'Ah she's grand,' he replied. 'Doesn't venture far these days, all the same. Too busy with them brushes and paints.'

'Is she still driving?' I asked him. In her last letter she had mentioned a problem with her hands.

Jimmy grunted and shook his head. ''Tis a rare occasion to get her behind the wheel now – thanks be to God.' He lowered his voice confidentially, and added, 'Even the birds do be taking to the trees when they see her coming!'

Again I hid a smile, happy at least to be back in Ireland.

The village of Rathegan had spread in the past ten years. Identical-looking houses had sprung up around it, and a factory sprawled where once green fields had been. The main street had been widened so the trucks could pass through it on their way south; Christmas lights were strung across it, and dusty bunting flapped in the breeze. Yet in spite of this there was a deserted air about it, as if everybody had decided to stay home in front of the fire.

'They're all jollificating,' Jimmy informed me. 'It being Christmas week and all. . . .'

I thought of happy families sitting around Christmas trees singing carols, then he added, 'They'll have taken to the pubs to drink – there'll be hell to pay on the roads, so there will.'

We passed Murphy's Lounge Bar, and I saw the outline of a Christmas tree lit up within, and noticed somebody had sprayed Merry Xmas on the door with fake frosting. Murphy's Food Store (formerly Paddy Whelan's) was now a small supermarket, and there were four petrol pumps outside it where once there had been two. Now we were out of the village, driving past the green fields and hedgerows towards Heronlough.

We turned up the drive, splashing along the muddy track

beneath an arch of shedding beech trees, Jimmy humming to himself now, the sad business of cousin Aggie forgotten. Everything looked colourless in its winter setting, the trees dark and skeletal against an iron grey sky. We crossed the humpback bridge over the swamp, and I saw the rushes had keeled over, to lie limply in the swollen weed-choked water. Then we rounded the last bend to the house.

The paintwork was peeling slightly, revealing the grey stone beneath, and a few more tiles were missing from the roof, but it was otherwise as I remembered it. Smoke drifted from the chimney, and the windows had misted up.

Aunt G came out onto the porch as we drew up. She was dressed in her winter woollies, a mohair shawl, and thick stockings. She held out her arms, and I rushed into them, smelling the familiar lavender smell of her skin. 'Into the kitchen with you, child, and get yourself warmed up.' She examined me, exclaiming, 'But you've got so thin! There's hardly a pick on you.'

I had noticed vaguely that my clothes had started hanging loosely on me, but I never seemed to have much of an appetite these days.

The kitchen table had been laid for a feast, with a cooked ham, various cold cuts, home-made chutney, potato salad, and thick slices of soda bread. On the Aga, a vegetable soup simmered. For the first time in ages, I felt a stirring of hunger. Bridget came out of the pantry, cheeks flushed, and greeted me shyly.

'We'll have our sherry in the drawing room,' Aunt G instructed her, leading me away. The drawing room fire had been lit, and the curtains drawn, making the room seem even more cosy and cluttered than I remembered. I looked around, admiring a couple of oil paintings I hadn't seen before. The artist had managed to capture the mood of the bleak coastline that stretched below Heronlough.

I turned back to Aunt G and said, 'Jimmy says you've been painting again. I'd love to see what you've done.'

'Ah, there's time enough for that,' she replied, sitting down heavily on the worn sofa. She patted the space beside her, gesturing for me to join her. 'I want to hear how you're getting on, first. How are you feeling, Emily dear?'

'I miss them terribly,' I said, staring fixedly at the Persian rug in front of the fireplace.

She lit a cigarette, and handed me the packet. 'I know,' she said softly. 'It's as if somebody has cut you in half and stolen the pieces. The pain eases, but you never get over the loss.'

Our eyes met, and, aware of an unspoken empathy between us, I remembered she too had loved Mother deeply.

We sat for a while longer sipping our sherry and chatting, then she said, 'Come on, let's get some food into you, girl, otherwise you'll fade away to nothing.'

We spent most of that week in the kitchen, warmed by the heat from the Aga, drinking tea and discussing the future, while Bridget bustled around us. Did I plan on staying in London, Aunt G wanted to know? It was a lonely place for a single girl, she emphasised. She was right. Once, I had been able to escape to the Isle of Wight and Mother and Father . . .

When I didn't answer, she said, 'Don't forget, there's always Heronlough. You must think of it as your second home.'

One damp afternoon, she took me to the attic to show me some of her recent work. She had just completed what was perhaps her best piece, an oil painting which she'd named 'Three Old Biddies', whom she likened to herself, only these women were poor and dressed in long tattered skirts and dark shawls. They were walking along a narrow boreen, bent forward against the wind. I liked it almost as much as I liked 'The Railway Cottage'.

'It might well be my last,' she told me as I stood there admiring it.

'Why?' I asked, then moments later noticed her hands. They were hunched, the fingers blue and swollen, the blood no longer circulating there.

'Arthritis,' she said. 'They say a copper bracelet is meant to help, but it doesn't work for me!'

She sat down in front of her easel with a sigh.

'That's awful,' I said, distressed, for painting was one of her greatest joys.

'Oh, I'll find something else to keep me busy,' she said dismissively. 'A big old house like this. . .'

'Perhaps you should have an exhibition,' I suggested, not fooled by her overbright tone, and remembering she had held one in the past. 'You have quite a collection.'

She laughed. 'Old souvenirs, that's all they are,' she said. 'Just clutter.'

'I'd buy every one of them, if I could afford to,' I told her. 'I'd love to have my own collection one day. Why did you stop selling them?'

'I needed the money, then,' she answered briefly. 'By the way, I meant to tell you in my last letter – "The Railway Cottage" is yours. Consider it your birthday present. I know how much you like it. You'll have to work out how to get it back to London, of course.'

'Thanks, Aunt G,' I said, touched beyond words.

She got up to leave, and I was about to follow when I spotted a portrait of a handsome young officer amongst her canvases. He was dressed in a khaki service uniform, with badges of rank on his shoulder. I stared at it curiously.

'Who's that?' I asked, wondering why she had never shown it to me before.

She turned around, saying shortly, 'That's a young man I used to know.'

Curiosity got the better of me. 'What happened to him?' I asked, sensing I shouldn't.

'He was killed in the battle of Alamein in 1941,' she told me.

'Were you in love with him?' I ventured, calculating that she must have already been in her thirties by then.

She frowned, and I was afraid for a moment that I'd angered her, but she said, 'Any more questions? If so, I'll sit down again.'

'I'm sorry,' I said.

'Yes, in answer to your question – we were to be wed, only he was killed in action.'

So that was why she'd never married, I thought.

'You must have really loved him,' I said, wondering why it was that the people you loved most were taken away from you.

'Yes,' she replied. 'But better to have loved and lost, as they say.'

'Was there nobody else?' I ventured. From the pictures of her as a young girl, she had been quite beautiful, with a mass of pale reddish hair, which she'd worn in a plait around her head.

She shook her head. 'One person doesn't replace another,' she said, as if it were as simple as that. 'We met rather late in life . . . I was already set in my ways. When he died, I knew there wouldn't be anyone else.'

I thought of the lonely years she must have spent. But there was no trace of regret in her voice.

She smiled suddenly. 'A bit like the Whooper swans who migrate from Iceland in the winter. One partner for life!'

I stared at her. 'But if their partner dies . . . ?'

'Ah, then, if it's not too late, they will most likely mate again.'

So it had been too late for her. Had she regretted not having children of her own, I wondered. As if she'd read my thoughts, she said, 'You know, you remind me so much of your mother at times. She was such a curious child . . .' She paused, then added, 'She was like a daughter to me.'

A lump formed in my throat.

She got up suddenly, walked over to a shelf, and took down a large dusty folder. Inside were a series of sketches of swans in flight, taking off and landing on the lough in a flurry of white spray – always in pairs. She'd called the series 'Swan Season'.

'They're beautiful,' I said in awe. 'You must frame them.'

'Maybe I will,' she said vaguely. 'They've been hidden away up here far too long. He once joked that he'd be back with the swans – but winter came and went . . . Anyway,' she snapped the folder shut abruptly, 'things worked out differently.' There was a catch in her throat, causing her to cough painfully.

Alarmed, I went over to the basin where she washed her brushes, and filled a tumbler with water.

'Dust,' she said, when it had passed. 'Come on, enough about the past,' she added briskly. 'It's chilly up here, and I could do with a cup of tea.'

I tried several times over that week to get her back onto the subject of Mother. I learnt that the 'rough diamond' had returned from foreign parts half pickled with the drink, and that one of the sons now ran the bar. I wondered briefly if it was the one I'd seen trespassing on the lough all those years ago, the one with the beautiful chiselled face. Twice I ventured into the village, but the pub was closed. In the evenings I was content to sit in the warm kitchen with Aunt G, while Bridget baked soda bread, as if nothing had changed.

But at night, I would lie in bed thinking about Mother, and her love affair with Tom Murphy. Why had it caused such a scandal? Things had been different in those postwar days, Aunt G had explained. Ireland had remained neutral throughout the war, and apart from the odd shortage – tea and petrol coming to mind – life had remained relatively trouble-free. Some of the Flavells had gone off and become officers, ending up serving in the Indian Army, and other Irishmen had joined the British Army, since jobs were scarce, while the Murphys had quietly prospered with their farmland and later the pub. Was it these differences that had driven a further wedge between the two families, or was it simply a class thing?

On Christmas day, Aunt G invited the daft cousins Lilly and Louise Flavell, whom I vaguely remembered from the memorial service, over for sherry and Christmas cake, and we all sat around yelling deafly at one another in front of a smoking wood fire.

At one stage, Aunt G left the room and the bossier of the two old ladies suddenly turned to me, her blue eyes glittering, and said, 'You're the spitting image of your mother, so you are.' She nodded disagreeably, as if the idea displeased her. 'I hope you've got a bit more sense in your head!'

I didn't reply, not knowing how to defend either Mother or myself. Only then did I finally understand what Mother must have gone through, and why she had been forced to leave like she had. I imagined the walls starting to close around her; sensed the cold wind of disapproval, the petty parochial censure echoing accusingly down the years.

Later, when I told Aunt G, she said, 'It's a people that cannot forgive nor forget, whose past encroaches on the present, a country where sorrow begets sorrow and old sins die hard.' As for the old woman, Louise Flavell, she added, 'She has led a little life, thriving on other people's misfortunes.' She urged me not to give it another thought.

After they had left, we exchanged Christmas presents. I had bought Aunt G a tartan shawl I could ill afford from The Scotch House, which she put on with great exclamations of pleasure, before handing me a large package wrapped in brown paper and tied with string.

' "The Railway Cottage",' I thought, tearing it open eagerly. And, with a jolt, saw Mother's face gazing back at me.

'But . . .' I gasped, 'I thought you said I could have "The Railway Cottage".'

'They're both yours,' she answered, 'but I wanted this one to be a surprise. I only hope it doesn't cause a squabble between you and Charlotte . . . But you're the one who wanted souvenirs.'

I hugged her fiercely. 'It's the start of my collection. But what happens when you become really famous, and your paintings are worth a fortune?'

'Then,' she said with a smile, 'you can decide whether you want to part with them or not.'

She also gave me some faded photographs of Mother as a girl, and a couple she had found of her and Father, sailing off in *Running Tide*.

'I don't know what I'd do without you,' I said.

She smiled. 'Well I intend hanging onto my perch for the time being – as long as I can be of some use to you.'

On the last day, we walked down to the lough together. It was a mild winter afternoon, the sky streaked with thin clouds. Aunt G had brought her binoculars, and was pointing out the various birds that nested in the salt marshes surrounding the lough.

As we reached the water, she spotted a group of swans some way away, where the sea merged into grassy swampland.

'Look at that!' she exclaimed, handing me the binoculars. 'Whoopers! You can recognise them by their slightly different bill pattern.'

But I was miles away, thinking of the handsome young officer who had never come back.

'They come to escape those fierce Icelandic winters,' she was saying, as I tried to focus on them. 'They're part of the changing seasons . . .' She looked at me meaningfully, and added, 'A reminder that life continues.'

Back in London, I began working on *The Love Trap* in earnest. And as I wrote Mother lived on, or so it seemed, her picture gazing down on me, providing a comfort of sorts.

Then, quite suddenly, everything changed. In the same way that memory can flick from winter to summer, one instant it was grey and hopeless, and in the next dazzling moment, there was Michel.

Chapter Six

I had been commissioned to write an article on fashions from France, and the women who were selling them. An interview had been set up with a young Parisienne called Florence Dubois, who owned a boutique in Bute Street, South Kensington. That interview was the first step into a glamorous world that was to change everything.

Florence Dubois was tiny, five foot at the most; one of those petite, compact women who tend to make one feel large and clumsy. She was dressed fluffily, in an appliquéd woollen dress and red suede pumps, and her hair, swept back from her oval face, was secured with a large red bow that matched the ones on her shoes.

The clothes that hung on the rails in her shop were classically French. Culottes with matching tops, blazers, cruise wear in nautical colours, safari suits and fancy cocktail dresses, all flounces and bows.

The interview went very well. She volunteered most of the information without much probing on my part, which was a relief – delving into people's lives was not my forte, nor was writing about them something I relished. As I was gathering my notes and preparing to leave, Florence swept her china blue eyes over me, taking in my old corduroy skirt and jumper that had gone bobbly with age, and said, 'If you would like something from the shop, I would be happy to offer you a discount.'

Taken aback, I muttered that I wasn't looking for anything at present (this wasn't true, I was always looking), but thanked her all the same. Even with a discount, the prices were extortionate. Besides, I never went on cruises or safaris, nor had many invitations to cocktail parties come my way.

'Have a look,' she insisted. She was one of those bossy, assertive little women whom you tend to obey, so I got up dutifully and went towards a rail where cocktail dresses glittered and floated on cushioned hangers, my mind still on the interview. I had learnt by then that her husband was a French psychiatrist with a practice in Harley Street, and the couple lived in a house in Chelsea.

'Anything you like?' she asked, coming up behind me.

'I'm not sure I'd find the occasion to wear such clothes,' I said inadequately, 'lovely as they are.'

She shrugged loftily, as if I had insulted her, so her next sentence took me completely by surprise.

'Come to my house for dinner on Friday night,' she said. 'I need a nice woman for my table.'

At the time, I couldn't understand why she asked me. I was hardly decorative compared to the elegant women who frequented her shop, and how she could have deduced whether I was nice or not from our short exchange was a mystery. I searched for an excuse, but came up with nothing. As I dithered, she scribbled an address on the back of a business card and handed it to me. 'Eight o'clock,' she said. '*Tenue de ville.*'

As I walked out of the shop clutching the address, I realised how foolish I had been not to take her up on her offer after all. One of those dresses would have been ideal. Now I'd have to fall back on the black crêpe dress I always wore when unsure of the occasion.

I arrived at the house in Sydney Street at eight-thirty that Friday evening, and nervously rang the bell. A black-coated waiter opened the door and greeted me formally in French, then ushered me into the drawing room as if I were royalty. A group of smartly dressed people stood in the centre of the room, yelling French loudly at one another.

My first reaction was to backtrack, and I wondered if there was some way of slipping past the bowing waiter and out through the door again. This was going to be an ordeal, I thought, trying to sum up the remnants of my school French. I took a step back, but suddenly Florence Dubois appeared out of the group and came towards me, looking like a china doll in a black ruched party frock.

'I thought you weren't coming,' she said directly.

'I'm sorry I'm late – I had trouble finding a taxi,' I improvised.

'Come with me,' she said linking her arm through mine, and led me into the throng of guests, who parted politely to let us through. 'There are a couple of English people over there,' she said, gesturing toward a chattering group, then led me in the opposite direction, towards two men who stood apart from the rest, deep in conversation.

The dark-haired man had a broad athletic body, almost black hair, and greenish eyes. He held his drink in his left hand, waving it around in accompaniment to his words, while the other hand remained buried in his pocket. I was aware that the other man had red hair, nothing else; I was so transfixed by the dark one.

His face wasn't particularly handsome, on closer inspection. The features were uneven, and the nose bumped at the bridge. He had that rugged look I often read about in novels, but seldom encountered. His mouth was slightly crooked when he smiled, but there was a mesmerising quality of easy confidence about him when he spoke. He wore a navy blue blazer and dark trousers, yet somehow managed to look more casual than the other men around him.

Through a haze, I heard Florence say 'Gerard Mesclain,' and was aware that I was shaking the red-haired man's hand, while my eyes remained on the dark one. 'And this is Michel Gautier.'

He smiled unevenly, deepening the creases around his eyes. '*Enchanté*,' he said, taking my hand. And for one glorious, spellbound moment, it seemed that he really was.

We had no sooner exchanged pleasantries than dinner was announced and we were ushered into a dining room, where a table was set for twelve. I was placed between Gerard Mesclain and a serious-looking Englishman called Robert Ellis, who spoke perfect French, directing most of it over my head at Gerard, who had to lean forward each time, as if I were an obstacle in his path. Michel sat opposite, sandwiched between two beautiful French girls, as thin as sticks, who punctuated each course with cigarettes – keeping Michel, who didn't appear to smoke, busy with the lighters. They seemed to be carrying on in the same way as my neighbours, conducting a conversation between them that criss-crossed over Michel's head. I caught his eye once or twice, and once he winked at me in silent acknowledgement of this extra-ordinary breach of etiquette, but remained apparently unfazed.

We were served some sort of raw fish salad to begin with, coquilles in a piquant vinaigrette. I emptied my wine glass each time it was filled, and listened half-heartedly to the different conversations around the table. They were a sporty, competitive crowd, who skied in glamorous resorts in the winter and migrated down to the Riviera in the summer. At the top end, where Florence reigned, they were discussing a power boat race in the South of France the year before that had ended in disaster. At my end, Gerard and Robert were in the middle of a business discussion, both now leaning forward, while Hervé Dubois talked to Michel about a yacht called *Jolie Brise* on which they had raced last season. The name rang a distant bell, but I couldn't think where I had heard it before. I sat there miserably, wondering if I was destined to listen to boating talk for the rest of the evening.

It was proving to be more of an ordeal than I had expected. I must have stopped listening after that – I'd recently developed a habit of blanking out things I didn't want to hear – for suddenly the conversation had moved on. Hervé had tilted his chair back in a listening attitude and was watching the two Frenchwomen, who now seemed to be vying for Michel's exclusive attention. They were talking about somebody called Marguerite, who was expected tonight but had suddenly left for New York.

'*Qu'est-ce qu'a passé entre vous deux?*' the one on his right was saying. She lowered her voice confidentially, while the other girl leant forward to listen.

'*Je ne sais pas,*' Michel replied shortly.

Hervé lifted his eyebrows, as though he knew something they didn't. He was a small balding man with an open enquiring face and the same intense gaze as his wife. I learnt later that he was a brilliant psychiatrist, and one of Michel's closest friends.

The girl on Michel's left said, in rapid French, 'I thought you were engaged to be married.'

There was an uncomfortable silence. Hervé shifted in his chair. I could sense immediately, as he had sensed, that Michel didn't want to talk about it; his face had taken on a curiously closed expression. He met the girl's inquisitive gaze with a hard look, and said, 'Well you thought wrong.' At least that was what I thought he said, but my French being limited, I couldn't be sure.

The plates were finally cleared away and a great serving dish, piled high with what looked like bones, was placed with relish in front of Florence.

'*Lapin,*' she announced, making my heart sink. I'd always been too sentimental to eat a rabbit. I wasn't the only one, it seemed. I noticed the Englishman beside me flinch at the news, and when the dish came around he held his hands up protestingly before passing it on to me. Not wanting to let the side down, I helped myself to a small amount, and soon we were all picking our way through clumps of bony meat without much enthusiasm. I tried to strike up a conversation with the Englishman, but he tilted backwards this time, and resumed his chat with Gerard.

It was then that I did something totally out of character, acted in a way that perhaps set a seal on the future. Fortified by the wine, emboldened by the look that had passed between Michel and myself, and furious at the behaviour of the two men on either side of me, I said loudly, 'Look, why doesn't one of you swap places with me? Robert, please take my place,' I ordered, 'then you won't have to talk over my head!'

There was silence around the table. You could have heard a pin drop. Everybody's eyes were fixed on me. It was a diversion from the faltering conversation and questionable food.

Gerard's face had turned the same colour as his hair. 'I'm so sorry,' he said finally, still in shock. 'How rude of us.' Robert cleared his throat and looked away, hoping perhaps that it would blow over, like a bad smell. But it was too late for either of them. I had scraped back my chair and stood up. Manners forced Gerard to his feet, and Robert sheepishly followed suit: amidst confusion and embarrassment, our plates were exchanged and Robert and I swapped places.

It was only later, when I dared look up again and meet all those eyes that were still on me, that I saw Michel wink again. He smiled briefly, causing my heart to continue hammering, only now it was partly from excitement over the silent rapport that had formed between us.

'*Chapeaux*,' he said, as we walked away from the dinner table. 'I should have followed your example. I must say, you took us all by surprise!' He touched me lightly on the elbow, making my heart lurch.

'I didn't mean to go quite that far,' I admitted, 'but well, we are in England . . .'

'I apologise for my compatriots' behaviour,' he said gallantly.

'One of them was mine,' I reminded him, thinking of the Englishman who had balked at the sight of the rabbit.

He had an excellent command of English, with only a trace of a French accent. I learnt he had gone to college in America, and moved to London a year ago. He was Swiss, not French, he told me; his family were from Lausanne, he had a real estate business in Geneva, and had come to London to start a second branch.

It was a good time for property, the early eighties; the pound was growing stronger, and interest rates were low. He had a Dutch partner, with whom he was in the midst of a project to build a shopping centre. I remembered that dreadful night with Shariffi and Jeddi, when they had talked of similar projects, and tried to blank out what had followed from my mind.

We were now back in the main room, perched on elegant chairs while coffee was passed around. Michel sat next to me, removed from the general conversation that filled the room. They were now talking about a slalom competition that had taken place in Courchevel.

'Tell me everything about you,' he said, sitting back comfortably, so his arm grazed mine.

'Oh you wouldn't want to know everything,' I replied diffidently.

'Yes, I would. I want to know where you get your temperament from!'

'My mother was Irish,' I told him, 'although not the red-headed temperamental type – in fact she had a far nicer nature than me.'

I told him then a bit about Mother, of the family feud and how she had fallen in love with the dashing Tom Murphy, causing a great furore. I moved on then to the Isle of Wight, and Father's dream of sailing away; of Toddy Freeman, who had realised it and never come back; and how it had all ended for Father on the way to the Fastnet Rock last August.

'I think Mother died partly from a broken heart after that,' I finished.

He stared at the ground for some moments, apparently at a loss. Then he said, 'You have a lot of courage – I find it admirable.'

I smiled. 'I'm afraid I don't. The last few months have been absolute hell . . . Although I've been feeling a bit better recently. Writing about it seems to help,' I added, explaining briefly about the novel.

It was then that he told me about the boat he kept on Lake

Geneva, christened *Jolie Brise* after the famous French boat that had won the early Fastnet races. So that was why the name had sounded so familiar! His boat, he explained, giving me another jolt, was a wooden sailing boat designed by William Fife.

It seemed to me, in my heightened state, that our meeting was more than a coincidence; some sort of twist of fate. Father would have been in his element to hear of another classic boat enthusiast, I thought. I was aware of a sudden swell of loss, as a vision of the two men deep in conversation flickered then faded away.

I told him, then, about Father's adventures on *Running Tide*, and how close he'd come to disaster on the Barrier Reef.

'Where is the boat now?' he inquired.

'She was sold, when the boatyard went. One of Father's colleagues bought her . . .' To my embarrassment, my voice wavered. I cleared my throat and took a deep breath. 'She's probably still out there somewhere, sailing across the Solent.'

He leant across and put his hand over mine, sending a tremor through me. His hand felt like a lead weight, pressing me to the ground, and causing heat to flood my face. Any moment now I would burst into flames, I thought. He was watching me closely, as if he too had sensed some kind of bond between us.

It was Florence who broke the spell – she had got hold of the coffee pot, snatching it out of the waiter's hand, and now she hovered above us like some sort of stunted sentry, her dress rustling as she waved it indignantly. She said something in French about anti-social behaviour, smiling falsely, as if she didn't really mean it. She didn't like the fact that I had not only disrupted her dinner arrangements, but also managed to distract one of her guests with my antics. She glared at me before bustling away, depositing the coffee pot awkwardly with the waiter on her way, so he burnt himself on the hot silver.

Imagining it was solely to do with my earlier *faux pas*, I said to Michel, 'I must apologise for behaving so badly – it's not as if I know her that well.'

He shrugged. 'Forget it,' he said. 'She's annoyed with me too, because I'm not being sociable.'

'Apart from skiing and sailing, what other sports do you do?' I asked him.

'A lot of watersports. I used to be a scuba diving instructor,' he told me. 'And when there's no snow, I go rock climbing, or hang gliding. What about you?'

'I didn't even qualify for the school hockey team,' I told him wryly.

'Then there's a lot I am able to teach you, if you'll allow me?' he said, causing my heart to start pounding again. The rest of the gathering seemed to have faded away, leaving Michel and me alone in the room.

'Can I drive you home, perhaps?' he asked some time later, as couples started to drift away.

'Yes,' I replied automatically, getting up.

I was hardly aware of anything else, as I floated across the room to where the Dubois were saying goodbye to their guests.

Florence accepted my apology gracefully, shrugging it off as trivial. She seemed more upset that Michel had offered to drive me home. It was as if she now regretted having led me directly to him earlier, and I wondered if it had something to do with the girl called Marguerite, whom I was meant to be only temporarily replacing. She kissed him twice on both cheeks, then stared at him suspiciously.

'*Elle rentrera de New York, non?*' I heard her ask and Michel, who seemed to be given to stock answers on the subject of Marguerite, replied, '*Je n'en sais rien.*'

I noticed again that closed expression, as if everything had shut down, so there was no point asking any more questions. It worked on Florence, as it had worked on the two girls at dinner. She went silent.

He leant forward and kissed her on both cheeks, closing the subject with a placatory smile and a squeeze of her hand, before turning away. As he led me out into the cold night, I was aware of her hard blue eyes watching us go, as if somehow I was the one who had displeased her.

He drove a dark green Mercedes, holding the wheel with one hand and my hand in the other. I didn't dare speak, lest I break the spell, but as we were approaching Marble Arch, I said, 'Who's Marguerite?'

'Marguerite?' he repeated, and the way he pronounced her name made it sound all the more lovely, 'was my fiancée. She was meant to accompany me tonight, but left for New York instead – in a bad mood.'

'Oh,' I said, my heart sinking. 'That's bad luck.'

'I consider it good luck,' he replied, without taking his eyes off the road, 'since you were there.'

I remained silent, unable to come up with a suitably flippant reply. Although curious, I didn't dare ask more.

'Will you have dinner with me tomorrow night?' he asked, breaking the silence.

By now, we were approaching Swiss Cottage and the Finchley Road.

'Yes,' I replied. 'But what about Marguerite?'

He pulled up outside the block of flats, as I had instructed, and turned towards me, his face partly concealed in shadow. 'I asked you, not Marguerite,' he said.

I hesitated. 'There was just one moment back there, that I had the impression you were already committed?'

'Officially, we are still engaged,' he admitted. 'That's something I'm going to have to sort out.'

He spoke as if it were only a detail, a bill he had forgotten to pay.

'What do you mean?' I couldn't help asking.

'I mean I'm not going to marry her,' he replied. 'Any more questions, or can we continue?' He spoke in a lighter tone now, and I noticed a smile hovered around his mouth.

'I got the impression Florence wasn't too happy that you offered to drive me home,' I said, after some moments.

'Florence has a habit of interfering,' he replied. 'How would you say – stirring the pot?'

I smiled. Was that why she had asked me tonight, I wondered; to stir things up? Banking on the fact that I wasn't glamorous enough to lure Michel away, but enough to cause a distraction?

I knew I was pushing it, but I ploughed on. 'Why did Marguerite rush off to New York in a bad mood in the first place?' I asked.

I sensed I'd gone too far. Back was that closed expression, and it seemed to me, in the semi-darkness of the car, that a curtain had been drawn between us, for I could barely see him now.

Then he said, 'She couldn't . . . how can I explain, mix into the life here. . . ?'

'Integrate?' I supplied.

'Yes – I had always suspected that.'

66

'Where is she originally from?' I asked.

'Geneva,' he replied, 'although the family is Swiss Italian.'

'London can be a difficult place to live,' I said, 'even for the English.'

'She speaks the language perfectly – besides, she didn't have to integrate, we have a lot of French-speaking friends. She didn't have to do anything, except be happy – and she even failed at that.'

Happiness, I reflected – sometimes elusive, often unrecognisable. I'd only realised how much I'd taken it for granted since Mother and Father had gone.

He sighed irritably, then changed the subject. 'So? Dinner, tomorrow night? I'll pick you up at eight?'

'Yes,' I said, my heart racing. 'I live on the third floor, flat number twenty-eight; my surname is on the door.'

I moved to go, but he reached over and pulled me back.

'Wait a minute, you haven't said goodnight.' He leant across and kissed me on both cheeks, as he had kissed Florence Dubois, then softly on the lips. He smelt of the mixed scents of Provence, of wild herbs, bringing a vivid memory of a holiday in St Tropez to mind.

'. . . à demain,' he was saying, bringing me back to the present.

I got out of the car, and stood watching him drive away, my lips still burning from that brief kiss.

I lay in bed that night too keyed up to sleep. There were, I thought, a number of conflicting things about him that were hard to separate.

He came across as conservative without being conformist; highly principled with a tendency to break the rules; resolute, yet flexible. Charlotte would have called him 'straight,' in its most derogatory sense – I saw it more as disciplined.

It was as if he got his highs from clean mountain air and panoramic views. There was about him a heady sense of adventure that dulled everything else around him.

Yet a shadow had been cast that intimated past complications, the impulsive and bad-tempered Marguerite, and the meddling Florence Dubois being only part of it.

It struck me that he might well be a moody, difficult person, with hidden secrets that he would never divulge. Yet if this were the case, if it was dark moods that silenced him, they passed almost as quickly as they had come. But they left behind the uncomfortable feeling of having intruded.

I could only sense part of this, however. Never, over the lovestruck, turbulent time that followed, did I allow these doubts to intrude; never did I admit to myself that I might be rushing headlong into the kind of trap Mother had hinted at, by falling in love with somebody from a different world.

Chapter Seven

He rang the doorbell at eight o'clock the following evening, as he had said he would, and I opened the door to find him standing there holding a transparent box tied with satin ribbons. Inside was a mauve orchid, the first of many gifts, which I later preserved by pressing it dry under a pile of novels, as a reminder of that golden time.

He was elegantly dressed in a Prince of Wales check jacket and dark trousers, and strode through the flat, peering into each dingy room with interest. Although the flat was more orderly since Amanda's day, the furniture was beginning to look old and worn, and the walls were badly in need of a coat of paint. I had spent most of the morning hoovering and dusting, yet seemed to have made little impact on the place, and now, seeing it through his eyes, it looked even more grey and shabby.

The fridge was stocked with a variety of mixers for once, and I had bought a bottle of gin and one of whisky, hoping he drank one or the other. But he asked for Perrier water, which I never bought, considering it an unnecessary luxury. Michel, I was to learn, drank rarely and moderately. His father had died of cirrhosis of the liver five years ago, he told me, although I think that was only part of the reason he abstained. He claimed alcohol slowed him down, and keeping fit and active were vital to him.

He settled for tonic water, so I poured two glasses (adding a large quantity of gin to mine, ice and lemon to both), and brought the drinks into the living room to find him standing by the window, gazing out over the Finchley Road. I handed him a glass, searching for something to say, but he spoke first.

'You need a study,' he said. 'Somewhere quiet to work, with shelves for all your bits and pieces.'

In spite of my efforts to tidy up, my desk was a mess, with reference books piled high, unfinished articles, a tattered dictionary and an assortment of pens and pencils contributing to the general disorder.

'That would be nice,' I admitted, 'although my flatmate is never here during the day, so it is very quiet . . . Besides, you don't find many flats with studies to rent – affordable ones, that is. I'll just have to add it to my list of dreams.'

He turned around and smiled, making me catch my breath. 'Then, I'll have to build you one,' he said.

'You could throw in a small balcony, while you're at it,' I joked.

He thought for a moment, then said, 'How about a penthouse with a roof terrace overlooking the whole city?' He waved his arms expansively, as if anything were possible.

'That sounds even more out of reach,' I replied.

'It depends how far you're prepared to stretch.'

'What do you mean?' I asked curiously.

'I searched for the ideal place for years,' he told me. 'I spend my time looking at property, but it's difficult to find the right combination – somewhere private and central, quiet, with a nice view. It's not a lot to ask, but it took me years to find it.'

'Where is it?' I asked, fascinated.

'Overlooking Lac Leman, or Lake Geneva, as it's better known. The view is spectacular. I'll take you there one day.'

A picture of a deep blue lake framed by jagged mountains formed. Around the lake, large stone houses would be dotted, with mossy steps leading down to the water's edge.

'It sounds lovely,' I said, wondering, in the light of this, what he must think of my dingy dwelling. An impression of wealth was forming, but I was to learn that, like a lot of people in real estate, Michel walked a tightrope on which large amounts of money were precariously balanced. 'Is somebody living in it at the moment?'

'Yes, I rented it out when I left Switzerland, four years ago. But I could move back any time under the present contract, providing I give a couple of months' notice.'

'Would you like to go back?'

He considered this for a moment, then said, 'No. The apartment is perfect, but I'm not ready to go back to Switzerland yet. I'm very happy in London, it's got a lot to offer.' He stared at me meaningfully, as if I were one of the things on offer.

'You must miss the skiing and sailing, and the other sports, all the same?' I ventured, a dismal picture of scuba diving in the English channel coming to mind.

'I still manage to go skiing from time to time,' he told me. 'It's just a question of organisation.'

We were sitting on the sofa now, with only a small space between us. He seemed to lose track momentarily of what he was saying, staring at me intently, as if for the first time.

'You're very lovely, Em-i-ly,' he said slowly. 'Eyes that change colour with the light, like the sea, silky hair – *chatin*, we call it in French . . .' He reached over and touched my cheek with the tip of his finger. His hands were smooth and brown, with long blunt fingers. I felt a tremor go through me.

'Flattery will take you a long way,' I said, smiling to cover my confusion.

'It's not flattery,' he stated. 'It's the truth.'

We were kissing; deeply, passionately, as if our bodies were synchronised, and I was aware of the blood pounding in my ears, like water falling from a great height. At last we eased away from one another, as though by a mutual consent, a desire to prolong the moment, and continue where we had left off exchanging fragments of the past. I felt limp suddenly, a piece of driftwood caught up and carried away by the current, only to be washed up on the shore. Glancing at my watch, I saw an hour had flown by without my noticing it.

'Shouldn't we be going?' I said halfheartedly. 'It's getting late.'

'What's the hurry?' He took my hand in his. 'Are you afraid I might dishonour you, or something?'

I laughed. He had a peculiar, old-fashioned turn of phrase that might have been used in jest, only he spoke seriously. At times like this, he would seem quite foreign to me.

'I don't know,' I said teasingly. 'Why, were you thinking about it?'

'No,' he replied, after a pause. 'Relationships are a bit like doing business. If you move too fast, you risk losing the deal. Although it had crossed my mind,' he added. 'So perhaps we had better go.'

We had dinner in a small bistro at Camden Lock, where the waiters spoke French and the food was rich and delicious. The evening passed in a haze, heightened by the wine, which he chose (and I drank most of), and by the growing rapport between us.

I talked more easily of Mother and Father now, and of trying

71

to come to terms with suddenly finding myself alone.

And what about my sister, he wanted to know? I realised then that I seldom thought about Charlotte. It was almost as if she were the one who had faded away, while Mother and Father lived on.

'We never got along when we were growing up,' I explained, thinking of the 'double betrayal' as I spoke. 'Since she's been living in Paris, we've become completely estranged. We don't communicate at all any more.'

'Perhaps you should go over and visit her,' he suggested. 'It might crack the ice.'

I thought of the last time I had seen Charlotte, at the memorial service, and remembered with a dart of dread the indifference that had lain between us. 'Maybe one day,' I said finally.

He spoke briefly of Marguerite towards the end of the evening. I learnt that she had a twin sister called Séverine, with whom he had had a fleeting relationship some years ago, before shifting his attention to Marguerite. They were known as the 'magnificent di Maggiore sisters'. Séverine was an aspiring actress, and undoubtedly the more beautiful of the two, but also more complex and demanding. She was looking for fame and fortune, he concluded, and had apparently found the latter with his wealthy and influential, but by no means handsome, cousin, Gregoire Gautier. Like Marguerite, Séverine had tried unsuccessfully to leave Switzerland to pursue her acting career, only to return and settle with Gregoire. The couple had been living together for almost three years in a beautiful apartment in the old part of Geneva; there was much speculation about the relationship.

'I secretly call them *La Belle et La Bête*,' he said with a grin. 'Séverine is probably one of the most beautiful women I've ever laid eyes on, while poor Gregoire looks a bit like one of those lizards – *un iguane*, in French. It's a mystery.'

I smiled. It didn't seem mysterious to me. I thought of Amanda, the compromises she had made in her quest for riches, and wondered if Séverine too was using Gregoire's wealth and influence as a stepping stone to better things.

Reading my thoughts, Michel said, 'I don't think the reasons are as commercial as everybody thinks – at least I hope not, for

Gregoire's sake. He's not that easy to get on with, but once you get to know him he's very . . . how can I put it – solid?'

'Down to earth?' I suggested.

'Yes, and very generous.'

'Are Sévérine and Marguerite identical twins?' I asked moments later.

'No,' he answered. 'They are different physically, although you'd guess they were twins.'

Sévérine was more beautiful in the classic sense, he explained, but Marguerite had 'these extraordinary purple eyes'. By the end of his description, I didn't know which one I feared most – Marguerite or the beautiful Sévérine.

I also gathered, from those vague references to his ex-fiancée, that she was a talented interior designer, who had started a successful business in Geneva before leaving it to come and live with him in London. She had made little effort to find work here, opting (for social reasons, he emphasised) to get married and have a child. Michel, however, had balked at this conventional route – marriage was one thing, he said, but children quite another. There were so many things he wanted to do, so many places he wanted to see. They had been together off and on for five years and engaged for the last one, although no wedding date had been set. This had been one of the many bones of contention. Michel had procrastinated. I also gathered that this was not the first rift between them but one of many, and that each had followed a similar pattern, with Marguerite leaving after delivering a series of threats and ultimatums, only to reappear, some weeks later, contrite and ready to start all over again. She had not been happy in London, he stressed; the relationship had become strained, she'd started drinking too much and become involved with a crowd of wealthy French-speaking Arabs. Through one of them she had landed a lucrative contract in New York. This had been the final straw, this 'shaky period', the end of all his hopes for them. Only there was still one detail left hanging in the air.

'What about the engagement?' I ventured, losing my appetite for the Crême Brûlée in front of me. Had she not ended it before leaving?

I had a vision of this raven-haired beauty, her purple eyes glittering as she threw the ring back at Michel.

'No,' he answered. He filled his glass with Perrier water and his face hardened. Having threatened to end it for months, he explained, she had apparently forgotten that detail at the last minute. Now it was up to him.

How could I possibly have gone into my own 'shaky period' after that? I was to ask myself later. And even when the opportunity arose again, I still remained silent. But if I had attempted to blank it out, built a wall to block out the past, then he had surely laid the first bricks. If he was determined to see courage where there was none, a woman emerging unscathed from the wreckage of the past, then I wasn't about to contradict him.

Yet, as is always the case when a structure is built on shaky foundations, it is only a matter of time before the first cracks appear.

Chapter Eight

He lived on the corner of a street that ran parallel to the King's Road, a quiet residential avenue lined with cherry trees. Opposite was an Italian wine bar, where people sat outside on wooden benches when the weather was good, while further up the street, past a row of pink and grey houses, was a green, around which small old-fashioned shops were dotted.

His flat was on the top floor, with a view over the rooftops towards Fulham. The rooms were so spotlessly clean and tidy that I wondered briefly whether he was subject to the same obsessive behaviour as Mother.

The main room was decorated in natural hessian shades, and looked like a photograph for *Ideal Home* magazine. The shelves were filled with books that somehow managed to be the same height and shape, as if they were a false front for a secret room. Even the flowers in identical vases looked too glossy and perfect to be real. Not a speck of dust was visible, not an object out of place. One room had been designated as a store, and was full of equipment, rucksacks, sleeping bags, a tent, climbing boots and ropes piled against the wall.

'Is it always this tidy?' I asked, as he led me back through the main room into the rest of the flat.

'I have a *femme de ménage*, who comes in to clean,' he told me, 'and most of my bric-à-brac is locked away – I hate living with too much clutter, yet I find it difficult to part with anything. Hervé claims it's an inability to let go of the past, filling your life with souvenirs. But I don't have to live with my possessions – I just have to know that they're still there.'

'Do you think it *is* to do with not wanting to let go of the past?' I asked curiously, thinking of my own clutter.

He shrugged. 'Hervé has a theory for everything, even if you're not looking for one. It's his job to analyse human behaviour . . . None of this furniture is mine, of course,' he digressed, as we moved through the rooms. 'It came with the apartment. I wouldn't have chosen it myself.'

75

Yet it was nice furniture, in an understated sort of way. Basic hardy materials in dark colours, chosen to survive the wear and tear of many occupants. I wondered what his own taste was like – conservative and elegant like his clothes, perhaps.

The bedroom was the least formidable room in the flat. The bed was covered in a pale continental quilt that matched the curtains, while on either side were two wooden tables on which tall lampstands with wide hessian shades stood. On one bedside table there was a glossy hardback book with a photograph of the Alps on the cover, and vivid paintings of snow scenes hung on the walls. Above the bed was a framed collage of photographs: Michel wearing climbing boots standing on a rocky cliff face; on skis poised on the slopes of a mountain; at the helm of a sailing boat squinting against the sun; several of him in the midst of a group of tanned and laughing people.

I didn't take in much more, for he suddenly folded me into a crushing embrace, tipping us sideways onto the bed. And in that heated passionate moment, I knew without a shadow of doubt that I loved him, that there would be nobody else . . . Then I drifted into a dreamless sleep. So it wasn't until I awoke the following morning, still in a lovestruck trance, and watched the dawn breaking over the rooftops of London, that I noticed the photograph.

It stood in the shadow of the lamp beside me, but as the room grew lighter, I could make out the subject quite clearly. It was a black-and-white shot of a dark girl with shiny hair, caught up in a side ponytail that lay like a stripe over one shoulder. She stared unsmilingly at the camera, a black beret cocked at a jaunty angle on her head. The face, otherwise unremarkable, was transformed by eyes that were huge and dark, almost hauntingly lovely, framed with thick black lashes. It was as if the rest of her face was set in an expression of blank repose to show off those eyes. I knew instinctively that it was Marguerite, and seeing her photograph there brought back the unpleasant knowledge that I had been trying to blank out all week. He was still engaged to her.

He woke up moments later and stared at me, his eyes heavy with sleep, then reached over and pulled me into his arms. But the sight of that photograph had momentarily frozen my desire. I couldn't stop thinking about those luminous eyes watching over us, as if it were only a matter of time before she returned to him.

Over the next weeks hardly a day passed when I didn't see him, an hour when I didn't think about him. We had dinner together most evenings, and lunch most days. We went to the theatre and the opera; we combed the art galleries, discovering a mutual love of paintings; and I showed him some of my own haunts – ethnic restaurants where you could eat for next to nothing, delicatessens where you could buy unusual food. At weekends we'd sometimes drive out of London, to Bath or Stratford upon Avon, staying in quaint little hotels and exploring the towns. He was like a chameleon, blending effortlessly into every setting. I marvelled at his zest for life, and his consuming interest in everything around him.

In those early days, I seemed to be drunk all the time, not on wine but on emotion. Unable to concentrate on my work, I'd walk the streets of London unaware of the bitter chill, in a haze of happiness. Once I had to stop and sit on a park bench for a moment, and wait for the world to stop spinning and the grass to stop rippling under my feet.

I started to spend more time in his flat, letting myself in in the early evening to sit by the window gazing out over the bare cherry trees, waiting for him to come home. He often brought a gift with him – a bunch of early freesias, a hardback book, a leather-bound dictionary, a satin cushion filled with goosedown to sit on while I worked, and once a butterfly on a chain from Van Clef and Arpels, with a diamond-studded body and onyx wings.

'What I love about you,' he said once, as I tore the wrapping off yet another gift, 'is the fact that I can spoil you.'

Marguerite had had it all, apparently; the designer clothes, the jewellery. One day I discovered her clothes still neatly folded in the drawers and some dresses, the type of garments that hung in Florence Dubois' boutique, still hanging in a wardrobe. That same week, I learnt through Florence that she planned to return at the end of the month – in less than three weeks' time.

I sensed Florence didn't approve of the way things had turned out. The four of us were having lunch together in the Italian wine bar one Saturday, and Michel had ordered a rather rough bottle of wine which only I was drinking. Florence suggested immediately that we send it back, then she spotted my almost empty glass and said, '*Ce vin est imbuvable*! How can you drink it?'

'I don't find it bad at all,' I replied, defending Michel who had chosen it, and myself who was quite enjoying it.

She glanced at Michel then back at me, as if our relationship was a mystery to her, then without beating around the bush said, 'You know Marguerite is coming back at the end of the month?'

I lit a cigarette, aware that my hand was shaking slightly. 'Yes,' I said, although I had not known.

Michel must have heard her too, for he stopped talking in mid-sentence. 'That would be keeping to the schedule,' he said in English, so it was quite clear to all of us, but his voice was cold, freezing any possible follow up.

I knocked back the rest of my wine, aware that they were all looking at me now, and saw Hervé's pale eyes, beaming down like searchlights, as though he knew only too well why I kept on drinking.

So it seemed we all waited for the showdown to commence.

I started putting her photograph face down in the drawer beside the bed, but the following day it was always back in its usual place – the cleaning woman seemed to think she was coming home too.

The month was coming to an end, the weather growing brighter, and I saw the first buds on the cherry trees below and felt the change in the air. I waited uneasily for the phone to ring, a taxi to draw up, dispensing her and her suitcases at the door, and the dreadful scene that would follow. But there was still no word.

One evening, when the thought of her was weighing on me more heavily than usual, I said, 'Michel, perhaps you should get in touch with her, at least tell her about us? It could save a lot of embarrassment.' But he cut me short with a gesture of irritation, as if it were no concern of mine.

As time passed and everything remained unchanged, I began to feel frantic, living in a kind of permanent limbo, where nothing would ever be resolved. If he noticed my anxious state, he said nothing. I moved through the days, restless and distracted, my nerves on edge like Mother in one of her dithers, waiting for an appropriate moment to bring up the subject.

It was Michel who provided it, in the end. He suggested we

return to the bistro at Camden Lock one Saturday evening, in what seemed like a symbolic gesture of our meeting one another. A new beginning . . . But the old one had to end first. I put a bottle of champagne in the fridge, hoping I could persuade him to drink more than one glass, then waited anxiously for him to return from work.

He was in particularly high spirits that evening. We fooled around, laughed a lot, and long lingering looks passed between us. He drank a couple of glasses of champagne, and I finished the bottle. I almost decided against bringing up the subject of Marguerite after that. What did it matter, I thought, elated by the champagne and the evening. We're so involved with one another now, her coming back won't change anything. And perhaps, if I hadn't drunk so much, I might have left it as it was, thereby avoiding that first bitter argument between us.

We were at cross purposes over dinner. I longed to talk about Marguerite – he wanted to discuss *Running Tide*. He never seemed to tire of hearing about Father's adventures. Once again, I talked about the regattas, of Father's more ambitious voyages, and of the times I had accompanied him.

'You didn't race much on her, it seems?'

'No,' I replied. 'I've never been very keen on competitive sailing. The regattas were important to Father – he had his favourite crew, and he and Toddy often raced together . . .' I paused. I didn't feel like continuing; it brought back too many painful memories. 'Michel,' I digressed, moving to the issue that was still burning under the surface. 'About Marguerite – ?'

His face immediately changed. 'What about her?'

'I think we should talk.'

'I didn't realise she was here with us tonight,' he said crossly.

I ploughed on. 'You may have blanked it out, left the situation unresolved, but it doesn't mean she's gone away.'

He took an angry breath. 'How did we get on to this?'

'Michel, her clothes are still in the wardrobe; I keep putting her photo away, but the cleaning woman keeps taking it out – Don't you think you should call her? Tell her I exist, at least?'

I was aware that my voice had gone high and shaky, taking on that domestic tone he hated.

'I don't think that would be appropriate,' he said tightly.

'I'm beginning to think you don't want to do the dirty deed!' I lit a cigarette, watching him closely.

'Shall we go?' he snapped, for he hated scenes in public places.

'Fine, if you want to evade the issue again, let's go,' I said furiously. I tried to rise, but my head spun, so I sat down again.

He beckoned to the waiter for the bill, looking away, removed from me now.

I don't remember much of what I said on the way home. It was the wine talking now, garbled sentences that bounced off him as off a wall, cutting through the silence.

'Look, perhaps you'd better take me back to Swiss Cottage, tonight,' I said finally, 'if you're not even prepared to talk about it.'

It seemed to me, in that desolate moment, it was all over before it had even begun.

He made a dangerous U-turn in the middle of the road, narrowly avoiding a cyclist, his face set.

As we reached Swiss Cottage he said, 'I'm leaving for New York in a week's time. I have a couple of business affairs to tie up. I will be doing the "dirty deed", as you call it, then.'

I stared at him in confusion. I had been all set to make a dramatic exit from his life on a note of justified outrage, and now I found myself at a loss.

'I wish you'd told me,' I said after a silence.

'I thought you trusted me.'

'I did.'

'Then you should have believed me when I said it was over.'

'Why didn't you tell her before?'

'I didn't want to do it over the phone,' he replied, 'and there was no reason to involve you . . .'

I stared at him in frustration. Surely he had sensed my feelings? After all, there had been a pattern of this – they had been together off and on for five years. Michel and Marguerite – even the names went well together. Or was it, as he had insinuated, a lack of trust on my part; my own insecurity that had led me to doubt him?

'You've always managed to get back together in the past,' I said finally. I had read somewhere that stormy relationships were more resilient than any other kind.

'Yes,' he replied. 'Only now I've fallen for you.' He reached over and squeezed my hand. 'Partners again?'

I nodded dully, still trying to shake off a slight feeling of unease.

'Can we go home now?' he asked, as if everything had suddenly righted itself again, 'or are you intent on leaving me alone tonight?'

'No, let's go home,' I replied.

He flew to New York a week later to do the 'dirty deed', and when he returned, informed me it was over between them. I noticed her photograph had disappeared, and her clothes and other belongings had been placed in cardboard boxes in the spare room, with all the sporting equipment.

It must have ended amicably, for he referred to her as an old friend, saying 'bygones were bygones'. But I would have preferred it if he had said goodbye to her once and for all, and she had gone out of his life forever.

Neither of us mentioned her afterwards. It was as if an unspoken pact had been made between us not to acknowledge her, in the hope that she would fade away.

Later, I found a ring – the engagement ring perhaps – in the silver box beside his bed with all his other memorabilia, like some sort of consolation prize. A beautiful pear-shaped diamond, surrounded by purple stones, the same liquid colour as her eyes.

Chapter Nine

'So, what do you think?' I demanded impatiently. We were lying in bed one wet Saturday morning, listening to classical music. Michel had asked to read *The Love Trap*, and I had somewhat reluctantly handed over the completed chapters. He'd read a couple of my articles but had so far remained noncommittal. 'My English isn't perfect,' he said, 'but the style seems good. I'd like to read some of the novel.' Now I wondered if it had been a mistake to agree. I felt as if I had opened a window to my soul, where all the doubts and confusion lay.

He put down the last page and smiled at me.

'So?' I urged.

'So,' he mimicked teasingly.

'So what do you think?' I repeated.

'I think I love you,' he said.

'Michel . . . please . . .' I hit him playfully with a pillow.

'Oh, this?' he said, picking up the script like an afterthought.

'I think . . .' he said slowly, 'that one day you'll be signing copies in bookstores.'

'Do you really?' I said, elated.

'I've said before, I'm no literary judge, and I don't read a lot of fiction, but I find it very readable. The sentences flow beautifully. It'll take time, of course,' he added, glancing at the last page again, 'but if you want it badly enough, I would guess you'll get there.'

'I've been dreaming about it for years,' I told him.

'Dreams do come true!' he stated. 'Perhaps the trauma of losing your parents has released it,' he added gently.

I lay back and stared at the ceiling. He doesn't need to read what I've written to know me, I thought.

'And now,' he said, eyes glinting, 'I'd like to honour you.'

I smiled. 'It would be my honour,' I replied, moving into the circle of his arms.

Afterwards, he got up and went into the kitchen to prepare

lunch. He came back with a tray of exotic looking cheeses, a jar of salmon eggs – which he called poor man's caviar – some slices of crusty bread and a bottle of chilled white wine. This was one of our weekend rituals; picnic lunch in bed. In the evenings, he'd sometimes prepare a cheese fondue, spending hours stirring in the different cheeses. Those were the best times. He'd light the petrol lamps he used for camping trips and we'd sit at the kitchen table, dipping new potatoes into the melted cheese, and talking of all the places we would visit one day.

Now he placed the tray on the bed, and turned over the record. 'To your novel,' he said, opening the white wine with a flourish, 'and to us.'

His words, the strains of Verdi's *Aida*, and the wine seemed to flood my senses. I lay there in a glow of happiness, thinking how much my life had changed. In the weeks since I'd met Michel, I'd slowly emerged from a cocoon of grief to find spring had arrived. The dark period had receded like a distant nightmare, part of another era.

At the end of April, we started living together. He cleared a space in the spare room and put in some shelves, creating a small study where I could work, so now I had a view over the quiet street and could watch the people going in and out of the wine bar across the road. Work was starting to pour in – since the interview with Florence Dubois, other interviews had followed, and I had been contracted to write short stories for one of the better-known magazines. It seemed that my career was taking off.

Michel was, I discovered, surprisingly well connected in London, and soon we were caught up in a treadmill of cocktail parties and dinners, expensive restaurants and formal nightclubs, until I felt permanently hungover from it all, and longed for the evenings we had once shared together. My wardrobe was now filled with silk shirts and cocktail dresses, tailored jackets and evening gowns – the type of clothes I had so recently dismissed as inappropriate to my lifestyle.

Summer came and went. He started fly-fishing with a couple of friends he had met through work. One of them owned a house in Scotland with fishing rights on the River Tay, and often invited us to go salmon fishing. We would set off early on the Friday with a crowd whom I named 'the jolly Brits' and spend a long weekend there. I would take long walks in the surrounding hills, or sit on the banks of the river with my book and my thoughts.

I remember the rest of the season as a series of hot days, and a trip to the south coast and Portsmouth, taking the ferry across to the Isle of Wight for Cowes week.

At first I had been reluctant to go; it was still so recent. We drove past the house that was no longer part of my life, but still full of memories, then on to the boatyard, where I introduced Michel to the new owner. It looked quite different now, more orderly than in Father's day. They'd modernised the entrance and created more space. Two men were working on a GRP day boat with a wood trim.

Michel asked for news of *Running Tide*, and we learnt that she had won a couple of regattas this season but didn't manage to see her, as she was out at sea.

As we drove away, Michel said, 'Not everything's lost, *cherie* – you still have your *souvenirs*. Nobody can take them away from you.'

He was right, I thought, glad now that we'd come. Somehow, the visit had brought Mother and Father closer again.

One morning towards the end of autumn, I woke up to find him sitting on the end of the bed, watching me. A sharp morning light poured into the room through the pale curtains – I had overslept again.

'What time is it?' I asked groggily, for it had been yet another late and drunken night.

'It's time you married me,' he said pushing a small black box across the bed.

I sat up, wide awake now, and opened it. Inside was an exquisite emerald ring, a fiery green rectangle surrounded by a crust of diamonds.

'To bring out the green of your eyes,' he said, slipping it on my finger.

I stared at it in awe. It was unquestionably beautiful, but somehow alien. The type of ring other women wore – expensive women with coiffeured hair and mink coats. Besides, weren't emeralds supposed to be unlucky?

But he was saying, 'Emeralds are a symbol of faith – they

84

represent immortality. So don't go losing faith in me again! Partners for life?'

Like the Whooper swan, I thought dazedly.

He was adamant about not having children. He said the world was already overpopulated, and he didn't want to contribute further. He was worried about the environment, and what he considered a 'rapidly deteriorating quality of life'. He didn't want to bring children into a world that was already black with people, he said. He, who believed that anything was possible, was surprisingly pessimistic about the future. I wondered if there were other factors, the main one being that children would impose on his time, time spent skiing down 'La Vallee Blanche' or racing across Lake Geneva. None of this really bothered me then, however. I didn't particularly want the burden of a child myself, although a whole lifetime without one seemed somewhat bleak. But I put it aside for the time being. He suggested I start taking contraceptive pills, saying, 'We don't want any nasty surprises,' so I rather reluctantly made an appointment with the doctor. I'd recently written an article on the pros and cons of the pill, and had come to the conclusion that there were healthier, if less reliable, methods.

'I can't imagine taking pills for the rest of my life,' I said, having made the initial concession.

'You won't have to,' he replied. 'I'll go and have an operation – it's easier for a man, and it's only fair.'

I stared at him uneasily. 'That seems pretty final.'

'It is final, but it's the best solution.'

'I'm not sure,' I said doubtfully. 'What if you change your mind?'

'I won't.'

'Maybe I will?' I ventured.

'I hope not,' he said.

After that, I went and got a supply of pills, hoping it would at least give us more time to decide before he took that irreversible decision. But the pills made me feel nauseous, so I threw them away and started looking into alternative methods.

It was Michel who decided we should get married sooner rather than later, suggesting a registry office service before Christmas. Having procrastinated for so long with Marguerite, he now seemed intent on a quick wedding.

'Why so soon?' I asked, rather overwhelmed by the way things were turning out.

'You never know what's around the bend, especially in my business,' he answered vaguely. I knew he had been having problems at work recently – the business was highly leveraged, and interest rates had soared; one of his partners was talking of pulling out. But I had no idea quite how bad things were.

It occurred to me, briefly, that I was rushing headlong into the unknown. I had only a sketchy picture of his past, while he had a censored version of mine. I hadn't even met his mother. But when I pointed out this detail, he said dismissively, 'My mother hardly knows me either. She's completely gaga.' (I had learnt that she was suffering from a form of dementia.) 'I'm afraid I can't provide a whole backup system as proof that my intentions are honourable.'

I laughed. As usual, he had guessed what was going through my mind. 'That makes two of us,' I said, knowing now why people spoke of 'taking the plunge'. At times you had to fall back on instinct alone.

'How about the middle of December?' he suggested. 'Then I can take some extra time off over Christmas for the honeymoon.'

'But that's less than two months away!'

'It could be next week as far as I'm concerned,' he replied.

I wrote to Aunt G straight away and told her our plans.

'We have decided on a registry office wedding,' I wrote, 'since neither of us has much in the way of family . . . I do hope you'll be able to come. I had hoped that you'd meet Michel before, but things have been a bit hectic for him at work, and are still rather shaky. I know you'll love him . . . We're very alike in some ways, in that we share the same views about life, sense of humour, all the things that really matter . . .'

I remembered Mother's ghostly advice, and added, 'He's almost more English than the English themselves, and I don't know when I've ever been so happy. I only wish Mother and Father could have met him – I know they would have loved him too. So it's a happy ending after all,' I concluded. As though I had reached the summit of a mountain after a particularly long and arduous climb, and now all I had to do was stand there and admire the view.

Aunt G replied, promptly as usual, her handwriting worse than ever, saying how delighted she would be to come to the wedding.

'I'm so happy for you, Emily dear, and look forward very much to meeting your young man.'

I hadn't told Michel much about Aunt G and the large part she had played in Mother's life. The only time I had spoken of her was after he had read those few chapters of *The Love Trap*; Michel had listened intently when I explained how Aunt G had been the only one of her family Mother could turn to. But as I rewrote Mother's story, it was becoming confused even in my own mind, until I could no longer discriminate between fact and fiction. Michel only knew Mother as I had described her in the book – a shadowy, insubstantial figure who had been brought up in a remote village in Ireland – while Aunt G must have seemed like a caricature of a colourful and eccentric spinster, living alone in that crumbling Georgian house overlooking the lough.

And so it must have remained for him, for quite suddenly everything changed, disrupting all our plans.

Michel came home from work some days later, and announced that he was closing the London office. I stared at him in alarm. 'What now?' I asked.

'There isn't much choice. It means going back to Switzerland.'

I sat down on the sofa, trying to absorb this sudden change of plan.

He saw my face, and said, 'It's not the end of the world. I'll teach you to ski, and you'll finally have your roof terrace. Is it your career?' he asked, when I didn't reply. 'If so, I've been thinking about that – this will give you a chance to concentrate on your novel. And maybe you could continue with the magazines by correspondence.'

'How soon?' I asked.

'Ideally before Christmas – there's not a great deal more I can do here.'

'But what about the wedding?'

'Can't we bring it forward?'

'I suppose so.'

'It's not as if it's going to be a huge affair.'

'No,' I said, not wanting it to be a small detail, quickly dispensed with, either. 'I've already given Aunt G the dates. I just hope she can get over sooner.'

I knew I was being trivial, but I couldn't help it.

'Call her,' he said.

'There's Charlotte, too.

'Pick up the phone,' he said, and there was an edge to his voice.

He's got all these problems, I thought, and I'm just making things worse.

'I suppose we don't have to get married right away,' I said vaguely, not really meaning it.

'It would be nice to start our married life in Switzerland,' he pointed out, making me wonder for a moment whether he was doing it out of desire or a sense of convention. 'And I've had an idea – I told you about my cousin Gregoire's villa in the Caribbean? Well, he's there with Séverine for six weeks or so. I thought we could fly over and go diving. A sort of honeymoon *à quartre*. Then we'll have a couple of weeks to pack up and leave London.'

My heart sank. It was not exactly my idea of a honeymoon. I had been nurturing a secret hope that we might spend Christmas at Heronlough, but he seemed to have made other plans. It struck me that the wedding was being planned around the honeymoon, rather than the other way around. And weren't honeymoons supposed to be for the bride and groom alone? I was to learn, however, that Michel seldom did anything without the company of others. I stared at him in a turmoil. On the one hand, everything was moving too fast, yet on the other, it was like a dream come true. I thought of the hapless Marguerite, waiting five years for such a proposal.

'I'll make those phone calls,' I said.

But when I called Heronlough House Bridget answered, and informed me that Aunt G had slipped on the driveway the day before and cracked her hip bone. She was still in hospital, not expected home for another two weeks, after which there was no chance of her travelling for a while. She would not be able to come to the wedding now, whatever date we decided on.

Sick with disappointment, I then rang Charlotte, dialling the number in Paris she had given me. A strange female voice answered the phone.

'*Oui, allo,*' she said.

'*Je voudrais parler avec ma soeur, Charlotte,*' I said, slipping easily into French after all my practice with Michel's friends.

'She's not here,' the girl replied in English.

I left my number with her, and said I would try again in an hour.

But Charlotte rang back fifteen minutes later, saying, 'Emily? What's the problem?'

Did we only speak when there was a problem?

'No problem,' I said. 'I rang to tell you I'm getting married.'

'Don't tell me – to a tall dark handsome foreigner?' she said immediately.

'Swiss, actually. How did you guess?' I replied, trying to keep my voice level.

'You've always had a penchant for foreign men – remember Marco, the Italian count!' she answered.

I laughed on a forced note, wondering if she was remembering Mother's advice. I never thought of Michel as foreign, nor did I consider our differences an obstacle.

'We're getting married in a registry office,' I continued. 'Can you come? I'm afraid it's rather short notice.'

'When?' she asked.

'At the end of the month.'

'You're not pregnant, are you?'

'No,' I laughed. 'Neither of us wants children – at least, he doesn't.

'I can't get away this month,' she told me. 'It's our busiest time, coming up to Christmas. The restaurant's expanding.'

'I see,' I said, wondering if she was expanding too. 'That's a pity.'

'Why don't you get married in Paris?' she suggested, as if that were the obvious answer.

'Because most of our friends are here.'

'Fine,' she said coolly, intimating that I placed more importance on my friends than on her. 'I can't make it, then.'

Since that seemed to be that, I moved on. 'So how are you keeping?' I asked dutifully.

'Ticking along.'

That was Charlotte all right. The most she would do was 'tick along'.

I was going to ask about her social life, then realised she hadn't asked about mine and the man I was about to marry, so said instead, 'Well, I'd better be going, lots to do . . .'

89

I felt a sudden longing for something that could never be – a glamorous sister, a soul mate, who would receive my news with pleasure; a handsome brother to give me away. I imagined him proudly and somewhat jealously handing me over to Michel. Wondering if I would ever have a family of my own, I was brought back to the present by Charlotte saying, 'Have a good wedding.'

'Thanks,' I replied. 'Have a good Christmas.' But the phone had gone dead by then, and I was talking into thin air.

I turned back to Michel and said, 'We could get married tomorrow, as far as I'm concerned – there's nobody else I want to invite.'

Florence Dubois gave me a beautiful silk cream suit from her shop as a kind of peace offering; Hervé was a witness, and there were others, who were connected with the Dubois, as well as a few mutual friends.

Afterwards we stood on the steps in the shadow of the building while photographs were taken, and I remember feeling quite giddy with happiness. It was only later, over an elaborate dinner at Blake's Hotel, that I glanced around the table, hearing a babble of French voices, and back at Michel, looking so handsome by my side, that I felt a flicker of doubt.

Soon we would be living in Switzerland, leading a different kind of life – Michel's old life, amongst all those glossy, smiling people I had seen in his photograph albums. I thought of the penthouse apartment overlooking the lake, and wondered what it would be like. I would miss our Chelsea flat, and all our familiar haunts. But most of all I would miss London, which in the last few months had finally become a home.

But by the time we were alone together in the honeymoon suite upstairs, the doubts had flown, and I knew that I would follow him to the ends of the earth, if that was where he led me.

Chapter Ten

The day before we left for the Caribbean, there was an unexpected and unwelcome confrontation with the past.

It was a brilliant winter's day, with a sharp nip in the air. Michel wanted to buy some diving equipment for the trip, so we had set off early that morning, walking the length of the King's Road to a diving shop he knew, close to World's End.

It was a long walk to the shop, then a long wait while Michel looked at masks, snorkels and fins, explaining as he did so the principle of neutral buoyancy.

'What if I don't like scuba diving?' I said, in an effort to dissuade him from investing in equipment I might not use again.

'I think you'll love it,' he replied. 'It's like being in another world.'

That was what I was afraid of. A cold, airless world – a deathtrap. I remembered Father talking of 'the great deep', that place below the sea where there was no life, no oxygen, no sound, nothing. Was that where he had ended up, in that cold and sodden silence?'

In the end, Michel bought a couple of diving knives, a pair of flippers and a mask for me, saying that Gregoire and Sévérine would provide the rest. We left the shop clutching our purchases and walked slowly back along the King's Road.

We had reached the side street that led to the flat when Michel stopped to look at a pair of climbing boots in a shop window. I waited beside him, trying to identify the heavy beat of a rock song that thumped from a boutique further up the street, which for some reason had vaguely unpleasant connotations. A couple were arguing loudly behind us. 'You're such a bloody liar,' she was saying, angrily. 'You're still seeing her, aren't you? I don't believe a word you say any more . . .' The man hung his head sheepishly and stared at the ground, and I remember thinking that Marguerite, the past and all its problems, no longer existed for us.

Then I saw Amanda.

She was walking towards us, arm in arm with the same small hairy man with the gold tooth I had seen her with in Harrods. Only then she had looked radiant; now she seemed pinched and distracted, with the discontented air of a woman who has sacrificed herself for material things. The greed that had once flickered in her eyes was dulled by compromise. Her heels were lower, to accommodate the man who walked beside her, and she wore a huge pale fur so lustrous it looked fake, swinging open to reveal a tight petrol blue dress beneath. She had permed her bleached hair, so it stood up like a tangle of barbed wire on her head.

The man, who must have been all of five foot four, strutted along beside her like a pouter pigeon, all emphasis on his swelling chest to compensate for his lack of height. A gold Rolex stood out on a hairy wrist and a thick chain sat on the bed of frizz at his neck. For one moment I thought she hadn't noticed us and tried to melt against the shop window, but Michel was moving forward, taking me with him, and as we moved, Amanda saw us.

'Emily! How are *yoooou*?' she exclaimed, bringing back a flood of unwelcome memories. She swooped down on us, smelling of hairspray and scent, and planted a sticky kiss on my cheek. Then her eyes landed on Michel. At that moment I identified the music – the same band that had been playing the night of Shariffi's party, when the police had come crashing through the door.

'This is Diaz,' she was saying, pushing forward the hairy little man, still gazing at Michel. I could see her taking in the foreign looks, the expensive but subtle clothes – then her eyes widened with disbelief as she spotted the emerald ring. 'You're engaged,' she said incredulously.

A cloud had covered the sun, causing the temperature to dive suddenly.

'Married,' I replied, keeping my voice level. The ring seemed to have hypnotised her. Her eyes remained riveted, as if caught in its beam, and her voice turned indignant and simpering.

'Well, aren't you going to introduce us?' she inquired.

'This is Michel Gautier,' I said warily, and watched her go through the ritual of eyelash-batting and hair-tossing as he shook her hand.

'*Enchanté*,' he said, making her preen even more, but I could tell he wasn't.

'*Comment allez vous*?' she emphasised, with an appalling French accent, then turned back to me. 'I don't remember receiving a wedding invitation, Em!'

Her use of that old nickname made me flinch. A warning bell went off in my head, but I could not bring myself to walk away. I stood there dumbly, watching her mouth move as she formed her questions, then, since she wasn't getting any response from me, she answered them herself.

'How are you keeping? Rather well it seems! Moved up in the world since Swiss Cottage, have we? You know that Shariffi and Jeddi ended up doing time? Perhaps you don't! It was all in the papers – they called it the Lebanese Connection! We got off lightly, with a suspended sentence – seems to be quite fashionable these days . . .'

She giggled, and I was aware of Michel standing rigidly beside me, but didn't dare look at him. I tried to move away, but as I did so, she took a step forward, so I could feel the warm mist of her breath on my cheek. In an ominous silence, she grabbed my arm and said peevishly, 'What's wrong, Em? You're not still cross with me over what happened, are you?'

Her tone, with its many implications, make me freeze.

'I'm quite all right,' I said, trying to shrug her off.

'Well, good for you,' she replied, retrenching now, stung by my tone. She glanced at Michel, and I stiffened at the glint in her eye. 'You were in a bad way, remember – I was starting to worry about you . . .'

Now her tone was plaintive, appealing to the side of me that wanted, but had no right, to forget. '. . . looks like it's all behind you now.' She winked at Michel. '. . . rescued by a knight in shining armour . . .' Her eyes did a tour of my body, taking in my new cashmere coat and expensive shoes. 'A knight with all the right credentials, it seems! Looks as if you're back on the straight and narrow?'

This kind of talk was quite alien to Michel. He wasn't attuned to clichéd innuendoes, 'a nod's as good as a wink' type comments. He stared at her, giving nothing away, but I could tell he didn't like her.

Then he was saving the day, taking my arm and preparing to leave. We had a lot of shopping to do, he said charmingly. The weekends weren't long enough. He nodded curtly to Diaz, who stood there bemused, his gold tooth glinting in the wintry sun, and started to pull me away.

'Well!' Amanda gasped, as if we had betrayed her. She pushed a manicured hand through the tangle of her hair, and her eyes narrowed to pale slits.

'. . . if you can't even spare a few minutes to catch up with an old friend,' she exclaimed, causing passers-by to stop and turn. 'Too good for the likes of me now? I get the feeling you still blame *me* for what happened!'

I remember thinking that this was the kind of thing that happened in soap operas, bitter painted women destroying one another with vicious revelations about the past. I had a sudden mad urge to plunge the diving knife I was still clutching into her chest, and watch her sink down in a pool of blood. She must have read my thoughts and sensed the tension in the air, for she turned abruptly on her heel and strode away, her body listing slightly like a boat caught in a gust of wind, one hip bumping against Diaz's waist while his long arm encircled her behind.

I started walking too, gathering speed as I went so Michel had to keep pace with me across the shopping precinct to the flat. Michel's face was grim as we reached the entrance of the building.

'What the hell was all that about? What an awful woman – *une vraie mante religieuse . . .*'

That was appropriate, I thought grimly, for didn't praying mantises feed off their prey until they died?

He appeared to be in a state of shock, and I wondered how I'd ever be able to explain it all to him. Tension made me say harshly, 'I used to share a flat with her. She's a money-grabbing social climber, who uses . . .'

'She doesn't appear to have climbed very high, if you want my opinion,' he cut in.

'That's because she always gets involved with the lowest of the low, and tries to drag everybody else down with her,' I said furiously.

He went silent, and I noticed with a pang that he had drawn away from me. We didn't speak again until we were inside the flat, then I said, 'God, I could do with a drink after that!' I went into the kitchen and took a bottle of wine from the fridge. Michel followed me.

'Don't you think you're drinking too much?' he said. He leant against the door and watched, puzzled, as if witnessing a scene in which everything was running rapidly out of control.

'No, I don't,' I retorted.

'I do,' he said quietly.

I poured the wine clumsily into the glass, ignoring him.

'I don't know how you can drink that,' he said in disgust.

'Why? What's wrong with it?'

'It's been open for five days!'

I glanced at the bottle, and remembered he had used it for a cheese fondue.

'Why should it bother you?' I said. 'I'm the one who's drinking it.'

'Because it brings out a very ugly side of you,' he replied chillingly, then turned and walked towards the bedroom, closing the door behind him.

When he had gone, I flung the wine into the sink and sat down, reaching for the packet of cigarettes and lighting one shakily. Anger coursed through me – not so much against Amanda and her insinuations, but at Michel for having been open to them. I didn't owe him any explanation, I thought. After all, he hadn't gone into the details of his past, so I was not obliged to give a blow by blow account of mine.

My thoughts continued along this track for several minutes, until I was brought up short by the cold realisation that he hadn't demanded an explanation. All he had said was that I was drinking too much. My anger changed course, coming straight back at me like a slap in the face. I stared out of the window at the pale sky, and realised I had made a stupid mistake by omitting to tell him. Now it had been blown out of proportion, so it was no longer easy to explain away. It would lie like a shadow between us, turning the past murky and full of other unanswered questions. This is the kind of thing that destroys marriages, I thought fearfully. Somehow, it had to be clarified and brought back to its proper dimensions.

I headed for the bedroom, afraid he might have locked the door. He hadn't. He was pulling his clothes out of the wardrobe, and piling them neatly on the bed, in the centre of which gaped an empty suitcase.

'What's going on?' I asked in a cracked voice.

'I'm packing,' he answered.

'What for?'

He stared at me as if I were quite mad. 'For the trip, what else?'

'Of course,' I said, sinking down onto the bed. I was losing control I thought, had to get a hold of myself.

'I was thinking of taking these for you,' he said, handing me a pair of diving gloves. 'They should fit – try them on.'

Marguerite's, I thought, but said nothing.

'Are you all right?' he inquired.

'Yes,' I hesitated, then said, 'I'm just sorry I didn't explain before.'

'What was it all about?' he asked casually. 'Don't tell me you're part of an international drug ring or something?'

He continued with his packing as if unperturbed, but his voice had a hollow ring.

'I was afraid you'd take it badly,' I said.

'Am I that intimidating?' he replied, placing half a dozen perfectly ironed handkerchiefs on top of the pile. We had a full-time maid now, who did the ironing as well as the cleaning.

'I didn't want you to think you were out of the frying pan and into the fire,' I said with difficulty.

'Meaning?'

'After Marguerite.'

Afraid now that he would think I was trying to incriminate his ex-fiancée, I added, 'After what you told me . . .'

'Marguerite?' he repeated, sounding puzzled.

'There was the odd parallel,' I said evenly.

He stared at the pile of clothes on the bed, saying, 'I doubt that very much.'

I took a deep breath. 'Just after Mother and Father died, I went to a party in Mayfair with Amanda, her Lebanese boyfriend, and another man . . .' I paused, waiting for this to sink in.

'Go on,' he said, and now I felt as if I were in the dock, while he sat in judgement, waiting to pronounce sentence.

'There were some drugs there – mainly grass, that type of thing.'

'Oh,' he said in a controlled voice, and I knew then why I had been so unwilling to tell him. I could sense his disapproval like a pocket of cold air between us. His shoulders stiffened, and he

96

seemed to lose concentration on his packing.

Guilty! I imagined him saying with a tap of his mallet. For him all drugs, hard or soft, were taboo, illegal and moreover lethal to the health. Sensing the way the conversation was going, I took a defensive stand.

'This is the nineteen-eighties, Michel,' I reminded him. 'People are doing far worse things out there than smoking grass, for heaven's sake. Where the hell have you been in the last ten years?'

'In all the wrong places, it seems,' he replied drily.

I was about to say, 'You're acting as if it were a crime', then remembered that it was, and that I had a criminal record.

'Go on,' he said again.

I spoke rapidly, the words tumbling over each other. 'There was a police bust – they arrested everyone . . . Amanda and I spent the weekend in jail – it was a Saturday,' I added, as if that explained it all. 'That's all, really. They let us out on probation and that was the end of it. We were just in the wrong place at the wrong time,' I concluded, wishing he would loosen up a bit.

'Perhaps it would have been better if you'd told me before now,' he said.

'Why, what would it have changed?' I asked fearfully. I sensed it might have changed everything.

I stood up, folding my arms across my chest, as if against the recriminations that were about to follow.

'It doesn't change anything for me,' he replied.

Not sure what he was insinuating, I said, 'Well as far as I'm concerned, it's all behind me now.'

'How do I know?' he replied with a shrug.

Frustration made me snap, 'I've no intention of repeating the incident, if that's what you mean.'

There was a silence, then he said oddly, 'I worry about it coming back at you later on, that's all.'

I was so taken aback, I didn't notice the glint in his eye at first.

'Why should it come back at me? Nothing happened; it's over. I'd forgotten all about it . . .' I was starting to feel panicked, out of control again. Then I saw his face. Back was that teasing smile he sometimes used to rile me.

'Does it mean that if you commit a second offence they'll put you behind bars?' he inquired with mock seriousness.

'Probably,' I replied, the panic subsiding, 'but I'd hope you'd come and bail me out.'

'Any more surprises?'

I looked at him closely. 'For a moment, I had the feeling it really bothered you.'

'You did take me by surprise,' he admitted, 'but it makes no difference to how I feel . . . Come here,' he said, pulling me into his arms. 'You know, you have a bad temper for such a sweet girl,' he said. 'Remind me not to get on the wrong side of you. I thought you were going to murder that woman.'

'She lied,' I said crossly.

'It's all right,' he replied. 'I believe you.'

As after a storm, the air was clear again, it seemed – but the echo of distant thunder remained. His reaction had, like a lot of things about him, been contradictory, I thought afterwards.

'I wish you'd told me,' he'd said, as if that were a crime in itself, and I had somehow arrived at this point of our marriage not on a wing or a prayer, but on a lie.

Chapter Eleven

We flew to Miami the following day, and after a night's stop-over took a private jet on to the Dominican Republic, where Gregoire's villa stood on the edge of a luxury resort. This was a special service for VIP clients who owned property on the island, Michel explained, and from there on we entered that exclusive private world that is only accessible to the very rich.

An emerald golf course stretched down to the sea; there were polo fields, tennis courts, salt and fresh water pools, even a shooting range – Michel had arrived in paradise. Luxurious villas sprawled along the coastline, shiny convertible sports cars cruised the tree-lined roads, even the people looked as if they had been carved from some rare and expensive material. Thinking back to that magical setting, and to my first encounter with Marguerite's exotic twin sister, it all seems slightly unreal now, and although it was meant to be our honeymoon, I never think of it as such.

Michel talked animatedly throughout the long flight. He looked fresh and relaxed, already caught up in the holiday spirit, yesterday's drama forgotten. He was describing a past holiday on the island, the four of them together – the two cousins and the twins – and listening to him, it seemed to me he spoke of an idyllic time that could not be emulated. They had organised a diving expedition down to a wreck that had been discovered a mile or so off the coast, which, from his account, had been the highlight of the holiday.

'What was down there?' I asked, shivering at an image of bloated rotting wood, rust and decay.

'It was an old cargo ship – originally carrying liquor! It went down during Prohibition. They brought up crates of whiskey and rum, still intact.'

'I wonder why it went down,' I said dully.

'There's a rock close by – known as Turtle Rock, because of its shape. You can only see it when the tide is low. Judging by the hull of the ship, it must have struck head on.'

I tried to blank out the image of splintering wood and chaos as the boat was sucked down into the sea. The business of diving now loomed over me, taking on terrifying proportions. But I was determined I was going to keep up with them – 'come hell or high water', as Father used to say.

Nor was I looking forward to meeting Marguerite's beautiful twin sister. I knew I'd never be able to compete with the glamorous Séverine, just as I'd never be able to fill the bright space that Marguerite had occupied. I also wondered what sort of a welcome I'd receive as Michel's wife.

Gregoire had sent his chauffeur, a young Dominican called Santiago, to meet us at the tiny landing strip. He had a broad shiny black face, which broke into a gleaming smile when he saw Michel.

'Good to see you, man,' said Michel, patting him fondly on the back. He picked up our cases and led us towards a white convertible jeep, and soon we were driving through a lush green landscape where jacaranda and oleander grew. It was a hot, windy day, low clouds billowed across the sun, and I saw glimpses of the sea between the trees like turquoise sheets, waves breaking the surface.

Gregoire's villa was close to the beach, hidden from the road by a cluster of waving palm trees. A guard appeared to open the heavy metal gates and we swung into the entrance, up a short gravel drive past showers of amethyst bougainvillea, and parked behind an identical, but brown jeep. The sun came out from behind a cloud, bleaching the villa a dazzling white and throwing long shadows over the open veranda that encircled it, and in this dappled light I saw the shadowy outline of a person appear.

'*Salut!*' Michel called, as we drew to a halt. '*On est arrivé!*'

The outline lifted an arm in greeting, but did not reply.

I climbed out of the car and followed Michel towards the steps that led up to the veranda. There were two figures standing there now, but the sun was shining directly into my eyes, so I couldn't make out their faces properly. They stood several feet apart, waving and calling.

For one bizarre moment, an optical illusion changed the whole picture, so it seemed that Michel's description had been reversed. It was Gregoire who looked like some sort of bare-chested

Adonis, tall and muscular, a statuesque figure carved by the shadows. He wore dark glasses and his hair was hidden under a white cap. Whereas Séverine stood concealed in the shadows, her black hair scraped back from her face like a skull cap, a shadow casting a hole where one eye should have been.

Then she moved forward into the light, and the picture altered dramatically. She made a beeline for Michel, arms outstretched, while Gregoire followed in a more dignified manner behind her, and I was immediately struck by the contrast between them.

Séverine had jet black hair with the consistency and sheen of spun silk, and in the sun blue lights shone off its surface. She had tied it back with a bright blue scarf, as if fully aware of those dancing lights. She was tall and fit looking, with long slender limbs; her skin was a burnished olive, her eyes dark purple. Not the same shade as Marguerite's, though; more the colour of fine wine in a dusty bottle. Around her neck a sapphire necklace sparkled incongruously in the sun. I smelt her perfume on the breeze, a hot spicy scent that has become so reminiscent of her that I cannot bear to smell it now. Then I dragged my eyes away and looked at Gregoire.

Michel's description had not been far off. His face was like that of a large toad, elongated. A fuzz of wiry hair sprang out from beneath the white cap, while the skin on his chest and shoulders was a warped mass of freckles, with clusters of brown moles raised like hillocks along a rocky outcrop. He took off his sunglasses, and protruding brown eyes stared at me with an expression of benign indifference. I waited for Michel to introduce us, anticipating with dread the usual double kiss on both cheeks, but to my relief he took my hand instead, shaking it briefly. His hand was rough and dry like a dead leaf.

Séverine's greeting was equally brief. She brushed her soft cheek against mine, and said sweetly, 'Hi there,' in a stage American accent, '*Bienvenue*.' But for some reason, I didn't feel at all welcome. She turned and led the way up the stairs onto the cool veranda, and we stood beneath the vines, everybody suddenly talking at once.

Glasses were produced, a bottle of champagne opened, and Séverine made a toast – not to our marriage, but to the news of Michel's return to Switzerland. I saw now that there was more than a slight resemblance between her and her sister, although it was hard to compare the animated version with a photograph. There was something wildly exotic about her, with her black hair and eyes glinting against burnished skin like jewels in a crown. Yet at other times, she had the slightly furtive look of a geisha girl. She was filled with a restless energy, flinging her arms about as she spoke, laughing delightedly at her own exuberance, ignited by the conversation she led in the direction she had chosen – the type of woman who needed a constant audience. She was telling Michel about a party of guests that had been staying at the villa, whom she had been obliged to entertain – it was because of these people, I gathered, that they had not been able to come to our wedding. It had all been a dreadful ordeal, she said theatrically, pausing in midstream to ask if I was following. I nodded vaguely, although I had stopped listening a while back, since the people of whom she spoke meant nothing to me.

After a while I managed to extricate myself, and wandered over to the edge of the veranda, where there was a spectacular view over the sea. Below lay a kidney-shaped swimming pool, to the right a tennis court, while beyond a narrow sand track curved through the palm trees to the beach. I stood there, overwhelmed by the beauty and luxury of the place, wishing more than ever that Michel and I were alone. But the next moment they were all standing behind me, and Michel was trying unsuccessfully to bring me into the conversation.

Later, we left Gregoire and Séverine and went into the cool interior of the house. The rooms were spacious, furnished in the colonial style, with dusty-looking furniture in dark wood, polished parquet floors and wooden ceiling fans. The main guest room was on the first landing, the master bedroom directly above it. A maid was already unpacking our suitcases and putting our clothes away. When we entered, she left discreetly, motioning she would return later. I went over to the window, pulled back the shutters, and stood watching the waves break over a rock far out to sea.

'That's Turtle Rock over there,' Michel said, following my gaze. 'The wreck is somewhere to the left of it. I'll take you diving down there at the end of the week, depending on how you get on with the lessons.'

Cold fear washed over me, so the sea appeared dark and storm-tossed, the sky threatening. But Michel didn't seem to notice my withdrawal. There was a familiar restlessness about him, as if he were keyed up and raring to go. He pulled me into his arms and kissed me passionately on the lips, but I could tell it was a gesture spurred on by a surge of his own excitement, like a person who has just received good news turns to embrace another.

'So how do you like it?' he inquired.

'It's out of this world,' I said, unable to shake off that sense of unreality. 'I can't get over how different Gregoire and Sévérine are,' I added. 'They make an odd couple.'

'She's the extrovert,' he said, making me wonder if Marguerite was the introvert.

I smiled inwardly, thinking that she was the sort of woman who would get away with murder – her joie de vivre masking a caustic streak, her beauty and wit exonerating her bitchiness. Men would be fooled by her, women left floundering. I was sure I had seen through her at a glance.

I'm going down to join them,' he said, a little later. 'I want to find out what the programme is. Come on down as soon as you're ready.'

When he had left, I took off my crumpled clothes and found a swimsuit, thinking longingly of a cool swim in the pool. I pulled on a white cotton sundress, then went into the adjoining bathroom to wash my face. The bathroom resembled the inside of an oyster shell. Everything gleamed like mother of pearl, a row of expensive looking toiletries lined the shelves, and a pile of glossy French magazines were placed in a rack beside the sunken bath. I wiped off the traces of the morning's make-up and applied more, brushed the tangles out of my hair, then, wishing I didn't look quite so pale and uninteresting, went down to join the others.

They were sitting on rattan chairs overlooking the swimming pool, and Sévérine was still holding fort. She had changed into a white bandeau top, over which a chiffon blouse floated, with the same Bermuda style shorts she had greeted us in, and silver pumps on her feet. They all had drinks in front of them, and Gregoire was smoking a thin cheroot.

Sévérine stopped talking in mid-sentence when she saw me, her face breaking into a contrived smile.

'How are you?' she called unnecessarily, while Michel waved

and beckoned me over. Only Gregoire paid no attention. I had a sudden childish urge to run away, but Michel was getting up and smiling encouragingly, as though he sensed my fear. Feeling somewhat superfluous, I moved across to join them.

They had been talking about Marguerite, I knew instinctively, and now Gregoire made no effort to change the subject.

'I had no idea she was so unhappy,' he was saying. He glanced at me with the same benign expression he had greeted me with, and I felt a rush of dislike for him that made me tense all over. Then Michel was moving the conversation away from the past to the future, and the next moment plans were being made for the following day. The weather forecast was bad, Gregoire announced, there was no question of getting out to Turtle Rock for the next couple of days . . . Besides, there was a beginner amongst us.

I could feel the tension mounting. 'Please don't let me stop you,' I said. '*Je vous en prie* . . .' I lit a cigarette and stared at the three of them challengingly.

'In any case, I'm going to organise for Emily to have some lessons,' Michel said. He turned to me, adding, 'I'll go with you.'

I shot him a grateful look, and heard Gregoire say, 'Why don't you teach her yourself?'

'Because then if she doesn't like it, she won't blame me,' he replied, smiling at me fondly.

Gregoire shrugged as if to say 'suit yourself', but I could tell he thought I was a hindrance. Not only is he hideous, he's also unpleasant, I thought, wondering why on earth Séverine was with him. Was she so dazzled by his wealth she didn't care about the rest, I wondered?

Séverine suggested we bring our drinks into the dining room, as it was time for lunch – although nobody had offered me a drink. I got up and followed them inside to where the table was already laid. A waiter poured white wine, and a uniformed maid brought in a terrine of avocado soup and ladled it into our bowls. The soup was followed by an exquisite lobster dish with saffron rice and more wine was poured, while Séverine babbled on, acting out some sort of charade, using people, places and situations unknown to me as props, causing Michel and Gregoire to laugh and the waiter to come hurrying in at each click of her finger.

Cheese and a bowl of exotic fruit followed; the conversation moved on to business and the property market, and Séverine grew restless. She turned to me and said, 'We are a very sportive crowd, especially Michel – you must try to follow.' She smiled sweetly, making me wonder if this was a friendly piece of advice on how to keep him, or a veiled threat that if I couldn't keep up, I would lose him.

Michel must have heard part of the conversation, for he said, to Gregoire, 'What about the spare tanks, by the way? Have they been checked recently? If not, I'll rent a couple for the fortnight.'

'They've all been checked,' Gregoire answered. He glanced at me, adding, 'She could use Marguerite's.' Now he seemed to be testing me.

Michel looked at me too, raising his eyebrows.

'It's fine by me,' I said with a shrug, intimating that I couldn't care less; that I was used to following in the wake of Marguerite, used to her presence hanging around, her photograph, her clothes. Why not breathe from her tank, while I was at it?

'*Bien*,' said Michel, since everything was now resolved, and resumed his conversation with his cousin.

After lunch, Gregoire and Michel went down to the boatshed to check the equipment, Séverine disappeared in the direction of the bedrooms, so I made my way to the pool. In spite of the wind it was too hot to stay in the sun, so I dragged a chaise longue under a palm tree and lay down in the shade. I heard Michel and Gregoire's voices coming from the shed, then I must have dozed for a while, for when I woke up everything was silent. The sun was lower in the sky and the wind had dropped; there was a smell of frangipani and lemon in the air.

I sat up, but the world spun, so I lay down again feeling slightly sick, then rose dizzily and went towards the dark entrance of the shed. When my eyes adjusted to the darkness, I saw lifejackets hanging on low hooks, fishing rods, tackle and diving equipment neatly piled up in one corner. There was a row of dullish yellow oxygen tanks lined up against the wall, four of them initialled in black and one unmarked. G, S, Mi and Ma, – Gregoire, Séverine, Michel and Marguerite. I turned away feeling oddly excluded.

Michel and Gregoire had gone out, it seemed, for the brown jeep was missing. I went into the house and upstairs to fetch a towel, still fighting waves of dizziness, and drank thirstily from a bottle of mineral water beside the bed. Then I went into the bathroom to splash cold water on my face, but the floor seemed to be pitching and heaving like a ship on the high seas. Alarmed, I picked up a magazine and lay down on the bed. I remembered Mother's dizzy spells, and how her nerves had got the better of her in the end, before putting it down to the heat and the amount of wine I had drunk at lunch.

I flicked through the magazine, which was a kind of 'Who's who in Swiss society, full of photographs of coiffeured woman at cocktail parties, and suddenly found myself staring at a photograph of Sévérine and Gregoire. They stood in the midst of a group of people who seemed to have turned with one accord towards the camera. Sévérine's black hair was woven into a chignon at the nape of her neck, and she smiled not at Gregoire, but at the tall, handsome man to her left. Gregoire, on her right, seemed oblivious, looking very much at ease amongst the beautiful people, in a dark tailored suit and bow tie. Underneath, the caption read, 'Sévérine de Maggiore, beautiful star of *Chateau Lunns*, at the Cartier Ball'. I remembered Michel mentioning she had a part in a current soap opera.

I glanced at the other photographs – a whole series had been taken at a yacht club dinner, where once again the women were decked up and bejewelled – and wondered if I were about to enter the kind of glittering lifestyle which had taken up so much of our precious time in London, destined to accompany Michel to functions such as these. 'Hobnobbing,' as Father used to put it, with the rich and famous.

The dizziness seemed to have passed, so I went downstairs to find Sévérine lying beside the pool, wearing a shocking pink bikini and matching sun visor. Her body was shiny with oil, her hair slicked back from her face. She looked like a seal basking in the sun.

'You sleep a little bit, yes?' she inquired amicably.

'Yes, too much food and wine at lunch!'

'Me, I always take a siesta,' she informed me.

'Where did Michel and Gregoire go?' I asked her, sitting down and dangling my legs in the aquamarine water.

'To the Marina, to check the boat. There is a problem with the engine.'

'Oh,' I said. I had learnt that Gregoire owned one of the luxurious boats that lined the harbour, which he used for deep sea fishing, diving, or just for cruising around the island.

Sévérine stared at me curiously, and said, 'You are Irish, Michel say?' She appeared to speak English only in the present tense.

'Half,' I said. 'My mother was Irish, my father English.'

'Where you meet Michel?' she inquired, squinting at me suspiciously.

'I met him through the Dubois,' I told her.

'*Ah oui?*' she said as if trying unsuccessfully to place me amongst them.

'Yes, it was quite out of the blue,' I added.

She considered this for a minute, then said, 'And now you move to Geneva to live?'

'Yes.' I wondered uneasily if there was something behind these questions.

'I speak with my sister in Geneva, this morning,' she said, sounding a warning bell in my head.

'Oh yes?'

'You meet her, no?'

'Not in the flesh,' I said wryly.

'*Pardon?*'

'No, I haven't met her.'

She made a strange sound, a sort of 'pooouf' that is peculiar to the French language, and looked moodily away. 'She telephone here, looking for Michel.'

All my senses were alerted, but I forced myself to remain calm.

'I thought she was in New York,' I said.

She shook her head. '*Elle est rentrée* – she return to Génève now.'

'Oh? Why's that?' I inquired evenly.

'Because of Michel,' she stated. My heart started thumping.

I stared at her. 'What exactly are you getting at?' I asked coldly.

'She follow,' she shrugged simply.

Indignation coursed through me, and the horrible suspicion that this was some kind of threat.

'Be careful,' she was saying. 'She can break everyzing.' She demonstrated this by making a cracking sound with a sharp nail against her front tooth.

I reminded myself that she was an actress, with the ability to play a multitude of parts. But I couldn't decide if she was confidante or adversary, or perhaps some kind of double agent, with secret designs of her own on Michel.

'She'll have a hard time breaking us up,' I said icily. 'It was over between them before he met me.' But I wondered, as I spoke, if that was altogether true.

'It was over because of London,' she said swiftly, quite fluent all of a sudden. 'Now London is finished.'

This is ridiculous, I thought. What is she trying to say – that now Michel is going home, everything will be resolved between them, discounting me as no more than a stopgap in his life? Was that why she hadn't even bothered to toast our marriage?

I wondered then if there was something else Michel had omitted to tell me, if the woman had some kind of hold over him that I didn't know about. All these thoughts raced through my mind, posing unanswered questions.

'I'm going for a walk,' I announced, although I wasn't sure my trembling legs would carry me very far, and made my way down the sand track to the beach.

The beach was almost deserted, bathed in an orange glow. An old man with skin like leather swept away the seaweed that the tide had brought in, a dog paced along by the water's edge, and a couple gathered up their things and walked arm in arm towards their villa. The sea was calm, although black clouds gathered on the horizon, and I thought briefly of tomorrow's diving lesson but felt no fear now, so preoccupied was I by Séverine's revelations.

I must have stayed there for some time, for it started to grow dark, and when I looked around I saw Michel coming towards me, looking wildly handsome in a pair of black faded shorts and a white shirt, his face already tanned. He carried his shoes in one hand, and strode across the sand with concern on his face.

'Em-i-ly, *cherie*! I've been looking all over . . . Sorry I was so long,' he said, sinking down beside me and taking my hand. 'We had to drive miles to find a spare part for the engine, and you were sleeping . . . Is everything all right?'

'Fine,' I lied. 'I just felt a bit dizzy – too much sun!'

'Be careful of that lovely skin of yours,' he said, stroking my cheek.

I looked away.

'Are you sure you're all right?'

'Yes.' I hesitated, then added, 'I don't think I'm hitting it off very well with the others, though.'

'Why's that?' he asked, sounding surprised.

'I don't know, just a feeling.'

'It's the language barrier, that's all,' he said reassuringly. 'Be patient; you'll be fluent in French in no time, then it will be a lot easier. Gregoire's a bit awkward at first, *pas bien dans sa peau*. He's always very shy with people he doesn't know.'

I smiled inwardly at this allusion to Gregoire's skin. But I knew it was more than a language barrier – rather a great ocean of differences that lay between us.

'Sévérine just informed me that Marguerite has left New York, and is back in Geneva,' I said casually.

'That's correct,' he replied, without much interest.

'She said it was because of you,' I continued. 'Actually, it was awful, the way it came across – as if I didn't exist!'

'It's got nothing to do with me,' he replied. 'It's because of the business. New York was only an interlude.'

Like Sévérine had insinuated I was?

'I thought she'd given up the interior design business to follow you to London?'

'It's a partnership,' he told me. 'She kept her share all along.'

'Oh.' I traced a pattern in the sand, trying to come to terms with the fact that soon we'd all be living in the same city. 'It was almost as if Sévérine was threatening me,' I said after a silence.

'Don't pay any attention to that,' he replied irritably. 'Sévérine plays the loyal sister act when it suits her, but the truth is there is no love lost between them. Don't look too deep for hidden motives – it's all playacting with Sévérine.'

Yet he seemed to be entertained by it.

'I wonder why Marguerite was looking for you here?'

'It was probably something to do with the apartment,' he answered, 'sorting out the wheat from the husk.'

I grinned. 'The chaff from the wheat.' I remembered they had been together off and on for five years – their breaking up was almost a divorce.

'I sometimes feel that we'll never be free of the past,' I told him.

He reached over and took my hand, 'That's ridiculous. Marguerite is just a friend now; you're my wife.'

'I know,' I said, wondering why he had to hang on to everything that passed through his life, and if I would ever be able to take her place in this tight-knit group, or would be forever blamed for having upset the status quo.

I smiled, as if reassured, but Séverine had unnerved me, bringing back all the doubts again.

'How about a swim?' Michel suggested, as if he had sensed my thoughts. We got up and raced each other into the sea. It was pitch dark now; the sea had turned black, and lights shone from the villas between the palm trees.

'Race you to that boat,' he said, taking long powerful strokes through the water.

I swam after him, but he reached it way before me. He pulled me into the boat, saying, 'What kept you? I thought this was meant to be a race?'

'Just you wait,' I said breathlessly. 'One day I'll overtake you.'

'I don't doubt it,' he replied.

I felt his wet body against mine and saw the Milky Way above us, and Marguerite, Séverine and Gregoire seemed to fade away as if they belonged to another time and place.

Chapter Twelve

The following day the sky was dark with clouds as the storm gathered around us. Michel said it made no difference, as under the waves it was always calm.

Séverine was all sweetness and light once again, greeting me with smiles and kisses as if yesterday's dialogue had never taken place. Gregoire was her target now. She snapped at him twice over breakfast, before announcing she would spend the day alone, while Michel and I went off to the beach where I was to begin my lessons.

The diving school provided all the equipment and the instructor explained the basics, but it was Michel who showed me that diving was not the terrifying ordeal I had imagined it to be. I discovered there was something quite peaceful about being beneath the waves, with only the sound of my echoed breathing, while the storm rumbled above us and rain fell like silver drops on the surface of the sea.

We dived together every afternoon for a week, until I became familiar with the equipment and had learnt the basic skills. I followed Michel and the instructor over the coral beds, where pale sea anemones shifted with the current; through luminous shoals of tiny sprat-like creatures, angel fish; over the eel beds and into deeper water where giant underwater forests grew. Séverine sometimes joined us, darting hither and thither, her black hair floating behind her, while Gregoire disappeared on some mysterious mission of his own.

In the evenings we would dine together in one of the local restaurants, Séverine tanned and glowing in some diaphanous creation, Gregoire withering beside her. I would follow the conversation for a while, then drift off into my own thoughts. At times I longed for other company, to be amongst people who spoke my language. But most of the time I longed for the end of the day, when Michel and I would finally be alone together.

One evening we drove to a small village in the hills to watch the sun go down, and ate dinner in a restaurant overlooking a wide river that ran into the sea. The stormy weather had blown over, leaving the sky pale and streaked with thin clouds. We drank a bottle of champagne and ate river shrimps with lime, and afterwards Gregoire turned to me, and said, 'I hope you are ready for tomorrow's expedition to Turtle Rock?'

I nodded confidently. Although he seemed to have warmed to me slightly, I couldn't help feeling that this was some kind of test I must pass before I was finally accepted as one of them.

The following day the sky was clear and blue, but the wind churned up the sea, and waves broke further out towards the reef. Gregoire and Sévérine moved with feverish purpose, organising drinks and equipment.

I stood on the veranda listening to Sévérine issue orders to Santiago, who carried the four tanks out of the boatshed, sweat dripping down his forehead, and lined them up on the grass. Sévérine walked up and down like a general inspecting his troops, dismissed one of them as being the wrong tank, and sent Santiago back for a replacement. The equipment was then taken down to the marina, where the captain and crew of Gregoire's boat were waiting to take us out to Turtle Rock.

I stood on the jetty staring out across the sea, afraid suddenly. The rock seemed so far away, and large waves were breaking over it. Sévérine was swaggering along the jetty in a tight diving suit that showed off the perfect contours of her body; she carried another, less glamorous one, under one arm, which she threw at me. 'It is cold down there,' she said. I took it from her gratefully, not caring how I looked, for in spite of the sun I was already cold.

Finally we were all aboard Gregoire's huge Bertram, and heading away from the marina to Turtle Rock. The sea began to get rough as we went; the boat bumped over the waves and I smelt the fumes of the engine above us. As we drew closer, I saw the rock was far bigger than I had thought, like a giant turtle with a long sinuous neck. Gulls perched on its highest point, and the waves sucked and hissed around it.

We dropped anchor close by and the captain switched off the engine. The equipment was assembled, Gregoire issuing instructions to his crew, then he struggled into his wet suit and pulled up the hood, so he resembled some kind of creature from the deep.

Séverine was sitting on the rear platform, rinsing her mask in the sea. They seemed to have forgotten about Michel and me, leaving us to rifle through the flippers and masks that lay in the stern. Without a word, Gregoire put the regulator to his mouth and jumped into the sea. Séverine followed from the platform, dropping gracefully into the water, where she bobbed around for a couple of minutes before sinking below the waves.

I turned to Michel and said, 'Well, it looks like we're on our own!'

Michel didn't seem in the least put out by their sudden wordless exit. He pulled his mask over his head, saying, 'We normally dive in pairs. Now let's get you sorted out first.'

The crew had already assembled my scuba unit, which felt different from what I had become accustomed to during the lessons. Michel shifted the tank to a more comfortable position on my back, but it felt heavier somehow, and the motion of the boat was making me leaden and clumsy, so everything was an enormous effort.

'Remember not to hold your breath,' Michel was saying. 'It's no different from what we've already done – a few feet more, that's all. But if at any stage you feel uncomfortable, flash me the signal.'

I stood on the platform, swaying under the weight of the tank. The sea looked dark and bottomless but, flashing Michel what I hoped was a confident smile, I half jumped and half fell into the water. He was beside me in an instant. We swam to the anchor line, and he made the signal to descend.

I felt the pull of the current as I sank down in a rush of bubbles, and looked around wildly for Michel. He was already a few feet below me, his hair floating like seaweed around his face, his eyes beckoning me to follow. I cleared my ears, and tried to breathe slowly to calm myself, but what felt like a battering ram in my chest caused me to gulp the compressed air. The water was cold and cloudy, with a dusty look, quite different from the clear shallows I had become accustomed to. There was no sign of a sandy bottom, no bright shoals of fish, just a great expanse of turbid sea.

As we slowly descended into the murky depths, I began to feel oddly disoriented. A dizzying profusion of tiny luminous particles streamed towards us, making the visibility worse. As the pressure increased, I breathed faster, swallowing mouthfuls of air, panicked suddenly. Michel had left the anchor line now, and was swimming away from me. I forced myself on, trying to grab the tip of his flipper as it waved and danced in front of me. We must have entered a thermocline, I thought vaguely, for suddenly the water was icy cold, and had taken on a hazy, shimmering quality, like heat rising off an asphalt road. Again I tried to reach for Michel's flipper, but my hand struck out uselessly against a bank of water.

Then I saw the sea bed coming towards me, dark with weeds, and through the gloom could make out the rusty edge of the wreck, rising one moment, receding the next. My heart lurched at the sight of the broken vessel, and strange images swirled in my head – Toddy Freeman lying at the bottom of the ocean in the shell that was *Merryman* . . . Father, and how he had drifted away from me in that terrible dream . . . I stared in horror at the gaping hole in the ship's hull. Fish swam placidly in and out of it, and I wondered for a sickening moment if they had feasted off the dead crew.

I looked around for Michel. He must have gone around the other side, to try and access the hold. Then I saw the swaying beam of his flashlight and swam towards it. I was breathing so fast now I was sure I had sucked the tank dry of air – Marguerite's air, I thought dazedly, trying to get a hold of myself. I must have touched the sea bed with my flipper, for suddenly sand was swirling in a cloud around me.

As I reached the wreck, something swam out of the murky hull – something long and snakelike that seemed to be heading straight for my mask.

In a parody of a horror movie it opened its mouth, and I saw a row of sharp teeth. I started back, and as I did so the regulator fell out of my mouth. Choking and gasping, I groped around in the cloudy water in an effort to retrieve it.

In the chaos that followed I saw Michel's eyes, globulous like the eyes of a fish, staring at me. Then I was breathing again from some other air source, and the next moment he was guiding me slowly up the anchor line to the surface.

We surfaced in a cloud of bubbles, and one of the crew helped us on board. Once free of my tank and equipment, I collapsed in the stern, trying to catch my breath. There was a burning sensation in my chest and lungs. Michel loosened the zip of my diving suit and crouched down beside me.

'I'm sorry,' I gasped, as soon as I could breathe normally. I tried to sit up, then fell back again.

'Shh, *calme-toi*,' he said soothingly. He pushed the hair out of my eyes, saying, 'It was too much too soon! I shouldn't have rushed you . . .'

We sat there for a while, not talking, the boat rocking sickeningly beneath us. Then there was a splashing sound and Gregoire surfaced, water running along the crevices of his face.

'What happened?' he asked, spitting water as he came on board.

'She felt bad,' Michel answered.

'Why?' he inquired in a puzzled tone. He worked his way out of his scuba unit, which he handed to the captain.

'It happens,' said Michel loyally.

'You were afraid!' Gregoire stated simply.

'Yes,' I replied, equally direct. 'I was afraid.'

'*Mais pourquoi*?' he said turning to Michel.

Séverine suddenly appeared behind him. 'What the hell happened to you two?' she said, using a harsh French slang.

Michel was looking at me, as if waiting for an answer.

'It was the wreck,' I said to him. 'I kept thinking of the people who went down with it – who knows, maybe they're still trapped inside.' I lowered my voice and added, 'There were snakes in there . . .'

'That was an eel you saw,' he said soothingly. 'Remember the eel beds?'

'It looked different somehow,' I said, thinking of those sharp teeth.

'Everything's magnified underwater, remember . . . I think we should head back,' Michel announced, turning to the others.

'Fine,' replied Gregoire with a shrug. Even the back of his head looked annoyed.

Séverine was busy pulling off her wet suit. There was a strange expression on her face, a flicker of triumph in her eyes before she turned away.

Michel suggested I stay behind the following day, while they returned to the rock. 'It'll be rough out there,' he said. 'Besides, you've probably done enough diving for the time being.'

I'd been secretly hoping we would spend the day together on the beach – this was our honeymoon, after all. But plans had already been made.

I nodded, deciding to spend the day by the pool reading a book.

I watched them leave from the veranda, Séverine throwing her head back and laughing as Michel helped her into the jeep, and turned away with a heavy heart. I had no desire to join them, but at the same time felt excluded. Gregoire had planned to explore different parts of the reef every day for the rest of the week. There was no point accompanying them unless I was going to dive, he said flatly. The sea tended to be choppy out there, and it would be uncomfortable.

I lay down in the shade of the palm trees, and closed my eyes. It was peaceful there, in the frangipani-scented air, listening to the waves breaking on the beach below. Yet I could not shake off that dull feeling. I sensed the future would hold a series of challenges such as this, and wondered if I'd ever manage to keep up with them.

Michel didn't pressure me to join them the next day, when again I opted to stay behind.

'Are you sure you don't mind me going?' he said. 'We might not be back until lunch time.'

'No, go,' I said, with a forced smile. I knew he was torn in two directions. He had come here to dive, after all – it had all been arranged – he couldn't let his hosts down.

The weather had become more settled. The sun shone from a blanched sky, and the villa lay shrouded in silence, broken only by the sound of the gardeners clipping the hedges. Santiago brought me a rum cocktail as I lay reading by the pool.

'To our honeymoon,' I said, raising my glass in a solitary toast before tipping it back – and falling instantly asleep.

I dreamt I was swimming through a shoal of snakelike creatures with their mouths open. In my dream the sea was calm, but so hot it scorched my skin. I woke up dizzy and sweating, to find the sun was directly overhead, and dived into the pool to cool myself. I swam up and down, trying to shake off the mood, but the beauty and luxury of the place now seemed oppressive, only adding to my sense of loneliness.

I started to dwell on that conversation with Séverine by the pool, the first day. It did seem, now, that she had been making some kind of veiled threat, and I wondered vaguely if my first impression of Marguerite's beautiful twin sister, when I had seen her standing there looking dark and evil in the shadows, had been the correct one, as first impressions so often are.

Then they were back – I heard a babble of French conversation as they discussed the day's events, Séverine shrieking with laughter over Michel's antics below the waves, making me feel more isolated than ever.

Michel and I spent our last day together on the beach, while the others were out diving. A couple of new guests had arrived that morning from Switzerland, taking the pressure off us.

We lay together by the water's edge, not talking much.

'This is absolute heaven,' I said dreamily. Michel's skin was deeply tanned now – he looked very continental, Italian or Greek, I thought.

He smiled. 'It doesn't take much to make you happy, does it?' he said, kissing my hot shoulder.

'No, only you,' I replied.

Later, we swam out to the fishing boat that was still moored there, and lay sunbathing on the deck, rocked by the waves.

For lunch, Michel made a small fire on the beach and we cooked some red mullet, freshly caught that morning by the local fishermen: Gregoire's chef had made a salad, and there was even a bottle of chilled white wine, with fresh fruit for dessert.

'That was a perfect day,' I told him, as we made our way back to the villa.

He was quieter than usual – we were both dopey from the sun. Then the others were back, turning everything loud and hectic again, and Michel immediately changed. He became animated all of a sudden, as Gregoire described the day's events; he laughed, too loudly it seemed, and his face lit up. I realised then that, in spite of the wonderful day we had spent together, he was wishing he'd been with them.

'Are you OK, *cherie*? he inquired suddenly, as we were relaxing in our room before dinner. 'Have you enjoyed the holiday? I'm sorry we didn't spend a bit more time together.'

'It was lovely,' I assured him, hoping I sounded genuine. 'It really is a beautiful island.'

'Once we're settled in Switzerland, I'll take you away for a second honeymoon,' he said. 'We'll drive into the Bernese Oberland, and I'll show you some spectacular places.'

'I'd like that,' I said, hoping there would be no rocks he would suddenly want to climb, no distractions such as Sévérine and Gregoire to lure him away. He pulled me into his arms, and, once again, I forgot everything else and for those few idyllic moments there were just Michel and me and the sound of the waves breaking on the beach below.

Chapter Thirteen

I wasn't feeling well. We had been back from our honeymoon for a fortnight, and it already seemed as if we'd never been away. Some mornings I woke up feeling so lethargic I wondered if I'd slept at all. Now a new fear had started to keep me awake at night.

The move to Switzerland had been postponed until after Christmas, while Michel tied up his affairs in the London office. He left for Geneva, to prepare the apartment for our return amongst other things, and rang every evening to tell me the news, sounding relaxed and cheerful, pleased with the way things were progressing. He was having the apartment redecorated and some of the furniture replaced, he informed me. He had taken an afternoon off and driven up to the mountains with an old friend. The weather was cold but bright, with some early snow . . . He missed me and couldn't wait for us to be together again.

I was working on *The Love Trap* when the suspicion first formed. I had reached the part where Tom Murphy told Mother he couldn't go on seeing her; the family turning against her, Mother abandoned, forced to leave the country she loved. Had she become ill after that, I wondered, from misery and heartache? Then, suddenly, my thoughts returned to my own condition. I made a frantic calculation and froze. I could no longer ignore the symptoms now.

I went to a doctor in Harley Street, unable to face an anonymous National Health clinic, and did the test the same afternoon. Michel had no idea I was no longer taking the pill, and I'd taken the odd risk lest he should suspect. Now, as I waited for the results, I realised I had fallen into that foolish trap of believing it couldn't happen to me.

After what seemed an interminable wait, I was ushered into the surgery. The doctor looked up from a file on his desk as I entered, and motioned me to sit down. In a daze I heard him say, 'Congratulations, Mrs Gautier,' and for one mad moment I thought he was congratulating me on my narrow escape, rather

119

than on the fact that I was almost six weeks, pregnant. His beam altered to an expression of startled concern as I slumped back in my chair and burst into tears.

'Are you all right, Mrs Gautier?' he was saying.

'It's a disaster,' I said desperately, 'the worst thing that could possibly happen.'

I heard him say, 'There are alternatives. I suggest you go home, discuss it with your husband and weigh it all up carefully . . . In the meantime no cigarettes, alcohol, or too much rushing around.'

Then I was walking blindly out of his consulting room towards Marylebone High Street, in a state of numbed disbelief. How could I possibly discuss it with Michel, I thought in despair? He was not open to discussion. Hadn't this been one of the prerequisites of us becoming man and wife? Marguerite had wanted children and they had parted because of it. I knew he didn't want to be shackled with a child.

I realised then that he had never really paused to ask what I wanted; had assumed that I shared his views, since no maternal yearnings had come from me. Well, in a way he was right – it was hard enough trying to keep up with him, without going through the mystifying process of childbirth in a strange country, with a man who was dead set against it. Foiled on the way to the clinic for a vasectomy, I thought grimly.

I was brought up with a jolt at the sound of somebody calling my name, and saw Hervé Dubois coming towards me from the direction of his office further down the street.

'Emily, what is it?' he asked with concern. 'Is there a problem?'

'It's nothing,' I said stupidly, annoyed at this untimely meeting.

'You are upset,' he said. '*Tu n'as pas une bonne mine.*'

Was this all he could deduce from his great experience into human psyche, I wondered irritably?

'I'm on my way to lunch,' he told me. 'I'd be happy if you would accompany me.'

God knows why I accepted. Tempted by the thought of a listening ear, perhaps; desperate to escape from the silent reproach of an empty flat?

We went to a wine bar called Barrels, off Marylebone High Street. Inside it was so dark you could barely see what you were eating. Hervé ordered a bottle of wine, and I drank a glass wondering if I should be drinking at all. Hadn't the doctor said no alcohol? I was about to light a cigarette, then put it away again.

'How was the holiday? Michel tells me you had a bad dive,' Hervé was saying conversationally, easing his way gently into the subject.

'Oh that,' I said, not wanting to go into it with Hervé, and at that moment I made the connection. I had been pregnant! That explained the dizziness and nausea . . . Alarmed, I wondered if that dive had damaged the tiny cell that was forming.

'Oh Christ,' I said, slumping forward.

'What is it, Emily?' Hervé was looking at me oddly.

I groped for a cigarette thinking 'what the hell', inhaled deeply and let out a stream of smoke.

'Nothing, I'm fine now,' I told him, attempting to smile.

His pale eyes bored into me, like the blue rays of a strobe light in the dark room.

'It is my belief that you are still suffering from trauma,' he said bluntly. 'I've seen this kind of thing before – when a person suffers a loss in their lives, like both parents. They can become very destabilised.' He placed his fingertips together in the shape of a steeple, and added 'If there is any way I can help?'

He was on the wrong track, of course. When I didn't answer, he said, 'Why don't you come in and see me one day this week – nothing formal, just a chat? Michel doesn't have to know, if you'd rather he didn't.'

I was suddenly overwhelmed by the idea of unburdening the real problem, but knew he was the wrong person.

'. . . think about it, anyway,' he was saying. 'Remember it's my job to help people find their peace of mind.'

I'll never know why I went in the end – perhaps if Michel had returned from Geneva sooner, or if I'd been able to talk to Aunt G or somebody equally close, I would have thought no more about it.

Up until then, I'd always imagined a session with a psychiatrist as it is so often depicted in films – the patient lying prostrate on the couch, digging up significant memories of the past, while the psychiatrist sits mutely behind his desk jotting down notes on a pad in front of him. In that short and seemingly insignificant session with Hervé Dubois, it was the opposite. It was I who listened, while he sat, legs outstretched, and talked.

He talked about the loss of my parents, and the effects of such a loss. He gave examples of traumatised patients who had lost next of kin, and of the recuperation process that sometimes took years. He described a totally different world as he spoke, a world of fragile, damaged individuals whose behavioural patterns were diverse and in some cases destructive.

He moved on then to Michel, who, he said, was busy trying to deal with his own ghosts – his senile mother, his alcoholic father also lost to him, his lonely childhood. His way was to shut it all out, by surrounding himself with people with whom he had shared past experiences.

'Sometimes I feel totally hemmed in by his past,' I admitted, drawn into his confidence.

I told him briefly, then, of the conversation I had had with Séverine that day by the pool, and how she had made those threats of Marguerite returning to him.

'Michel's a very social person,' he said unnecessarily. 'He finds it hard to let go of anything . . . He tries to make his old girlfriends his friends – like Séverine di Maggiore. He hangs onto his past like people hang onto old clothes.'

I remembered that first time Michael had taken me back to the flat, and said, 'I find it impossible to part with anything.'

'. . . as for Marguerite,' Hervé was saying candidly, 'she is an attractive but foolish woman who had become obsessed with the idea of a child.'

I froze. This seemed to have turned from a professional exchange into a gossip session. I knew I couldn't confide in him now.

'There's nothing wrong with wanting a child,' I said instead.

'No, of course not, only it wasn't what Michel wanted.'

I looked away, feeling for once some empathy for the thwarted Marguerite, and a sudden anger against the uncompromising Michel.

'One thing, off the record,' (Did that mean that everything else was *on* the record?) 'I have never seen Michel so happy before – forget about the past, concentrate on the present and the future.'

Yet what would the future hold now, I wondered?

'How do you feel physically?' he moved on. 'You seem to be showing some signs of anxiousness.'

'Anxiety,' I corrected him.

'Yes,' he replied. 'I can prescribe something that will help. You're not pregnant, I hope?' he added with a smile.

'No,' I lied swiftly.

'Good.' He picked up his pen and wrote something on a prescription pad. 'I don't want you to consider this a tranquilliser, since it's very mild, but it will help with the difficult time ahead.' He smiled sympathetically. 'It's hard to change countries – I know that better than anybody.'

The move had been the last thing on my mind – now I remembered we were leaving at the end of the month.

'I don't want to take pills,' I said. I felt like telling him that no pill could possibly make everything right, but he was handing me the prescription.

'Take it,' he urged. 'They will help – you'll see. And ring me next week to let me know how you are feeling. I assure you I will be discreet.'

I took the prescription, and got up to go. It was this last sentence that I was to remember later, and conclude bitterly that promises, ethics and integrity went flying out of the window when the chips were down.

Michel came back from Geneva at the end of the week. He walked in swinging his briefcase in front of him, and loosened his tie before slumping down on the sofa beside me.

'I missed you,' he said.

'I missed you, too.'

'The apartment is looking respectable, are you all set for your new life?'

I stared at the ground, trying to find the words to explain.

'What is it?' he asked, taking my hand. 'Is it the thought of leaving London?'

'No,' I replied, although that bright vision of Switzerland I had once had, with its lakes and mountains, was now clouded by the shadows of Sévérine, Gregoire and Marguerite.

'Then what? You seem depressed.'

I opened my mouth, but the words wouldn't come. I thought, he'll consider it a trap . . . I took a deep breath, and said, 'I'm pregnant. I've just found out.'

He went completely still, as if shock had turned him to stone. 'How did it happen?' he asked finally, his voice heavy and doom-laden.

'It must have happened before we went away.' (I had pin-pointed it to our wedding night, the ultimate cliché.) 'I've been feeling unwell for a while – perhaps that's why I kept imagining things.' I was searching for the right words – a buffer against the shock, anything to bring him back to life again.

'You've always imagined things,' he said.

He looked, I thought, like a condemned man from whom the last remnants of happiness had flown. The creases around his eyes seemed deeper suddenly, and I noticed for the first time a few grey streaks at his temple.

'I thought you were taking pills,' he said.

'They made me feel sick. I've never liked taking pills.'

He laughed on a false note. 'I bet you feel a lot worse now!'

'It's a different feeling,' I said. 'I didn't exactly plan it,' I said a little later. 'I'm as shocked as you are.'

'It's a shock, all right,' he replied. 'A child was never part of my plans.'

'Perhaps it was part of mine,' I said. 'In the long term, that is.'

'I didn't realise.'

'You never asked.'

'When?' he said finally, as if counting the precious time that was left to him.

'Theoretically July.'

'You'll miss the skiing season!' He rubbed his forehead in a characteristic gesture of despair.

'There'll be other seasons.' But there wouldn't be other babies, I thought. He would make sure of that.

But I had to know how far he wanted me to go.

'What do you want me to do, Michel?' I asked desperately.

The silence in the room was almost tangible. We had become strangers suddenly. He must have realised, then, what I was going through.

'You must do what you think is right,' he said at last.

'You'd like me to get rid of it, wouldn't you?'

'I haven't asked that.'

'I can't,' I said.

'I know.' He sounded resigned. He took my hand and squeezed it gently. 'I realise that.'

'So now what?' I felt as though I were the one who was trapped.

'Well,' he said, trying to lighten up, 'I suppose one of us gets what they want.'

'What about us, though, the marriage – how will it affect us?'

I was watching him closely, trying to deduce whether he could ever adapt to this new situation.

'Ah, now you're asking the key question,' he replied, 'and that, I'm afraid, nobody can answer.'

We stared at one another in silence, our eyes locked, considering the great gamble of the future, and whether we would beat the odds.

The chances that it would cost us our marriage were slim, but they existed. And if that was the case, I concluded fearfully, there would be no alternative but to pay the price.

I thought of Mother then, and how she used to say, 'You pay your money and you take your chances.'

PART TWO

Chapter Fourteen

Switzerland, the winter of 1982

The Alps were hidden by dense snow clouds the day we landed, and a thick grey mist hung over the city.

Cold dry air seemed to come up from the ground, freezing all extremities within seconds. It bit into the ears and numbed the fingers and toes. Facial nerves ached from its impact. In spite of my thick coat and the layers of clothing beneath it, I shivered as we waited outside the terminal building for Gregoire, who was meeting us, to arrive. I saw then how unprotected I was against it. The people who passed by wore sheepskins and furs, puffy ski jackets, scarves wrapped Cossack style around their heads, fur-lined boots or heavy walking shoes with thick soles. Michel, dressed for a wet English day in a light beige raincoat, didn't seem affected, however. Instead he appeared rather invigorated by it, as he paced the pavement sending clouds of condensation into the freezing air.

'You don't notice the temperature after a while,' he assured me, as I stood hunched and shivering beside our cases. 'It's a dry cold – doesn't get into your bones. All the same,' he added, glancing at his watch with irritation, 'one shouldn't linger too long.' He shot me a worried look (he often looked worried these days), and at that moment Gregoire pulled up beside us in a black Jaguar. The window slid down, and he smiled his most beastly smile. He had stopped to collect the keys of the apartment, he said, explaining his late arrival.

Without his suntan he looked worse than ever. His eyelids, which had hung in baggy folds in the heat, seemed to have retracted, and his skin had a dry and flaky appearance, as if he were about to shed it.

As we drove through the silent streets, it struck me we were entering a ghost town – which the people had only recently vacated, for everything appeared to be still running. A bus attached to electric cables swung out in front of us, shooting yellow sparks into the air, while taxis sped past, the shadowy forms of passengers within. The shops were lit up, but the pavements deserted, in this no man's land that skirted the city.

But as we drew closer to the lake, towards an expensive shopping area that flashed brand names, banks and international hotels, there was more evidence of life. Here men in long dark coats like plain-clothes policemen and women in furs walked at a brisk pace. Nobody lingered for long at shop windows. They moved swiftly to escape the cold.

Gregoire lit a cigar, so I rolled down the window and breathed deeply, afraid of the nausea that was with me all the time now, and felt the cold air hit my lungs.

Michel hadn't mentioned the baby to anybody – it was almost as if he had blanked it from his mind. Apart from Aunt G, nobody else knew. But from time to time I'd sense him watching me closely, and he often asked how I was feeling, perhaps to make up for the words he couldn't bring himself to say.

We pulled up at a set of traffic lights and there was the lake, like a grey sheet stretching to the left of us. A few gulls wheeled overhead as we crossed the Mont Blanc Bridge, then we turned left along a wide avenue lined with bare plane trees, running parallel to the lake.

Michel said, 'Let's continue up to Le Nautique – I'd like Emily to see *Jolie Brise*.'

We followed the lake front for a while longer, towards the sailing club. A solitary jogger bobbed beneath the plane trees, and a woman walked a dog dressed in a tartan coat, but these were the only signs of life. Ahead lay a squat grey building, and long jetties built out into the water. Here boats covered in tarpaulins sat motionless on the water, like a still-life painting blurred in the mist. Gregoire slowed down, and pulled into the car park.

'There she is!' Michel exclaimed, pointing towards the jetty where a line of wooden sailing boats were moored. 'You can't see much – she's all covered up.'

He turned around and smiled at me, saying 'Another reminder?'

I couldn't see much from where I sat, but I smiled back.

'Emily's father owned a William Fife,' Michel explained to Gregoire.

'So you know how to sail, then?' Gregoire stated, interested now.

'Yes,' I replied.

'Good,' he said, as if it were one of the prerequisites for living here. Then he reversed and pulled out of the car park, turning back the way we had come.

We drove up into the town, past more lit-up shops.

'Where is everybody?' I asked curiously, as we glided through the empty streets.

'In the mountains,' Michel replied. 'There's a mass exodus from the city every weekend. Once you get above the clouds the weather is spectacular. We'll drive up there tomorrow, if you like.'

A plan had already been made that we would join Gregoire and Sévérine for the skiing season. Every year they rented the same chalet in Mégève, Michel had explained – only the crowd differed. Michel would ski, while I explored the town, wrote, or whatever took my fancy. Gregoire was now talking about the people who were there this season, reeling off names I had heard in the past; talking about runs they had done, restaurants they had frequented, dinners they had attended. I thought of sleek, bronzed women like Sévérine in designer ski suits, poised elegantly on the piste, and athletic men with mirrored glasses snaking down the slopes.

'You must take some skiing lessons,' Gregoire said, glancing at me in his rear view mirror.

Michel answered for me. 'Not this year,' he said. 'She's pregnant.'

Gregoire almost did a double take. He was silent for a moment, then swerved across the tram lines into the right-hand lane following the signs that read *La Vielle Ville*. '*Quoi*?' he said, incredulously, '*ce ne pas vrai. . . ?*' as if it were some rare and debilitating disease. '*Oh la la*,' he said, glancing at Michel curiously, as if trying to determine how he had fallen into such an unfortunate trap.

I felt as if I had arrived on an alien planet where procreation took place by laying an egg, so they could carry on with the challenging business of their lives without interruption.

131

We were now entering the old part of the city, where the streets were narrow and steep, lined with dark cafés, pâtisseries and art galleries. We passed the *Bourg de Four* in the centre of the old town, and then were suddenly into a residential area of tree-lined avenues, where tall buildings with jutting balconies stood. Miniature street cleaners with revolving brushes crawled along the pavements, spraying jets of water onto the already immaculate street, and cars moved slowly now, aware of the '*canari*', or radar, hidden in the trees.

We pulled up outside a dun-coloured building, and I looked up to the penthouse and saw the tip of a small pine tree, standing like a sentinel in the grey and freezing air.

Inside, the apartment was quite different from what I had imagined. It had a touch of contemporary elegance, but it was coldly done, with an eye to aesthetics rather than comfort. A tan leather suite crouched around a low marble-topped table, and there were other fashionable pieces placed in strategic positions throughout the apartment. But scattered amongst this prosaic assemblage were odd touches of beauty – two amber lampstands, glowing like dying coals, stood on matching coffee tables, and the dining table was an elegant Victorian piece, with eight spindly-legged chairs that had been in Michel's family for years. The floors had been carpeted in pale beige, and the walls were a startling hospital white. Through the shutters that opened onto a narrow balcony, I caught a glimpse of the mountains. I stared around in awe, unable to identify Michel's taste. He was pointing out the various changes that had been made since the last tenants had moved out. The carpet was new, the rooms had all been repainted, new furniture bought, and pieces like the dining table taken out of storage. Dust motes swirled around the room, settling on the pale carpets, and I thought of the immaculate streets below and wondered where they had come from.

'Well?' said Michel, turning to gauge my reaction, 'how do you like your new home?'

'It's very nice,' I said, hoping I sounded more enthusiastic than I felt.

I sensed Gregoire's eyes upon me before he spoke. They were round and staring, with the fixed gaze of a toad watching a fly before the whip of its tongue lashed out for the kill. 'It is much improved,' he said in French. 'This time she's done a very good job.'

It took a moment to register – the words banged painfully against my ears, as if they'd been refused entry. Of course, I thought with a sense of disbelief, Marguerite! A talented interior designer. Michel had asked her to take care of it!

I heard him say, 'I asked her to change those curtains as well – they're too light for this room,' and was aware of that presentiment again. I envisaged the two of them sitting cosily together, discussing colour schemes and furniture, that week I had stayed in London . . . Was this what Séverine had been trying to warn me against? Was there no getting away from the woman? I wondered crossly. I remembered that she had an apartment in the old town, along one of those narrow winding streets we had passed – only a stone's throw away. I took a deep breath and, forcing a smile on my face, repeated, 'It's very nice.' But they were still discussing the business of the unchanged curtains, and didn't hear me.

Later, Michel led the way up a short flight of wooden steps to the roof terrace. He unlocked the door and we all trooped out into the freezing air. A narrow bed of earth bordered the terrace, where the pine tree grew, while the rest of the beds were virtually empty. Only the stunted stems of a row of geraniums and a solitary winter rose, straggling out of the frozen earth, remained.

I walked to the edge and looked down to the courtyard dizzily far below, the conciergerie shuttered; beyond, I could make out the misty gleam of the lake. Gregoire was now playing the part of tour guide, pointing into the clouds to where the Mont Blanc stood, but the cold was making my face ache, so I left them and retreated below.

I went into the bedroom and lay on the king-size bed staring up at the white ceiling, still uneasy. Why hadn't he mentioned that he'd asked Marguerite to decorate the apartment, I wondered? Was it because of that silent pact we had made not to talk about the past, lest it should taint the future? And what had impelled her to take on the work in the first place? Had she offered her services as a final favour to an old friend, or was it a way of trying to hang onto him? 'We shouldn't have come,' I said out loud.

Exhausted suddenly, I closed my eyes and dozed for a while. When I woke up, I heard the mutter of voices coming from the other room. I joined them, willing Gregoire to leave, but he stayed for another hour, finally taking himself off in a cloud of cigar smoke, having issued various invitations to lunches and dinners in the coming weeks.

'I thought he'd never go,' I said, when we were alone in the sitting room at last.

'It was very good of him to have done all this,' Michel replied defensively. 'Picking us up from the airport, getting the apartment in order – he even stocked the fridge, so we don't have to go out and buy food. I couldn't have managed without him.'

Or Marguerite, I thought, looking around the immaculate room. But I vowed I would not say it.

'Come here,' he said suddenly. He picked me up in his arms, then carried me into the bedroom and threw me unceremoniously onto the bed. Kissing rather frantically, I felt my unease vanish at last.

We lay there afterwards still entwined under the soft quilt, until the daylight had faded. Eventually he extricated himself and left the room, coming back with a tray of thinly sliced smoked salmon decorated with slices of lemon, a baguette, a jar of caviar – 'The real thing, this time,' he announced – and a bottle of champagne with two glasses.

'To make you feel at home,' he said, opening the champagne with a flourish.

I smiled, saying, 'You've already made me feel at home.'

But looking around the stark room, I knew I'd never feel totally at home here. I would have to make some changes, I decided. I would hang Aunt G's paintings in the main room, and fill the bookshelves with glossy hardback books. We would eat our meals in the kitchen, I thought, which was cosier, and make a comfortable corner where the television was. Excited by my plans, I started unpacking our belongings, filling the wardrobes with our clothes, placing the familiar objects we had brought from London on the matching dressers.

But when I'd emptied all the boxes, I looked around with a sense of defeat. The room still looked large and alien, with the transient air of a hotel suite, and I wondered if I'd ever be able to change it.

Chapter Fifteen

The following day was one of those icy winter days that often follows a bad spell. I awoke to a flawless blue sky. Stripes of light filtered through the shutters. I reached across to Michel, but the bed was empty. He was already up, and had been out to the bakery. The smell of coffee and warm bread wafted from the kitchen.

'How did you sleep?' he inquired, pecking me on the cheek.

'Like a log,' I replied. 'I couldn't think where I was when I woke up.'

'Go and have a look,' he urged, motioning towards the stairs to the terrace.

I climbed the steps, opened the door and stepped outside. The cold was like a shock wave, the view breathtakingly lovely. Yesterday's clouds had lifted, so now I saw the lake like a tarnished coin stretching below, framed by the Jura. Everything was completely still and silent, the pine tree stiff with frost, and the street was empty of cars. The conciergerie was still shuttered, and there was hardly a breath of wind. I saw the white speck of a gull hovering above, but even it seemed motionless, frozen against the blue canvas of the sky. I stared, mesmerised by the icy beauty, like an exquisite painting in which everything had been slightly exaggerated.

In the spring I would plant rows of bright geraniums and delphiniums, I decided, looking at the empty beds, and maybe some herbs in boxes. I'd always fancied tending a garden of my own.

We ate breakfast in the kitchen. Michel had bought some *brioche* and another bread called '*une tresse*' – soft milk bread woven into a plait and baked to a dark mahogany. We ate it with unsalted butter and *Cenovis*, a yeast extract not unlike Marmite. I poured myself another cup of the strong Italian coffee and gazed out of the window. 'I'm never going to be thin again,' I said contentedly.

135

Michel smiled. 'It's a good life here,' he said. 'You're going to love it.'

After breakfast, we crossed the border into France and drove into the mountains on a narrow winding road, past wooden chalets with rooves weighted down with snow. Below us, valleys of a dazzling whiteness sparkled with a diamond edge. It was postcard material, I thought – beautiful, almost too perfect.

'Are you all right?' Michel inquired as we reached the top.

'Fine,' I replied bravely, hoping the road would be less winding from now on.

He covered my hand with his. 'Tell me if you want me to stop,' he said.

We were approaching a ski resort, where cable cars slid up the mountains, and people stomped through the snow with skis balanced on their shoulders. Then the village ended abruptly and we crossed a deep valley, through flatter landscape filled with pine trees and farmhouses. Michel turned off the road into an even narrower lane, and we got out and walked up a steep path to an auberge where people sat outside eating and drinking on the terrace. I sat down thankfully, glad to be out in the fresh air.

'This is where people come to cross-country ski,' Michel told me, pointing out a line of skiers in brightly coloured jackets ploughing through the paths below. The dazzle from the snow was almost blinding – I had forgotten to bring my sunglasses. 'Here take mine,' Michel said, handing them over.

'No,' I replied. 'I want to see it as it really is.'

He smiled, beckoning the waiter to bring the menu. We ordered a *raclette* – portions of melted cheese served with new potatoes – and '*viande sechée des grisons*'. Michel chose a bottle of Dezalay, a crisp white wine from the valleys.

'How many portions do they bring?' I asked, after the waiter had replaced our empty plates for the third time.

'It's a big piece of cheese,' Michel replied. 'You could go on and on, but I've just about reached my limit, too.'

Unable to contemplate one of the delicious *tartes* the waiter suggested, I sat back and looked at the view.

'We used to stay here overnight for the cross-country expeditions,' Michel was saying, pointing to the rooms above.

Inside, the reception area was all dark wood and low beams,

and behind the desk a cuckoo clock chimed the hour. I watched a man, dressed like William Tell in green breeches, coming towards us with a tray of frothy beers. 'Do you think he can yodel?' I asked Michel, for although we had crossed the border, the scene appeared more Swiss than Switzerland itself.

'This hotel is run by a Swiss family, so it's fairly typical,' he explained. 'Wait until we go into the Bernese Oberland, and see the real Switzerland.'

Our second honeymoon, I thought. He began to talk, then, of all the places we would visit and all the things we would do.

'There are some good runs on the other side of this valley I'd like us to do together,' he was saying. 'Next year, perhaps.' He made it sound as if everything had been put on hold before the real adventure began.

'We have time,' I replied.

'Yes, of course. We'll get an au pair so you can take some lessons – that's the only way around it.'

I nodded, and looked away. The baby would change everything, I knew that. There would be no more spontaneity, no chance to go where the wind blew us. He had known that before I had even considered it. Now a few doubts crowded in.

'It'll work out,' Michel was saying reassuringly. 'As soon as he can walk, we'll put him on skis – that's how I learnt.'

'I hope you're not banking on a boy,' I said, encouraged that he finally seemed to be acknowledging it.

'I wouldn't consider anything else,' he said with a wink.

We smiled at one another, and he squeezed my hand across the table, but even though the day still shone with a dazzling brightness, I was aware of a chill in the air, as if an invisible cloud had covered the sun.

The following week, Séverine called to invite me out to lunch. She would pick me up at eleven o'clock, she announced, and Michel warned me to be ready, as people were punctual in this country and expected the same from others.

A cold leaden day, it had snowed heavily overnight, bringing everything to a grinding halt. People moved through the streets in slow motion; cars crawled along, pumping clouds of exhaust into the´air; and a curious stillness descended over the town, broken only by the muted clang of a bell as a tram ground to a halt. Michel had bought me a Volkswagen GTI so I could get around more easily, but I was nervous of driving through snow and ice in a city I was still unfamiliar with.

Séverine was swathed entirely in fur. She wore a long silvery fox coat, with a matching Cossack-style hat. On her feet were kidskin boots trimmed with fur, and she had some kind of animal, a dead fox perhaps, wound around her neck. She looked like a character from *Dr Zhivago*. I smelt her cloying perfume as she pecked me twice on each cheek, and was aware of her mauve eyes running over my clothes appraisingly. Michel had bought me a goose-down jacket for the mountains, and I had some leather boots that had seen better days, but I was hardly equipped for elegant restaurants, her look seemed to say.

'There are many beautiful boutiques in the centre of town,' she said. 'I will show you where to go.'

'It's very good of you,' I replied. 'I'd also like to know where the best supermarkets are, and where to buy good meat and fish.'

'I show you,' she replied.

She was in high spirits that day. I was to learn that shopping had that effect on her.

We drove into the centre of town, she chatting gaily all the way, and parked down a side street close to the lake. Then she led me into an area filled with designer shops and famous brand name jewellers, hurrying me from one to the next. We went into a couple of shops, the kind of places where you have to ring the doorbell and be examined before they'll open the door, and she made her entrance with a flourish, causing all the assistants to jerk into action and rush forward to attend to her. I realised that she was the one doing all the shopping, as I watched her examine velvet trays of bracelets and rings, the shop assistants running hither and thither around her.

At last we were making our way back through the drifts of snow, laden with bags, pausing at the odd shop window in case she had forgotten something.

'You don't want to buy something?' she asked. She had problems with her th's, so 'something' became 'somezing'.

'I haven't see anyzing yet,' I replied quite by accident, wondering where the normal shops, where you could buy woollen

138

tights and thermal underwear, were. But apparently shopping was over for the day, for she said, 'Now we must eat somezing,' hurrying me back to the car. Large flakes of snow started falling around us as we walked, making me feel quite dazed, and I was numb with cold.

She piled the bags into the boot, and soon we were driving towards the lake front and across the bridge. We entered an anonymous underground car park on the other side, then took a lift up, emerging into a large shopping mall filled with more expensive shops. The restaurant was on the far side, overlooking the lake. Elegant women sat at the tables sipping white wine, talking in low confidential voices. They glanced at Séverine when we entered, and she smiled back graciously, as to an appreciative audience. It occurred to me that she was some sort of celebrity in this city, because of her part in the soap opera.

'This is nice,' I said politely, although I found it quite horrible – formal in the dullest sense of the world, and completely character-less.

'Yes,' she said. 'I come here very often.' She waved the waiter over and ordered her usual – some sort of salad with dandelion leaves and alfalfa, which sounded like a plate of mixed fodder, and a bottle of mineral water.

'I'll have a chicken salad,' I said faintly, 'and a glass of house wine.'

While we waited for our food, she talked of a party they had held the week before, to which everybody who was anybody had been invited, and of her part in the soap opera. I had already seen one episode – she played the tempestuous and shallow wife of a millionaire, who was in the throes of an adulterous affair with a musician. Most of it was filmed in an old château in Berne – hence its name, *Château Lunns* – and it was worth watching for the scenery alone, though the content was predictable, the acting exaggerated. Any day now she was going to get a break, she told me, nibbling on a piece of bread. It was only a question of time before she landed a movie contract . . . I wondered how much longer Gregoire and his contacts would be useful, if she was poised to hit the big time.

She suddenly switched topics, surprising me. 'You will be boring in the chalet, all day, without skiing, *non*?'

'I beg your pardon?' I replied, for I was still not accustomed to her bad grammar. 'Oh, I see – No, I don't get bored easily, being alone doesn't bother me. I'll go for long walks, and catch up on some reading.'

She stared at me oddly, as if all this sounded unutterably boring, and shrugged. 'You must learn to ski,'. she said.

'I will,' I replied, irritated, 'next year.'

We finished our salads in silence, then she gestured for the bill, saying 'I pay,' before rummaging in her designer bag and pulling out a handful of credit cards.

'Thank you,' I said, wondering if I should argue with her over it, then deciding against. It occurred to me that I might have misjudged her – she was as selfish and shallow as the part she played, but hardly the evil person I had imagined her to be. At least she was making an effort, which was more than I could say for the grisly Gregoire. It was all on her own terms – the shopping, the lunch – whilst the rest was perfunctory padding, but perhaps it was all she was capable of.

She drove me home through the old town, then doubled back down a steep cobbled street filled with galleries, pointing out a dim-looking café where all the writers and musicians went. She slowed down, and craned her neck to look up at the building opposite.

'This is where Marguerite lives,' she told me, pointing to the top of an old building, sixteenth-century perhaps, with narrow balconies housing window boxes. A row of plants had keeled over from the frost, and the fading green shutters were closed. 'We have a big fight,' she confided.

'It can be difficult with sisters,' I said.

'I like to kill her,' she declared, making me review my former conclusion. She glared at me malevolently, as if I had become her target.

It struck me that this would be a solution of sorts. 'What exactly happened?' I inquired politely.

'She try to take everyzing.'

I remembered Michel mentioning they had been fighting over their father's will. I waited for her to expand, but she was not forthcoming. Instead she said, 'Be careful of Marguerite,' making me wonder if they were the same veiled threats she had made in the Carribean.

I shrugged, feigning indifference, and tried to change the subject. But her good mood had gone. She drove aggressively up the hill, sounding her horn at everything in her path, caught up in some desperate scheme of her own. She was still muttering about the evils of Marguerite when we reached the apartment, making me imagine some dreadful siren with hypnotic eyes lurking behind the green shutters, waiting for a chance to lure Michel away.

Chapter Sixteen

The chalet was more like a small hotel, built on a steep hill overlooking Mégève. It had eight bedrooms – which we drew lots for, and Michel and I won the room at the top; the nicest, in my opinion, because of the view.

There were seven of us staying in the chalet that season. Below us was a bachelor called Bertrand, whom I secretly nicknamed the robot because of the way he walked. He had the dull, bespectacled look of a banker, with receding hair and a bland expressionless face and moved as if he was programmed. It was a surprise to learn that he owned a private detective agency in Lausanne. I couldn't imagine him prowling the streets at night, taking photos of clandestine meetings. He chain-smoked Barclay cigarettes and was relegated to the bottom end of the table – 'smokers' corner' – with Gregoire. Rather than join in the rapidly changing dialogue around the table, he recorded everything by constantly taking photographs, blinding us with his powerful flash. It was my opinion that he was secretly in love with Séverine, and hoarded pictures of her away in his smoky room.

On the same floor as the robot was a couple, Dominique and Nicholas, of whom I could never decide which was which. She was another beauty – not in Séverine's league, for she was petite with swinging fair hair and a rosy complexion – while her husband was a good match with the same smooth blond hair and pink skin.

On the first floor was a bachelor called Antoine, whom I recognised as the handsome stranger in the magazine who had stood by Séverine's side at the Cartier ball. He had a string of girlfriends who came and went, put off by Séverine, who made them feel invisible as she gathered her minions tighter around her like a cloak.

Séverine was the pivot around whom the rest of us revolved, performing daily to a captive audience. It was hard to determine what was real and what was an act. Gregoire sat back like an indulgent uncle who has provided an entertainer for his friends, and let her get on with it. His friends, a wealthy self-indulgent group, fed off the rich fare he offered, the caviar and champagne, as if they expected nothing less. It struck me that he was quite ignorant in the ways of the world – he knew how to make vast quantities of money, but had no idea when to stop paying.

The evenings were hectic and unpredictable. We usually went to a restaurant in town, taking over the place with our raucous laughter and antics. Sévérine would start mimicking somebody known to the rest of the group, causing the laughter to grow louder as the dinner progressed. She would place herself between Antoine and Nicholas, who became prompters in her act, egging her on and, as the wine flowed and the restaurant emptied, we would still be there, sitting over the debris of dinner, until my eyes grew heavy from exhaustion. Sévérine treated the dinner table like a playground – firing a bread roll at Michel, using her napkin for conjuring tricks while the rest of us looked on with a mixture of admiration and disapproval. It was like watching the antics of a spoilt and privileged child. Michel admitted once that she sometimes went too far, but he entered into the spirit of her games, and often a quick-witted dialogue would pass between them, making him seem unfamiliar suddenly.

I didn't see much of the group during the day, since they left for the slopes soon after breakfast, leaving behind a blissful silence. I'd lie in bed until after they had gone, then have a bath and laze around reading magazines. Sometimes I put on my jacket and boots, and followed a treacherous path down to the town, stopping at one of the cafés for coffee and croissants. Other days, I caught a pony and trap and explored the town, listening to the swish of snow as we clopped along the roads. Michel urged me to meet them for lunch, so I would take the *télécabine* up the Rochebrune or Mont Joux to the restaurant and sit on the terrace in the sunshine, waiting for them to arrive.

Over those lunches, they seemed to talk only of the past – of previous seasons, other restaurants, and distant people. I heard the same skiing anecdotes over and over – how Gregoire had broken his thumb, Sévérine her toe, and how Michel and Marguerite had almost got caught in an avalanche high on the powdered slopes of Mont Joly.

During those weekends, I wrote to Aunt G, keeping my letters light and cheerful.

'Switzerland is very beautiful in a rather soulless way,' I wrote. 'I can understand why Byron and Shelley came here to write; here in the mountains, it's like being in another world . . .'

I went on to describe the crowd in the chalet, without sparing the details. By then the weekends were starting to hang over me – I longed for the season to end.

Aunt G now dictated her letters to Bridget, since her hands were too stiff to hold a pen. I looked forward to those letters more than anything.

'. . . a nation without a language is a nation without a soul,' she had replied to my last letter. 'I do hope, Emily dear, that you start making a few more compatible friends. Those actressy people tend to be a bit unstable. It's important to have some mutual friends – still it doesn't happen overnight, and in the meantime, you must observe and choose carefully. It's all part of life's rich pageant. Good material for your next novel, perhaps?'

But would anybody believe it, I wondered?

The Love Trap was slowly starting to take shape, the characters coming alive, but it was still a long way from being finished. Somehow the baby seemed to have taken over, sapping my energy and inspiration, and I was finding it increasingly hard to concentrate.

I had found a doctor whose practice was within walking distance of the apartment. He spoke English in a formal sort of way, and said that everything appeared to be progressing normally. On the last visit, however, he had announced that my blood pressure was high. I wondered if it had anything to do with the recent tension between Michel and me.

One Sunday evening, as we drove home from the chalet, I told Michel I'd prefer to stay behind in the apartment the following weekend to write, causing what was to be an ongoing argument between us. He couldn't understand why anybody would choose to stay in a deserted city, under a blanket of cloud, alone. Besides, we had been invited to the chalet as a couple; it would look odd if I didn't go. It struck me once again that he was afraid of breaking the rules.

In the end I gave in, but the weather was bad both days, and we spent the weekend trapped in the chalet, waiting for the clouds to lift. Unable to ski, the crowd were at a loss. Séverine complained bitterly, as if the bad weather were some sort of personal vendetta against her, and the atmosphere grew tense, as everybody lounged around in an aura of discontent. I tried to read my book but, sensing I was being anti-social, put it down again. Then Michel disappeared for the afternoon to do some cross-country skiing, leaving me alone with them.

By the time he returned, I had worked myself into a state of fury. Why had he dragged me here, only to disappear like that, I fumed? Had I been able to ski, it would have been different, he retaliated, to which I replied harshly, 'What do you suggest I do?'

'I suggest you try to be happy,' he replied coldly. 'That's all!'

Shocked by this allusion to the past, I turned away. After that I prayed for the weather to improve.

At last the season was coming to an end. The days were growing longer, the snow starting to melt as the sun shone on it later and later into the afternoons. It ran in muddy brown rivers, disintegrating under my boots as I walked.

Gregoire decided to end the season with a bang, with a grand dinner at the most expensive restaurant in town. The robot brought out all his photos, which were duly passed around and commented on, and Séverine drank too much champagne and tried to dance on the table.

I glanced through the photos curiously, struck by the contrasts. They might have been postcards, I thought, staring at the powder blue sky, the blinding snow, the jagged edge of the Alps. In the foreground were the figures of Séverine, scowling at Gregoire, Antoine looking on in amusement, his current girlfriend behind him, Dominique and Nicholas striking identical poses – while Michel stood a little aside, as if poised for flight.

In one of them they all seemed to be arguing, angry figures against a glittering backdrop, a great blot on an otherwise flawless landscape.

Chapter Seventeen

The end of March brought with it La Bise, a frantic north-easterly wind that churned up the lake and whipped through the city, making people burrow in their furs and swarm into the coffee bars; icy blasts that were held responsible for every sort of malaise. Women clutched their heads and complained of aching limbs and sleepless nights. Michel bought me a mink coat to keep out the cold, but like the emerald ring I never felt comfortable in it.

I was feeling well again, my former lethargy replaced by great bursts of energy. Now I rose early in the mornings and went for long walks through the empty streets – for the high winds kept people indoors – down to the lake where the yachts bobbed and swayed on their moorings. The sounds took me right back to the Isle of Wight, rushing down to the harbour with Father to check on *Running Tide*. Sometimes I'd take the long way home, walking up through the old town, stopping for coffee at one of the cafés there, but I kept away from the steep cobbled street where Marguerite lived behind the green shutters.

La Bise blew itself out after a week, and the temperature rose, so I went up onto the terrace in the short bursts of sunshine to tend to the flower beds. I planted some herbs in boxes, and filled the borders with geraniums and wild flowers that reminded me of the English countryside. Below, the lake turned inky blue, and snow still glittered on the highest peaks of the Jura. Pigeons landed on the walls of the terrace, and sometimes a sparrow would hop along, searching for food. I laid a trail of crumbs, and soon a number of them came to feed. It was peaceful up there, with the birds and the plants in that quiet interim between seasons, before the madness began again.

I rearranged the furniture in the apartment, and went in search of new curtains for the main room. The unfinished portrait of Mother now hung over my writing desk, 'The Railway Cottage' over the bed. Towards the end of spring, I started decorating the guest room for the baby. I found some wallpaper covered in animals that looked as if they belonged in a Beatrix Potter book, and pasted it over the white walls. If we had guests they would have to sleep in the other room, which was smaller and right next door to the kitchen. I sensed Michel wasn't keen on the results, although he never said so. He wanted more than anything for me to feel at home here.

Then, with the help of the *femme de ménage*, I cleaned and aired the whole apartment, as though to dispel the last of Marguerite's presence.

Now the weather had improved Michel had started playing tennis again, disappearing in the early evenings. Whereas I spent more and more time in the apartment, happy to be away from the fray, enjoying a certain kind of solitude.

One morning a woman came to the door, and asked if she could have a word with me. I recognised her immediately as the tenant of the apartment below us. She wore a dark tailored suit and shiny buckled shoes, and her hair was scraped back painfully from her face, forcing her eyebrows into an expression of permanent surprise. I realised after a moment that this was no social visit.

'*Excusez moi de vous deranger*,' she began.

'*Pas du tout*,' I replied amicably.

'You are English,' she said, switching.

'Yes,' I replied, annoyed that it had taken only three words for her to deduce that.

'I see.' She paused, then embarked on what seemed to be a string of complaints. It had been brought to her attention that I had been hanging garments over the balcony, was the first one. I remembered I had aired a couple of blankets during that spring-cleaning session, since they had smelt of Séverine's perfume. Unlike other places on the continent, she pointed out, that was not allowed here. There had also been noises, she said ominously. Was I aware that no machines were allowed to run after ten o'clock at night? I hadn't been, but was now, I replied, trying to remain calm. And finally, and apparently the last straw, I had been feeding the pigeons on the terrace. This was forbidden, since pigeons were pests, liable to 'foul the building'. Taken aback, I muttered an apology, explaining that I hadn't been aware of these rules, but would bear them in mind in the future. Apparently satisfied, she turned to go, clicking her heels in an alarming teutonic gesture of farewell before descending the stairs.

I closed the door and leant shakily against it, my feelings of contentment and solitude gone. Instead, I felt an Orwellian chill begin somewhere in my spine, and linger there as if somebody was watching my every move.

'Don't let it get you down,' Michel said, when he came back from work that evening. 'They're a bit like that here – overly protective of their environment.'

'She was like a policeman,' I told him, shuddering at the memory of those shiny buckled shoes.

'I know the type,' he said with a wry grin.

'Clean living is one thing, but when the *birds* are considered pests it goes beyond all reason!'

'Just be discreet,' he said. 'And by the way, you'd better take those plant pots off the terrace wall – that is illegal. They're meant to be tied down – and what with all this wind we've been having . . .'

'I was actually hoping one would fall on her head,' I said irritably.

He laughed. 'Then you really would be in trouble!'

At the end of March Michel took me to Paris, where I saw Charlotte for the first time since the memorial service.

We stayed in a small hotel off the Boulevard St Michel, and spent an idyllic long weekend exploring the city. We visited the Louvre and Notre Dame, then wandered up to Montmartre and had lunch in one of the cafés where the artists used to sell their paintings in exchange for a meal. We had our portraits sketched by a young Algerian artist, who caught an extraordinary likeness, only he'd somehow aged us ten years. I gasped when I saw it, and Michel grinned at my shocked face.

'It's us ten years down the road,' I exclaimed, not liking what I saw.

'So?' he said. 'We'll grow old together, what does it matter?'

I smiled, thinking Michel would age elegantly; his hair would remain thick with silvery strands, his body lithe and fit. I glanced down at my swollen stomach, wondering if it would ever go back to normal.

He took my hand then, and led me into a warm crowded café that smelt of roasting meat, herbs and garlic. The walls were covered with paintings of Paris scenes – wide boulevards lined with plane trees, Notre Dame at night, the Arc de Triomphe. A beautiful watercolour depicting two swans on the Seine, similar to Aunt G's style, caught my eye.

'This is the loveliest weekend of my life,' I told Michel.

He smiled at my enthusiasm. 'Have I told you lately how much I love you?' he said.

'I love you too,' I replied.

Afterwards, Paris, the café, Michel and I would all become one of those poignant reference points in a chain of memories.

Charlotte met us in the lobby of the hotel. She was very fat now, in an overblown, blowsy sort of way. Her thick ash blonde hair had dulled, her glands working overtime, and her features had lost all definition.

She greeted me perfunctorily, as if no time had passed, then turned to Michel and spoke in perfect French, extending her lips as the French do. I watched, fascinated by this unfamiliar side of her.

'So, Emily, how are you?' she inquired, staring at my stomach. 'You look fat,' she added with a grin.

I had written to her some time ago, telling her about the baby, but she hadn't replied.

Likewise, I wanted to say, but bit my tongue. 'I'm fine,' I replied, forcing a smile.

'Shall we go, ladies?' said Michel, herding us towards the door.

We went to a crowded bistro Michel knew, where the food was delicious, but the evening was a strain. Charlotte insisted on speaking her practised French throughout, while Michel alternated between the two languages, making the conversation seem forced and unnatural. The restaurant was hot and hectic, the chairs uncomfortable, and the service slow. Charlotte talked about herself and her life in Paris most of the time, directing it at Michel as if I wasn't there. She spoke as though she had done an extraordinary thing in making her home here. She was running the restaurant now, she told us, and going out with the head chef and owner. They spent their free time visiting the famous Relais Chateaux – 'like true *gourmands*,' she joked – sampling the finest

French food. No wonder she had got so fat. She had found one of her kind, as I'd always known she would.

As she talked, I started to feel oddly embarrassed. I was used to her total absorption in herself, but what must Michel think of her? I wondered. But Michel was his polite and charming self, apparently happy to let her ramble on, as if the evening were entirely for her benefit. I sometimes wondered if some of the most obvious human failings bypassed Michel. His was a nature, it seemed, that seldom dwelt on quirky behaviour. Or perhaps he was just being polite.

At last he was signalling for the bill and – to my further irritation – saying, 'Why don't you two meet up for lunch tomorrow? You must have a lot of catching up to do, and I have some business to attend to.'

I shot him an angry look. Didn't he realise we had no catching up to do?

But Charlotte was saying jovially, 'Good idea. I'll take her out to lunch – keep her out of mischief. Somebody can fill in for me at the restaurant for a change.'

My heart sank. I had been planning to explore some of the art galleries – I couldn't get the picture of the swans on the Seine out of my mind. But I forced another smile, and said, 'Fine, where shall we meet?'

'Oh, I'll pick you up and take you to one of my haunts – I know all the good restaurants in this city,' she said airily.

'Good,' said Michel, now that was settled.

Charlotte had bought herself a Deux Chevaux, like a true Parisienne. As she climbed in it tipped alarmingly, the under-carriage sinking down onto the cobbled street. '*Au revoir*,' she said, with a wave as she drove away.

'Did I say something wrong?' Michel inquired, as we walked back to the hotel.

'No, it wasn't you. I just didn't feel like meeting her for lunch tomorrow, that's all.'

'I sensed that.'

'Then why did you suggest it?'

'I thought it would be a good opportunity for you both,' he replied.

When I didn't answer, he said, 'Emily, she's your sister. She was

150

part of your life – she's a link with the past, with your parents. Don't let her go.'

'I know she's my sister,' I replied. 'She's just not a very good friend.'

'She wants to be your friend,' he said steadily.

'Oh, I don't know,' I said with a sigh. 'I had the feeling she saw me out of duty, more than anything else. She spent the whole evening talking to you.'

'She's afraid, can't you see that?'

'Afraid of *me*?' I exclaimed. 'If anything, it's the other way around.'

He shook his head. 'She seems to have a few problems,' he said finally. 'I think she was trying to impress you.'

Taken aback, I said, 'Well I am impressed with the way she handles the language, and the fact that she seems to have integrated so well here – but I find her terribly self-obsessed.'

'I felt sorry for her,' he said, surprising me. 'I also felt that I wasn't seeing the real person – there was a facade.'

'You're right about that. She's always shut me out – right from the beginning.'

'But if anyone can get through to her, you can.'

We walked on in silence for a few minutes. 'It's almost as if she's cut herself off from the past, and started a new life here – like Mother.' I wondered then if Charlotte was running away from something too. 'And she's got so fat,' I added.

Michel grinned and patted my stomach. 'Well at least you've got that in common,' he said.

Charlotte took me to a posh restaurant she knew, not far from the hotel, where the food was too rich, the decor dark and uninviting.

She ordered *andouillette*, which she explained was a kind of tripe. I asked for an omelette, but when it came it was so undercooked I could barely eat it.

'That's the way they eat them here, *baveuse*,' she explained, making me think of a drooling dog. She sat back and said, 'So how's life in Switzerland?'

'It's a beautiful country,' I told her, 'more beautiful than you could ever imagine. But I still don't feel at home there . . .' I paused, then added, 'Still, it's early days.'

151

'Really?' she said, cutting into what looked like a piece of inner tubing. She spoke as if she'd had no such problems. 'You could work on your French a bit.'

'You're obviously the linguist, of the two of us,' I said rather sharply.

She flushed, making me feel ashamed. 'So how do you fill the days?'

'I'm writing a novel,' I told her reluctantly, thinking of the last time she had read something I had written.

'You always said you would. What's it about?'

'It's a kind of love story,' I told her, 'loosely based on Mother's life.'

She took a large gulp of wine and waited for me to amplify.

'And the affair with Tom Murphy,' I added.

'Oh yes?' She thought for a moment, then said, 'That all seems so terribly dated now. Nobody gives a damn about nationality or religion nowadays. Poor Mother! She was born in the wrong century. Still, it does make an interesting story,' she added graciously.

She was right, I thought, thinking of our own situations. A French chef and a Swiss businessman. Neither of us had chosen one of our own nationality.

We were both silent for a minute, the memory of Mother bringing us momentarily together.

'That reminds me,' she moved on. 'I've been meaning to write to Aunt G. She's always asking me to come over, but for some reason – I don't know, too many memories.'

I thought it odd that, while I was trying to hang onto the memories, she was running away from them.

'Could you tell her, when you next write, that I've been busy with the restaurant or something? What do you want for dessert, by the way? They do an exquisite *tarte aux pommes* here.'

'Nothing,' I said, feeling a tightness in my stomach. 'Otherwise I won't be able to move.'

'Coffee, then?' It seemed she wanted to prolong the moment.

'With milk,' I said.

We drank our coffee and chatted about everyday things, then I said, 'Well, I must be going.'

We both hesitated, as though there were more to say. Only we didn't know how to say it.

She insisted on paying the bill. 'Try and keep in touch,' she said, throwing a wad of francs on the table.

'Of course,' I replied as I got up.

'And let me know when the baby comes.'

I nodded. 'Maybe you could come over and see us, next time?'

'I'll see how it goes,' she promised.

With a pang, I watched her waddle away – fat, familiar, belonging to another world. Just as I was now a remnant of the past for her.

Chapter Eighteen

In April, Michel put *Jolie Brise* back into the water. The weather was glorious now; clear sunny days, with only a slight chill in the air. People sat outside the cafés in the sun, or walked along the lakefront eating ice creams. The city had finally come alive. Now the weekends revolved around the sailing club, as preparations for the regattas began.

I'd wander down to the club in the late afternoon to find Michel already there, the Merc parked outside, (he had put a sticker reading 'Let's go sailing' on the back windscreen, now the season had begun). I'd sit there drinking coffee, watching him rig up the sails as I had watched Father, all those years ago.

Some of the skiing crowd spilled over into the sailing crowd. Bertrand 'the robot' was one of them, Gregoire and Séverine too, but I met some new people quite different from the ones who had adorned Gregoire's chalet. Father had always claimed that people who loved boats loved life itself, and sure enough there was a *joie de vivre* about the sailing crowd that seemed to stem from the natural order of things, rather than being guided by the fashionable dictates of society.

Gregoire owned half a dozen pointed speedboats and spent his time mucking about in one or other of them, while Séverine, back from filming *Château Lunns*, lay like a rag doll sunbathing on the deck. But I saw less of them now.

Michel was very friendly with an old man called Jean Jacques Lemont, who owned a boatyard further along the lake, and did all the maintenance on *Jolie Brise*. He called me 'la petite Anglaise', and once, after a few beers, said that I was the best thing that had ever happened to Michel. 'The Italian girl was an ill wind,' he said (he always used the elements to describe people), whereas I was a ray of sunshine. 'As for the prima donna,' he expostulated, waving his arm towards the harbour, where Gregoire and Séverine were circling, 'she is a hurricane who will one day wreak havoc on everything around her.'

154

'Hurricanes eventually blow themselves out,' I replied with a grin, relieved to know that I was not alone in my opinion of Séverine. But I wondered if there was some truth in his predictions.

As the weather grew brighter, I started exploring the old town, visiting the art galleries, stopping at the cafés to sit outside in the sun and watch the world go by. It was on one of these occasions that I met Jeanette.

I was sitting outside my favourite café in the highest part of the old town, in a strip of sunlight that filtered through a gap between the buildings. I had just ordered a *café crème* when I noticed this beautiful dark-haired girl struggling to light a cigarette with an empty lighter. She had what appeared to be the dregs of a whisky in front of her, although the sun was a long way off the yard arm, as Father used to say. Her hair was dark brown with a hint of red, her complexion so pale it appeared almost translucent. Her colouring immediately separated her from the healthy tanned people around her. She had a small oval face, blue-grey eyes, and a dusting of freckles over her nose. She kept trying to catch the waiter's attention, but without success.

'What the hell do you have to do to get a bit of service around here?' I heard her mutter. 'Dance a fecking jig?'

I grinned, realising then that she was Irish.

Although I no longer smoked, I still carried cigarettes and matches around in case the urge should come over me. Now I fumbled in my bag for the lighter, and handed it to her.

'They get annoyed if you sit here without ordering food,' I told her. 'They don't bother serving you.'

'In that case, I'm not moving,' she said immediately.

I smiled at her spirit. 'You can't stay here all day,' I pointed out.

'Nothing else to do,' she said. Then quite suddenly her expression changed. She grinned, saying, 'So what brings you to this graveyard? You don't look as if you're about to kick the bucket.'

'My husband's Swiss,' I told her, taken aback by her forthright approach. 'Besides, it's not that bad – it's a very beautiful country, in a slightly unreal sort of way.'

'Switzerland's not a country,' she said aggressively, 'but twenty-three cantons cobbled together by greed and money. You come to

155

Switzerland to die, not to live,' she added, taking a deep drag of her cigarette and squinting at me through the smoke.

I shivered, noticing the sun had moved off my table.

'That's quite a strong statement,' I replied, wondering what on earth could have made her so bitter.

'Ah, don't mind me, it's one of those days when everything seems blacker than usual.' She smiled sheepishly and said, 'When's the baby due?'

'Not for another six weeks,' I answered, glancing down at my huge stomach. 'It seems like forever.'

'Come and join me,' she suggested, 'then we can fight the waiter together.'

I hesitated. There was something shaky about her that reminded me of Amanda – the whisky, the harsh words: a front for some dreadful crisis in her life? Besides, I tended to steer away from unhappy people, lest their malaise should spread to me. But my curiosity got the better of me. She shot me a bright smile, so I picked up my cup, and moved across to join her.

'Jeanette Joyce,' she announced.

'No relation to James?' I asked as I sat down.

'No,' she replied. 'It was bad enough having to wade through his books at school, don't tell me you've read them?'

I smiled. 'My mother read all his novels; she was Irish. Emily Gautier,' I added.

'Nice to meet you, Emily,' she said, 'fellow saint and scholar.'

'Neither,' I said with a laugh. 'Just an aspiring novelist, who has only a hazy knowledge of Ireland.'

We sat there until the sun had gone down behind the buildings, toying with a plate of sandwiches to keep the waiter happy, rapidly exchanging life stories – eager to be done with the small talk so we could get down to the friendship straight away. Hers was an extraordinary story.

She had been married to a Swiss banker for five years, and divorced for the last two. There were two young boys – Christophe and Paul – who lived with their father and his new girlfriend in a converted farmhouse outside Geneva, while Jeanette had moved into a small apartment close to the French border. The divorce had been messy and acrimonious, she told me briefly, and after a certain amount of wrangling the court had awarded custody of the boys to the father. An arrangement had been made that Jeanette would live within a twenty-mile radius, so she could visit her children every other weekend, but while they were in her care, a court order prevented her from taking them out of the country. She had just driven them back to their Father's, only to learn that he wanted to take them away for a month's holiday in July with his girlfriend, who Jeanette referred to as 'Bony Maloney' because of her extreme thinness. She had come here to drown her sorrows.

'I can't see how I can stop him,' she finished, knocking back the rest of her drink. 'Where's that bloody waiter? I could do with another of these.'

I smiled. I knew all about drowning one's sorrows. 'How the hell did he manage to get custody in the first place?' I asked her. 'It's normally the mother, surely?'

'My situation is not exactly normal,' she replied. 'The law is different here – both the boys were born here and have Swiss nationality.'

'But you're the mother,' I cut in.

'Married to a Swiss living in Switzerland,' she pointed out. 'Didn't you know that this was the last country in Europe to give women the vote? Besides, he's the one with the money and connections; with the best lawyers. I didn't have a chance. They said I drank too much – the Irish are always being told they drink too much – but I never drank at all until this happened.'

I listened in amazement.

'There were other factors, too,' she continued. 'I used to smoke the odd joint – grew it in the garden, in fact.' She laughed adding, 'Fabian thought it was a weed and tried to pull it up! It wasn't quite so amusing when he found out what it really was and told his lawyer.'

'Good God,' I said, astonished.

'So there was this drunken Irish mother who smoked pot,' she said, with mock horror, 'and hadn't the means of supporting her children. It was a lost cause.'

'How awful for you,' I said with feeling.

'The worst part is being trapped here – because of the boys.'

So that was why she was so harsh.

'I'll be here until they're old enough to decide where they want to live – and that's a lifetime in prison terms.'

'Do you go home from time to time?' I inquired. Home, I learnt, was Howth in County Dublin, a peninsula that stretched into Dublin Bay.

'I used to go frequently, but I've only an aunt left in Ireland now. My mother died eight years ago – she had cancer. Da went soon afterwards. Besides, I'd prefer to stay close to the boys so I can keep track of them.'

She looked away suddenly. 'Anyway, it's not so bad. You can ski and go sailing – and as you said, it's a beautiful country, if you like that sort of thing. The weather's a good deal better than it is at home . . . And now,' she added without ceremony, 'I've met you.'

We started meeting regularly in the café at the top of the old town. She was often late – she had just missed a tram, lost her keys, or track of the time. I got used to it. I found her company exhilarating, for here at last was someone who was willing to break the rules. She parked her car in forbidden places and sent the bills to Fabian; she aired her clothes on her tiny balcony, never tied her plants down, and often left her stereo on all night. She was always being reprimanded for something or other by what she called 'public policemen'. I knew she would never conform. 'I've got nothing more to lose,' she'd say, when she had just related some particularly daring thing she had done. I never understood, however, why she wasn't willing to fight the legal system for custody of her children.

We'd wander down town to shop, stopping in one of the cafés for coffee and pastries, then return to the apartment to drink wine and watch Séverine in *Château Lunns*.

'She looks like an awful wagon!' Jeanette would say, as Séverine floated down the stairs in a filmy negligée on her way to a clandestine meeting with her lover. And I would laugh, and tell her of Séverine's antics in the chalet, and of Marguerite who forever hovered in the background, the unknown entity.

Jeanette's theory was that Séverine was hanging onto Gregoire with a view to marriage and divorce, so she could bleed him of his fortune, but I had come to the conclusion it was even more straightforward than that. Séverine stayed with Gregoire because she was afraid to leave. There were no movie contracts in the pipeline, no big breaks around the next corner. In spite of her beauty, she'd never be anything but a second-rate actress in a soap opera. Here she was the star of her own show, living a lifestyle she could never give up. I remembered Michel saying that neither twin was capable of integrating elsewhere.

Jeanette's apartment was in a gloomy neighbourhood, close to the tram station on the border with France. The buildings were all painted in dreadful colours – acid green and violent orange – perhaps in an attempt to brighten the area, only it had the opposite effect, giving it a sad and tawdry air. Her apartment looked out over a stone courtyard, where youths kicked footballs against a wall and mothers sat on benches watching toddlers stagger along the concrete paths. Jeanette seemed philosophical about her living arrangements, however. She said she was happy that the boys had plenty of space to grow up in, and that all she needed was a place to lay her weary head.

'I don't really live here, you see,' she once said mysteriously. 'Only in body, not in soul.'

It turned out that Michel knew Jeanette's ex-husband, Fabian Feroux – everybody seemed to know everybody in the city. He claimed he was pleasant enough in an unadventurous sort of way. But I sensed Michel didn't like Jeanette, although he never actually said so. For a start, he never remembered her name – he was bad with names, seldom registering the details of a person whom he was yet to meet or didn't like. He also claimed she drank too much, and once insinuated she was loud and overbearing.

'No more so than Séverine,' I pointed out defensively.

'Séverine's an entertainer,' he said. 'It's part of her personality – she's naturally funny.'

Only at other people's expense, I thought. It struck me that within this indolent society, where money spoke louder than words, people like Jeanette would always be passed over, or thrown to the dogs. Séverine, however, backed up by her social position, not to mention Gregoire's money, got away with being overbearing. The fact that she was an opportunist and a scavenger was never contemplated.

When I told Michel how Jeanette had lost custody of her children, he said, 'I'm sorry for her, I genuinely am, but remember there are always two sides to every story.'

Michel was busy with regattas now, so on the weekends when

159

Jeanette had the boys we'd prepare a picnic and set off for the lake to watch the yacht races. We'd take turns to dive into the cold, clear water, or lie on the sun-baked rocks watching the yachts set off across the lake like a flock of migratory birds.

Both boys had Jeanette's pale skin and dusting of freckles, and would turn red by the end of the day. They were quiet and well-spoken but subdued, as children of separated parents sometimes are. They clung to Jeanette like limpets over those weekends and Paul, the younger of the two, would cry hysterically when it was time to leave her. Jeanette would console them with promises of weekends to come, but I could tell she was as miserable as they were. She'd turn to me and say bitterly, 'Old Bony Maloney must have put the fear of God into them.' Christophe, the elder boy, referred to Fabian's girlfriend as the 'wicked witch', and once we found a fading bruise on Paul's arm that looked like the mark of rough handling.

It seemed to me that the court had made a terrible mistake in taking the boys away from their mother, swayed by power and money, and I urged Jeanette to find another lawyer and try to appeal, but she wouldn't listen. Normally a fighter, she seemed to have been beaten down this time.

One afternoon, we were lying on the terrace sipping lemonade (Jeanette was temporarily on the wagon), and talking about our families.

She spoke about the Northside of Dublin, a part that was unfamiliar to me. 'In the summer we'd often walk along Howth pier, on a Sunday, and look across to Ireland's Eye . . .' she reminisced. 'There's another smaller island next to it, called Ireland's Tear. I remember the last time my mother and I stood there, looking out across the sea. She was very sick by then – knew she hadn't much time left. She was worried about Da, afraid he'd spend the rest of his days in the pub. She suddenly said, "Keep an eye on him for me, Jeanette, will you?" We'd reached the end of the pier by then, and were watching the waves breaking against Ireland's Eye. The wind was fierce that day. It made her eyes stream. Then I realised it wasn't the wind at all, that she was crying. She was saying goodbye. We both stood there like a couple of eejits, sobbing into the wind. That was the last time we walked down the pier. She died a couple of days later, and my Da hit the bottle just as she'd feared. There was no stopping him at all. He was coming out of the pub one night, when a car hit him head on . . .'

She lit a cigarette and inhaled deeply. 'Thinking back, perhaps it was best . . . He would have slowly drunk himself into the grave if he'd had his way.'

I listened, thinking with a pang of Mother and Father, also lost to me.

'So what brought you here?' I asked.

'After Da went, I applied for a job as a *fille au pair*, working for a Swiss family in Vaux – the next canton. I've always loved children, and thought it would be the answer – a fresh start.' She laughed bitterly. 'I had this vision of lakeside walks with the children and playing in the snow . . . I ended up as general skivvy, cleaning the house, washing the dishes – the lot. It was a dog's life. Then I met Fabian by chance. I was in *Parc des Eaux Vives* with the children one afternoon, and he was sitting on a bench reading a book. He was so different then,' she said reminiscently. 'Really good fun – he hadn't been moulded by the banking world. I don't think he ever intended to marry me, but one thing led to another, and Christophe was conceived. I was madly in love with him, and he did the decent thing. Talk about a love trap.'

I felt my heart lurch.

'Of course deep down, he was as much a conformist as the rest of them, product of a strict Calvinist upbringing, from a family who spent most of their lives rehearsing how to live. Tons of money, but all stashed away in various banks for a rainy day. They almost disowned him for marrying me – but there was their grandson to consider, and Fabian redeemed himself by settling down and becoming a good banker.' She took a deep hopeless breath. 'They were quite right, though. I was the wrong woman for him. But for a while there, I thought we might make it. There was a lot of passion at first.' She shrugged. 'But like everything else, that flew out of the window. We both started compromising less and less . . . *et voilà*!' She raised her hands in the air – 'Here we are – divorced, the family in bits, an awful bloody mess.'

'Oh, Jeanette . . .' I squeezed her hand. 'You still have access to the boys, at least . . .' My words trailed off inadequately. 'Mother always warned me not to marry a foreigner . . .' I said, some moments later.

She put on a broad Dublin accent, making me laugh. 'Well she might have saved her breath to cool her porridge,' she declared.

'Tell me more about your family,' she said, switching suddenly. She was always quizzing me about Mother, and never seemed to tire of hearing about Aunt G and Heronlough. I had recently let her read some of *The Love Trap*.

'Perhaps you should go back and find out what really happened,' she suggested, when I told her how cagey Aunt G had been about Mother's relationship with Tom Murphy.

'I'm not sure anything did happen – it was just a love affair that never came to anything.'

'Hmm, the universal story,' she replied. She sat up suddenly and said, 'Emily, if ever we should become separated for some reason, I want you to promise to meet me on Howth Head, where Ulysses deflowered Molly Bloom, on exactly this day in five years' time.' She was given to impulsive ideas like this.

'Why should we become separated? We're both stuck here,' I said with a sleepy yawn – the baby was now a great weight pinning me to the ground. It was due any day now.

'Oh, you never know – I might just get up and go, one fine day.'

'You wouldn't do that. I know you, you'd never leave the boys.'

'I suppose you're right, but just in case, I want you to promise to meet me there in five years' time.'

'OK,' I said with another yawn, moving out of the sun lest the baby should suffocate from the heat.

'Just don't be late.'

We both laughed. That was how what we called 'the Howth Oath' came into being.

I closed my eyes and heard her say, 'Do me a favour, Emily – as soon as the baby arrives, put him or her on your passport straight away, and register it with the British embassy. Then if anything should happen, go back to England immediately, and get yourself a lawyer.'

'Hey, what brought this on all of a sudden?' I asked. I knew she wasn't that enamoured of Michel, although she was careful never to criticise him.

'I don't know,' she said moodily. 'Sometimes I think all this could have been avoided. Anyway, I don't want to talk about me, I'm a lost cause. But you're salvageable.'

'If there was ever a problem between Michel and me, I'd automatically get the child – that's for sure,' I said.

'You can never be sure of those things. Men are so unpredictable – I thought I knew Fabian so well. We were together for five years, for God's sake . . . Then I realised I didn't know him at all.'

'Michel will never change vis-à-vis the baby,' I said, 'even if he changes towards me.'

'It's my secret opinion that the worm will turn,' she replied.

'He doesn't want this child, Jeanette, it represents the end of all his freedom . . . . He'll do what's expected of him, of course, but no more.'

'I think you might be wrong,' she said.

'I hope I am, but I don't think so. I'm on my own in this case.' I laughed uneasily.

'No, you're not,' she said. 'You've got me.'

We smiled at one another, happy for the time being that we had each other.

Chapter Nineteen

Jean was born on a sweltering hot day at the end of July. He had Michel's dark olive skin and almost black hair, but his eyes were a deep indigo blue that everybody predicted would change colour. He was tiny but perfect. I took one look at him and melted.

We christened him Jean after Father whose full name had been Jonathon, although everybody had called him John, and I alternated between the French and English pronunciations.

To my surprise and delight, Michel turned out to be an excellent father – patient and gentle, handling Jean like an expensive piece of sports equipment. He always spoke to him in French, soothed him when he cried, and managed to lull him to sleep at night, when I was ready to drop off myself. Jeanette was right, it seemed: the worm had turned. He even cancelled the odd social engagement so he could spend more time with the baby, but he continued to enter regattas, and I never tried to dissuade him from doing so. He urged me to find a nanny so we could sail together, but I was reluctant to hand Jean over to a complete stranger at this early stage. Besides, I had Jeanette.

Jeanette came over almost every day to help. She was a natural mother, and taught me everything about how to take care of a baby. Jean seemed to have given her a new lease of life. 'You're a dead ringer for your mother,' she'd whisper in his ear, making me realise that people see only what they want to see – for the dark hair, the olive skin, and the occasional brooding expression were definitely Michel's.

I moved into Jean's room for the first couple of months, so as not to disturb Michel during the nightly feeds, but it wasn't long until he was sleeping through the night.

'Now we must get a *fille au pair*,' Michel said, for I had missed a number of social engagements and the yacht club ball was coming up. But still I procrastinated. Looking after Jean was one of my greatest pleasures. In the afternoons, I'd wheel him to the park and sit in the shade of a chestnut tree watching him sleep, or meet

164

Jeanette in the café at the top of the old town, from where we'd set off for the lake together. Jeanette's boys loved Jean, and would argue over whose turn it was to push the pram.

Perhaps it was Jean's arrival that finally spurred Michel to introduce me to his mother. He went to visit her regularly, but seldom spoke about these occasions, and had so far insisted there was no point in my accompanying him. His mother was beyond the stage of meeting anybody new, he stated. She even had trouble recognising her old friends. But maybe the sight of her grandson would trigger a connection with the past . . . or so he hoped.

We drove to Lausanne one hot afternoon, to the elegant lakeside apartment in Pully where Michel had lived part of his life. And although he had warned me over and over that she probably wouldn't know who we were, I still wasn't prepared.

There was about that apartment a faded but empty charm, as if, like Michel, she had put away all her bric-à-brac for fear of cluttering the rooms. We had brought a bouquet of exotic flowers, but they looked somehow out of place in those austere surroundings.

I'll never forget that bleak introduction, as long as I live. She seemed to stare right through us. '*Qui êtes vous?*' she demanded finally, in a wavery voice.

'This is my wife Emily, and our son,' said Michel steadily.

The old lady seemed confused.

'*Enchantée,*' I said, approaching warily. Then, in my best French, I told her how much I had been looking forward to meeting her.

'I don't understand what she's saying,' replied the old lady fretfully. 'Is she foreign?'

'Emily's Irish,' said Michel. 'Remember, I told you we met in London, when I was working there?'

'Is this her child?' she inquired, staring into the pram where Jean was sleeping, his face all crinkled and flushed.

'He's our son – we're married,' Michel repeated. He was so calm and patient with her, my heart ached for him.

A maid dressed in an old-fashioned uniform came in with a tray of canapés and some white wine in tiny liqueur glasses. It seemed like a standard gesture, rather hastily put together, as if she'd had no idea that we were coming.

Madame Gautier took a glass from the tray with a trembling hand, and put it clumsily to her mouth. I glanced at Michel. His face gave nothing away. No wonder he was so shut off at times, I thought, gazing around the cold room, and at the old lady who sat there, a thousand miles away from us.

We stayed for what seemed an interminable length of time, sipping the chilled white wine, trying vainly to get a conversation going, but eventually she drifted away from us completely, and Michel gestured it was time to leave.

On the way home, he was quieter than usual.

'I didn't realise,' I said inadequately.

'She might as well be dead,' he replied, in a voice devoid of emotion.

'How long has she been like this?' I inquired.

'Since my father went. The wine doesn't help,' he added grimly.

'No,' I said automatically. I shivered, remembering that blank look in her eyes.

'It's as if the past has been completely wiped out for her,' he said, in the same flat tone. 'That's the worst kind of death.'

I gazed out of the window. Was that why he clung so compulsively to his? I wondered.

He reached over and took my hand. He seemed oddly vulnerable, just then.

'Partners for life?' he said suddenly.

'For life,' I repeated.

Summer drifted into autumn, and the days grew cooler. At Michel's insistence, we hired a Dutch au pair girl called Delia to take care of Jean. She moved into the pokey room next to the kitchen, but I found her presence an invasion. I wasn't prepared to hand Jean over to her during the day, so there was little for her to do; mostly she lounged in front of the television between preparing occasional meals for Jean. But it left us free to go out in the evenings, Michel pointed out, and to do things together at the weekends.

But as the winter closed like a grey cloak over the city, Jean began to get the odd fever, and I didn't dare leave him for long. He would suddenly start crying, his temperature would soar, and his breathing became laboured. The doctor called them febrile illnesses and claimed they were nothing to be concerned about, but I worried all the same. I'd sit by his cot, listening to his gasping breath, fearing it would stop altogether.

As the temperature dived, Michel grew restless. There would be some early snow in the mountains, he said, and people were starting to take off to their chalets in search of the sun. Only now there was the problem of Jean. I didn't want to leave him, and felt uncomfortable about bringing him to the chalet with us. So I urged Michel to go alone, saying that there would be other times.

Jeanette was horrified. 'You mustn't let Jean come between you,' she said. 'Your marriage is equally important. You've got Delia now, and I'll drop in every day. You've no excuse!'

But as far as I was concerned, it was the perfect excuse.

'I was the one who persuaded him to go,' I pointed out. 'Besides, it's only one weekend.'

'As long as it doesn't become a habit,' she said.

'You can't expect somebody to pay the price for something they haven't ordered,' I told her.

She looked at me closely. 'I thought you were partners?' she replied.

I made a concerted effort after that, but although I enjoyed the skiing, I hardly ever saw Michel: while I struggled on the nursery slopes, he skied with the others through the powdered valleys above. The atmosphere in the chalet was bad that season. Séverine and Gregoire had started bickering – their arguments often taking place around the dinner table, so that once again we were the unwilling audience. Even Michel admitted it was becoming tedious.

'It's time we bought our own chalet,' he'd say from time to time, and I would briefly see an escape – a way out of this stultifying arrangement. But I realised after a while that these were only dreams he harboured. He never did anything about it.

After a few bad weekends, I opted to stay behind with Jean, thereby establishing a pattern. Although I didn't realise it then, we had already started leading separate lives.

The following spring, we began sailing together. We'd take off with Jean Jacques, or another couple, across the lake, stopping at one of the lakeside restaurants to eat *filets de perches* – succulent lake perch lightly sautéed in butter – returning as the sun went down. But I discovered that Michel was incapable of relaxing on board. He darted hither and thither, coiling ropes, tightening the jibsheet, his face set, as though fighting the elements alone. When I was at the helm, he'd issue instructions impatiently, as if it were an important race that we must win. We were completely at odds with one another, it seemed, and I began to wonder why he insisted I accompany him at all.

I found myself thinking back to those pleasant trips with Father in *Running Tide*. I remembered him explaining tactics and wind directions, his white hair shifting in the breeze. *Jolie Brise* seemed smaller than *Running Tide*, the deck a mass of ropes and stays, the cabin area set aside for storage. I'd sit there cramped and restless, watching the passing scenery – the sedate paddle steamers making their dignified way across the lake, the famous *jet d'eau* shooting into the sky like a celebration, the elegant yachts, and the bateaux-mouches taking tourists around the lake.

Michel was looking forward to an expedition he had planned, across the lake to stay overnight at Montreux, wind permitting. There was a lovely hotel he knew with a lakeside terrace, and an excellent restaurant that served the famous 'malakoffs', or cheese balls, that were a local specialty. The robot would be joining us with his new girlfriend, and Séverine and Gregoire would make up the rest of the party. As we would be away overnight, Jeanette agreed to take care of Jean. Michel didn't approve of this arrangement. He said there was no point in having full-time help if we weren't going to use it, but these were the only conditions under which I'd go. I'd never left Jean overnight before, I pointed out. Delia might not know what to do in an emergency.

A supply of food and drink was bought and packed away in ice boxes, and it was agreed that we would meet at the sailing club at seven in the morning.

I couldn't sleep the night before. I got up twice to check on Jean, who was sleeping soundly, then found a packet of cigarettes and went up onto the terrace to smoke one. It was a clear, moonlit night, with a strong breeze. The terrace door banged behind me, and the trees rustled in the courtyard below. I lit a cigarette, and sat on one of the damp chairs to smoke it.

Moments later, the peace was shattered by the roar of an

engine, and I saw a helicopter swooping down, as if it was about to land on the terrace, before it headed off towards the moonlit lake like some sort of deranged insect. I remembered the night Toddy Freeman had disappeared, and wondered uneasily if there had been an accident, for it was almost two o'clock in the morning.

The feeling of unease turned into an icy premonition that sent a shiver through me. I lit another cigarette, and stared at a light blinking far out on the lake. First Toddy, then Father. The words of John Masefield's poem suddenly came to mind, Father's favourite poem, from which he had christened his beloved boat.

'I must down to the seas again, for the call of the running tide
Is a wild call and a clear call that may not be denied . . .'

When the terrace door swung open, I jumped up in alarm, then registered the dark shape standing there as Michel.

'God, you gave me a fright,' I said, my teeth chattering.

'What are you doing up here? I thought I heard a door banging?'

'I couldn't sleep.'

'Neither can I – must be the full moon.'

'There must have been an accident,' I said, shivering in my thin nightshirt.

'It happens.' He stared across the terrace towards the lake.

'It reminds me of the night Toddy Freeman disappeared,' I told him.

Michel crouched down beside me and took my hand.

'I think Father lost the desire to live after that.' It was the first time I had talked about Father's death for ages. 'He wasn't swept overboard, that day,' I said finally. 'I know now that he jumped.'

Michel covered my hand with his. 'What brought this on, all of a sudden?'

'The helicopter, tomorrow's expedition – I don't know. I have a feeling something's going to happen.'

'Nothing's going to happen,' he said, pulling me into his arms. 'Come on, enough of these dark thoughts.'

We sat there for a while longer, arms entwined, neither of us talking. It was the closest we had been for weeks.

*

169

By morning the wind had risen, causing yachts to scud across the waves at great speed.

'Perfect conditions,' Michel said happily, 'and because of the wind direction, we won't be using the spinaker today.'

The others were already waiting for us down at the Nautique, drinking coffee and eating croissants. Séverine and Gregoire wore matching tracksuits with hoods, and Gregoire's hair was slicked back with something oily, in case the wind might turn it into a frizzy halo around his head. He reminded me of 'Slimy the Salamander' from nursery book days.

'Salut, salut,' they called lazily. I noticed the robot had his camera slung around his neck, ready to record the day's events. His girlfriend, a plumpish woman called Karine, seemed to be glued to his side, the two of them chain-smoking nervously.

'Bon pied, bon oeil!' they greeted us, as Michel and I sat down. We ordered coffee and I nibbled on a croissant, then the men wandered off towards the boat, leaving me to finish my coffee and Séverine her conversation.

I stared out beyond the neck of the harbour, where boats scudded along, listing into the wind. A race had apparently started, for gunshots blasted through the air – distant explosions had echoed across the lake, and a woman with a voice like a chipmunk repeated something inaudible over the crackling intercom. There was a sense of chaos in the air. Yachts creaked and swayed on their moorings, stays clinking in the wind. In the restaurant waiters rushed around with cups of coffee, paper napkins rose and flew away, and people seemed agitated, as if expecting something to happen.

Séverine's story was gathering momentum, Karine's eyes were wide as she listened. She was talking about the accident the night before. It was all in the newspapers. The helicopter had been searching for a body, as I had thought. A well known Italian lawyer had flung himself into the lake after discovering his girlfriend with another man. They had found his body caught up in the nets in front of the power plant, close to the Mont Blanc bridge.

The men had loaded the picnic on board now, and Michel beckoned us over – they were raising the mainsail, all set to go. We climbed aboard, Séverine establishing herself on the prow like a figurehead, while Karine and I sat like ballasts on one side. I glanced towards the petrol station, where a fat woman sat in a red-hulled day cruiser, with a tiny dog. She was decked up in a chiffon ensemble, with a matching pink hat. In spite of the noise, I heard the muffled explosion, saw a puff of white smoke, and what appeared to be the engine cover of the cruiser hitting the water with a splash, a few yards from the jetty.

Jean Jacques emerged from nowhere and unceremoniously hoisted the woman (who had grabbed the dog) onto the quay. He loosened the tenders then, to my horrified amazement, jumped aboard to the controls and thrust on the accelerator. The boat jerked forwards, smoke billowing from the engine.

People were gathering on the quay, aware of the danger. The restaurant staff lined the water's edge, still holding trays of coffee, watching the scene. The boat was only about twenty yards away from the petrol station when a second, much larger, explosion lifted the hull from the water. Jean Jacques was propelled forwards as if by a giant invisible hand, and his body disappeared overboard.

The cruiser was now engulfed in flames and billowing smoke. No longer under power, she was rudderless – and I realised, heading straight towards us.

'Get the sail down!' yelled Michel. The acrid smell of smoke was in my eyes and throat. I started to choke. Gregoire had already loosened the main halyard and leapt for the sail, which collapsed, covering the deck with slippery folds of artificial canvas. I heard the sound of police sirens draw closer.

Michel had grabbed the paddle and was plying it furiously.

'Shouldn't we have left the sail up?' I heard Karine say.

'No,' I replied. 'It'd catch fire and the boat would burn.'

'The tiller!' yelled Michel.

Karine beat me to it and, not realising what she was doing, veered *Jolie Brise* into the path of the approaching tornado.

'The tiller!' Michel screamed again.

'I'll take over, Karine,' I said, pushing her aside.

The robot just stood there, clicking his camera wildly at the scene through clouds of smoke.

'What's going on?' shouted Sévérine hysterically.

I knew what had happened. The fat woman in the cruiser had

filled up with petrol and forgotten to activate the blower before turning on the ignition. She could have blown the whole marina to bits. Father had warned me often enough it was an easy thing to do.

The siren sound was on top of us now – the fireboat from the *Ville de Genève* coming to the rescue, telling everybody to clear the area. I could no longer see the mast of *Jolie Brise*, the smoke was too thick, and there was a noxious smell of melting plastic in the air. I remembered Father's hatred of plastic boats.

Gregoire appeared next to me, his eyes on stalks. He had covered his skin with a monogrammed towel lest the sparks should singe his skin (I had read somewhere that salamanders could endure great heat), while the robot was still clicking his camera repeatedly, like a reporter at the scene of a crisis.

There was a jolt. I fell forward into the cockpit, and hit my head on the floorboards.

I lay there dazed for a moment, a searing pain in my right wrist. Then I heard Michel's voice above me. '*Cherie*, are you all right? It's over, they've towed it away.'

I sat up and stared at him. 'What was the bang?'

'We hit another boat. But it's OK, it's over.'

'Michel,' I said. 'Oh, Michel . . .'

'What is it?'

'It was Jean Jacques – on the other boat.'

Michel's face turned a deathly white.

'*Oh mon Dieu,*' he said.

172

Chapter Twenty

Jean Jacques died in hospital two days later from head injuries. His head had struck a metal buoy moored yards from where the cruiser had exploded.

The sailing season seemed to end prematurely with his death. At least for Michel, who had no choice but to withdraw from the last few regattas, while he waited for repairs to be done on *Jolie Brise*. He became moody and withdrawn, burying himself in magazines of great adventures of the outdoors, or pacing the apartment like a prison cell. Jean Jacques' boatyard was closed down, and Michel covered *Jolie Brise* with a blue tarpaulin that slowly whitened from the gulls' droppings, and started playing tennis instead.

I tried to shake him out of it, but he remained distant and preoccupied. He had problems at work too. He had lost a lucrative contract to build a series of lakeside apartments near Lausanne, and couldn't get planning permission for the second option he was working on.

But he wouldn't talk about it. 'Nothing's wrong,' he'd say, when a whole evening had passed and we'd hardly spoken. Depressed – and frustrated by my broken wrist, which prevented me from writing – I turned my attention to Jean. I sent Delia off most afternoons and took him to the park, or drove over to Jeanette's where we'd set off for the mountains, stopping at an auberge for lunch while the boys played on the slopes below.

I heard through the local grapevine that Séverine and Marguerite had settled their differences, and wondered if I would finally meet Séverine's twin sister. But she was part of another crowd now, who played golf in the spring and tennis in the summer, so still our paths did not cross.

That same year Jean turned one, and we heard that Florence Dubois was filing for divorce, claiming Hervé had been having an affair with one of his patients. She was trying to keep the house in Sydney Street, and a whole lot more. This came as a shock to both of us, and Michel flew to London to see his friend and offer what comfort he could.

He returned saying Hervé was in a dreadful state: so adept at sorting out other people's lives, he had been totally unable to come to terms with this mess of his own, Michel said. He and Florence had been drifting apart for a while, it seemed, and Hervé had stupidly got involved with a woman he had been treating for depression.

This news brought me up with a jolt. Michel and I were drifting apart too, I thought uneasily. How often did we really talk to one another? There was always some distraction – a problem at work, a regatta, a social function . . .

Then on top of everything, Michel's mother suddenly became ill, hovering between life and death for three days before quietly passing away in her sleep. They took her into hospital straight away, and we drove to Lausanne, leaving Jean behind, but this time she didn't recognise even Michel. She stared at him from watery unblinking eyes, without uttering.

I left them alone, knowing how painful it must be for him, and went and sat in the garden, in the shade of the chestnut trees, to wait.

When he came out, he looked almost jaunty, as if all were well, though I knew it wasn't.

'Let's go,' he said, in a forced, jovial voice that hid a whole lot of emotions. 'She's completely gaga,' he said, as we drove home. He shrugged. 'Didn't know who the hell I was.'

She died two days later, while he was on his way over to see her. She had left instructions that she wanted to be cremated, which seemed to upset Michel more than anything else.

'Gone without a trace,' he said when at last it was all over.

I watched him pace the room, rubbing his forehead in a characteristic gesture of despair. But he didn't cry.

'I'm so sorry,' I said, distressed, but not knowing how to comfort him.

He shrugged. '*C'est fini*,' he replied distantly.

I remembered my grief when Mother and Father had died, and wondered how he could be so restrained.

The old lady left the apartment in Lausanne to him, and most of her money, which was a small fortune. I suggested he sell the apartment and buy a chalet, as we had often talked about, but he wouldn't discuss future plans.

Months later, he still hadn't done anything about the apartment – it remained as it was, dusty and unchanged like Miss Havisham's wedding feast, as if he could not quite accept that his mother, who had effectively left him long since, had finally gone.

'Let's go away, just the two of us?' I suggested one evening, after we had sat through another silent dinner.

'Where would you like to go?' he asked.

'South,' I said on a whim.

Michel seemed to wake up suddenly. 'How do you feel about leaving Jean?'

'Fine,' I replied, knowing that Jeanette would take care of him.

'St Tropez?' Michel suggested, full of enthusiasm now.

Gregoire owned a villa in the hills behind St Tropez, which he was always urging us to use. We would have it all to ourselves.

'Sounds perfect,' I said, happily. 'Our second honeymoon!'

It was a long drive, and as we moved south it became fiercely hot. I stared out at the flat scorched landscape, thinking about the events of the last few weeks, and about Jean Jacques, who like Father had died so heroically, averting a major accident.

Shirtless men sped down the motorway in convertible cars, trucks rumbled along in the slow lane, and the road shimmered wetly in the heat. We stopped at a petrol station to buy cold drinks, then as we moved further south, evening fell, and it grew cooler. I smelt the spicy scents of Provence – basil and thyme and lavender –and heard the cry of cicadas in the trees. We drove along the Napoleonic Way, through cypress and olive groves, past stone villages where men in rolled-up shirtsleeves played boules in the square, then wound down a steep hill towards the sea. Insects splattered against the windscreen, and the night seemed to turn to velvet around us. At last I saw the lights of a town reflecting on the water below us.

Gregoire's villa was of bleached limestone with a terracotta courtyard and a swimming pool. It was built in an area shaded by olives and cypresses, and could have accommodated at least ten people. But we had it all to ourselves.

That first evening we drove into town and had dinner in one of the fish restaurants on the harbour. Beautiful couples paraded along the waterfront, artists sketched at easels, and vendors hawked paintings and hand-made jewellery.

'How about some champagne?' Michel suggested, glancing at the menu. He seemed to have come to life again.

'Great. What's the occasion?'

'Our second honeymoon,' he replied.

I smiled, thinking it was already a lot better than the first one.

'Long overdue,' I said.

He reached over and took my hand. 'I know the last few months have been difficult, but you can't live on cloud ten all the time.'

'Cloud nine,' I corrected with a smile. 'Although it was definitely cloud ten at the beginning!'

'So? It's a bit like maintaining a yacht. It needs a new coat of varnish from time to time.'

I laughed, thinking it was the kind of analogy Father might have used.

'Cheers, partner,' he said lifting his glass. 'To us.'

'Cheers,' I echoed, happy that everything was suddenly all right again.

That night we fell asleep in each other's arms.

Michel rose early most mornings and went to the boulangerie for a baguette. After we'd eaten breakfast, we'd lie on the baked tiles basking in the sun, dipping into the pool to cool ourselves, then wander down to St Tropez for a drink at one of the bars along the quay. I bought a couple of watercolours of the bay, which I framed when I got home. One afternoon Michel hired a windsurfer, and I lay on the beach amidst a bevy of bronzed beauties watching his blue sail scud along the waves. In the evenings, we'd eat at one of the many restaurants on the quay, or buy fish from the market and cook it on the barbecue. Michel met some people he knew on the beach and asked them to join us for dinner one evening, but I didn't mind. For it seemed that nothing could come between us, or break the momentum now.

Then, on a pale blue morning a few days before we were due to leave, the phone rang, bringing the idyll to an abrupt end.

Michel went to answer it, and I heard him say *'Bien sur, je suis ravi . . . C'est ta maison!'*

176

I listened with a sinking heart, guessing who it was before he told me. He came back into the room moments later and announced that Gregoire and Séverine would be flying down to join us. He suggested we call Delia and tell her we were extending the holiday another few days.

I stared at him, unable to reply. The ability to feign pleasure was beyond me. Instead I muttered, 'I don't believe it!'

'What's the problem now?' he inquired in a pained voice.

I couldn't help it; the words bubbled up and out before I could stop them. 'I thought for once we'd managed to get away from them.'

His good mood seemed to evaporate, like water on hot stones. 'It is their villa,' he said shortly.

'And there are fifty-two weeks in a year! Why do they have to pick this one?'

'What do you want me to do?' he asked helplessly. 'Ring him back and say he can't come to his own villa?'

I lit a cigarette and inhaled deeply. 'No, of course not,' I said, after a silence. 'Don't do anything. But if you don't mind, I'd rather go home the day we planned – for Jean's sake as well as everything else.'

As far as I was concerned, the honeymoon was over. If the worst came to the worst I would drive back alone, I thought.

'If that's what you want,' he said stiffly, as though *I'd* ruined our pleasure.

Séverine appeared to have brought her whole wardrobe with her. She was dressed as if for the Cannes film festival, in a huge floppy hat, a red linen dress and diamond-studded sunglasses. But in spite of her dramatic attire, she seemed somewhat diminished in these surroundings, amongst all the honey-coloured beauties who migrated here every year like a flock of exotic birds.

From the moment she arrived, I could sense something was wrong. There was an air of discontent about her, manifested in the odd comment that things were not as they had once been. Gregoire was aware of it too. They didn't argue so much now, as if they both knew it was over.

She complained about the heat, the temperature of the sea, and the state of the villa (this last comment was directed at me, for having given the cleaning woman time off to visit her sick mother), but she still played the court jester some of the time, making it hard to discern what was real and what was not.

Already resentful of her presence, now she ground on my frayed nerves like a welder on iron. Michel seemed oblivious to the growing tension in the air. He was out windsurfing a lot of the time, caught up in the holiday spirit, and didn't seem to notice that Sévérine was slowly poisoning the atmosphere.

Then, the day before we were due to leave, all hell broke loose. It was a particularly hot day; I thought the weather was about to break. Gregoire had decided to hire a boat so we could sail further down the coastline to an isolated cove he knew, but I decided not to join them; the thought of being cooped up on a small boat with Sévérine was more than I could stand. Michel didn't put any pressure on me to go, but I could tell he thought I was being anti-social. Then, just before they set off, Sévérine and Gregoire had one of their famous arguments, and the next moment she had decided to stay behind with me on the beach.

We spread our towels by the water's edge and I opened my book, but she wasn't going to let me read it: she needed an audience. She began with a long list of grievances against Gregoire. He was stubborn and selfish, she said. He had become so boring recently, stuck in his ways – he couldn't sunbathe any more, since he had all these problems with his skin. '*Grains de beauté*,' she announced, making me smile inwardly, for a mole was a mole in my book. They used to have such fun together. Once again, the past became a shimmering unmatchable time, halcyon days that could never be repeated. Before money had become commonplace, and luxury second nature, before Gregoire had started to see through her; back when the four of them had been one big happy family. From the way she spoke, it all sounded slightly incestuous.

'Now it is completely boring,' she said.

I felt irritation stab at me, like the sharp rays of the sun.

'You should have gone with them,' I said sharply, since I was apparently part of the scene she found so dull.

She shrugged moodily and looked away.

The words spilt out unchecked. 'If you're so unhappy with Gregoire, why don't you leave?' I said. 'It looks to me as if you're just using each other.'

As soon as I'd said it I regretted it, and prayed she would misinterpret my words, for like everything else about her, her English was shallow and limited. But she didn't. A look of fury crossed her face. I should have guessed she was devious enough to know that I had seen through her.

Even the dialogue was script material. 'You know nozing of Gregoire and I, *nozing*!' She shot up in a spurt of sand, and towered above me.

For a moment, I thought she was about to kill me, as she had threatened to kill Marguerite. The scene had merged into one of her soaps. She was tossing her head and flinging her arms about, so the other sunbathers sat up to watch us.

'Michel make a big mistake with you,' she said. 'What could he do with a woman who could not dive, who could not ski, who is afraid? You can bring him nozing, nozing,' she repeated. 'Now,' she added with a malicious grin, 'he have an *aventure*, with Marguerite.'

For one ridiculous moment, I had a vision of Michel and Marguerite trekking through the mountains with backpacks on a wild adventure.

'What are you talking about?' I demanded shakily, realising then that she meant an affair.

'They meet every day at the tennis club,' she told me slyly.

'You're a liar,' I said, holding my towel against my burning skin for protection. The woman was evil after all, I thought, and wondered how far she would go once the chips were down, and open war declared. 'You're the dangerous one,' I added, following her script, 'not your sister . . . You're an opportunist and a gold digger, and what pisses you off more than anything is the fact that I've seen through you. You may be a good actress, Séverine, but you're not that good . . .' I backed away, gathering my things as I went, leaving her shouting after me, and made my way up the beach towards a dark bar on the quay, where I sat down and ordered a double whisky.

Michel had no sooner walked in the door later that day, than I announced I wanted to leave. 'I can't take another moment of that woman,' I said.

'What happened?' he inquired with a frown. 'Don't tell me there's been another dinger?'

He never quite got words like humdinger right.

'She started her spiel again,' I told him. 'Said you were having an affair with Marguerite – the same thing all over again.'

'*Merde!*' said Michel.

'It was like something from *Château Lunns*,' I said. I paused, then looked at him closely 'You're not still seeing her, are you?'

He looked defensive now, closed off from me. 'Of course not. I see her from time to time at the tennis club, but she's got someone else now. We're not going to go through all that again, are we?' he said angrily.

'She was the one who brought it up,' I said. I stared at him helplessly. 'Michel, it's time we made a few mutual friends – who speak the same language.'

'Like your drunken Irish friend, I suppose?' he retorted. 'I don't particularly want to live like an expatriate in my own country.'

'I wasn't asking you to . . . Oh, forget it,' I said furiously. 'But since you brought it up, I'd rather not socialise with the so-called *crème de la crème*. It strikes me they've long since turned sour.'

'So what's the answer?' he asked.

'I don't know. There doesn't seem to be one.'

'You'd better start packing, then,' he said.

I stared at him, thinking of that long hot drive alone.

'You're staying, then?' I inquired.

'Hardly,' he snapped. I wondered if, once again, he was acting from social convention. It wouldn't look right to let me leave alone.

'Stay if you want,' I said with a beating heart.

But he slammed out of the room without replying.

Later I saw him talking to Gregoire. He raised his hands helplessly in the air, as if trying to explain the inexplicable. Then he came into the bedroom and started flinging things into his suitcase. I watched him, distressed. He was normally so careful with his clothes.

Gregoire and Séverine came to see us off. Séverine muttered goodbye, but didn't look at me. Instead she squeezed Michel's hand in a gesture of sympathy, then turned away, leaving a sickening wave of perfume on the hot air.

Gregoire didn't seem put out by the strained atmosphere between us. He must have been used to Séverine's explosions, and

180

knew better than to get involved. He merely seemed somewhat puzzled that we were leaving when, surely, the party had just begun.

As we drove away, I noticed him staring after me curiously, like the intricate mechanism of a clock that he'd never quite figured out.

Chapter Twenty-One

The seasons seemed to be melting into one another now. Michel went skiing, insisting that I was welcome as always, in spite of the latest drama with Sévérine, but I was reluctant to join them. One weekend, I suggested we go to Chamonix, from where you could take the *téléferique* up Mont Blanc, but the clouds were low that day, obscuring the view. Afterwards we skied a couple of runs together, but it was hardly the lively, challenging day Michel was used to. I sensed he missed the *après-ski* – those long evenings around the dinner table, discussing the day's events. Who knows, he probably even missed Sévérine and her dramas. At least, I concluded unhappily, as we ate our lunch in silence, she had given us something to talk about.

At the end of spring, Gregoire and Sévérine finally split up, and Sévérine flew to New York in a rage, as her sister had done three years before, only to return a few months later and move into a lakeside mansion with a television producer. Gregoire seemed to go into hibernation afterwards, while his minions slowly dispersed, no longer drawn by the lure of Sévérine.

That summer was a chain of endless hot days and blue skies. Jeanette and I spent the afternoons at the swimming pool, watching Jean and her boys splash around in the shallows, while Michel was busy with regattas once again.

One stuffy August day, when the wet towel smell of the lake hung over the city, I set off for the market to buy fish, and bumped into Gregoire. He was standing by a glass counter pointing to some vile delicacies behind it, discussing them with the *vendeuse*. They looked like bald baby birds plucked straight out of a nest. So he eats birds on top of everything else, I thought, trying to back away before he spotted me. But it was too late.

'*Bonjour*,' he said, politely. '*Ca va?*'

'Fine,' I replied. 'Just fine.'

'I didn't see much of you on the slopes this year,' he said, amiably.

'No.' I wanted to tell him that I couldn't have tolerated another moment of Séverine's company, then realised it might be tactless under the circumstances. So I said nothing.

'You must practise your skiing,' he said obliquely.

'So everybody keeps telling me!'

'For Michel.'

'It will take years before I can ski with all of you,' I pointed out.

He was still staring at me in an almost friendly way, but with a strange look in his eyes. I shifted uncomfortably.

'I'm sorry about you and Séverine,' I found myself saying, although I wasn't in the least bit sorry.

He shrugged. *'Plus ça change, plus c'est la même chose,'* he replied.

'Quite,' I said, in English. 'Well, I must be going.'

He leant forward confidentially, causing me to step back in alarm. 'You must accompany your husband,' he said in his awkward English.

I stared at him, wondering what was behind this. Then I realised that there were no evil motives. Gregoire was a victim of his own limited personality; a financial genius but a social failure, who relied on women like Séverine, for whom he was prepared to pay any price, to elevate him. In his clumsy way, he was only trying to help.

He was right, of course, I concluded. I should have put my dislike for Séverine behind me and accompanied Michel, even if we did ski at different levels. Maybe now Séverine had gone it would be easier, I thought.

I nodded. 'Next season, perhaps.'

'A bientôt,' he was saying, stuffing his dubious purchase into a carrier bag.

I felt a flicker of sympathy for him. He had been taken in by Séverine, and no doubt would be used again by the next woman who happened along. As he had said himself, the more things change, the more they stay the same.

'Au revoir,' I replied, forgetting what I had come for now.

Thinking back, it now seems an added irony that Gregoire, who appeared so naïve when it came to relationships, was the one to issue the warning.

*

Jeanette had started drinking heavily again. There were dark shadows under her eyes, and she had lost a lot of weight. The end of the summer always depressed her – she said she felt the walls closing in. I urged her to spend more time with me in the apartment. We watched the afternoon soaps together now, and saw with some satisfaction Séverine killed off in a fatal car accident in *Château Lunns*. She died beautifully, her face deathly white, her features composed. In some strange way, her disappearance from the television screen made her absence from the social scene seem like a real death.

Jeanette said, 'I knew the bitch would get her come-uppance in the end.' But all the same, the pleasure had gone from watching *Château Lunns* now.

I had finally completed *The Love Trap*, but had done nothing about sending it to a publisher, although Jeanette had urged me to do so. She had read it and called it 'a brilliant debut', but I still felt it was lacking. I'd written to Aunt G at the end of August, asking if she knew anybody in the publishing world, but she never replied to my letter, so I put the manuscript away for the time being and forgot all about it.

In the autumn, Fabian and 'Bony Maloney' announced they were going to cruise around Corsica in a sailing boat, and wanted to take the boys along. Jeanette was distraught.

'That's the bloody irony of the whole setup,' she fumed. 'The court takes the boys away from me because I grow my own grass and go on the odd bender, but he's allowed to take them on a cruise, when neither of them can swim.'

We were sitting in the Café des Artistes, opposite Marguerite's apartment, drinking *café renversé* and nibbling squares of Suchard chocolate. Jeanette had persuaded me to go there, saying it was time I dispelled the ghost. Marguerite and I had been living in the same city for two and a half years now, and still hadn't come face to face. I wondered if we ever would.

'Jeanette, I really think you should consider getting another lawyer,' I said after listening to this outburst. 'Perhaps I could help.'

'It's a lost cause,' she replied wearily.

'Even lawyers fight lost causes,' I said.

She smiled thinly. 'I couldn't go through all that again, Emily. I just couldn't.'

'That's not the Jeanette Joyce I know speaking!'

'Oh, it's all a facade with me. I'm a dreadful coward when it comes to the crunch.'

'You're about the bravest person I know,' I replied.

'And just look where it's got me – trapped here, without my kids, on visitation rights. Sometimes I feel as if I'm serving a life sentence.'

I had never seen her so wretched. 'What you need is a good night out on the town – preferably with somebody tall, dark and handsome.'

I knew she sometimes saw other men, but none of them seemed to last very long.

'The Swiss want their relationships to run smoothly, like their watches,' she had once said. 'My life is more like a machine that's gone haywire.'

'Not much chance of that,' she replied unhappily. 'I don't think I'll ever meet anybody now.'

'You're a survivor,' I said, trying to console her. 'You'll land on your feet – something or somebody will turn up.'

'Somebody on a white charger like Michel? I doubt it.'

'It only takes one encounter to change your life.' I thought of how Michel and I met, so unexpectedly, at the Dubois' that night.

'I used to say to myself that if I couldn't take it, I'd go out the back door.'

'I almost did, once,' I joked. 'Not the back door, though, but a window overlooking the Finchley Road.'

'And. . . ?'

'The telephone rang,' I said, with a giggle.

'Saved by the bell!'

We both laughed.

'You can't fling yourself out of a window when you have kids, that's the problem,' she said, lighting another cigarette.

'Come on, we're getting morbid,' I replied. 'How about a drink?'

Michel was involved in a new building contract, working later and later into the evenings. He seldom got home in time to see Jean, so I would go ahead and eat dinner without him. Now the dark evenings hung over me, waiting for him to come home.

So Jeanette and I started meeting in town for an evening drink that often stretched to dinner. We found an American bar that served cocktails, and would sit there picking at a plate of spare ribs and drinking Whisky Sours until we were quite drunk.

Michel was away on a trip when Jeanette went on what I called her 'bender'. We met as usual at the cocktail bar, and by the time I arrived she was on her third Whisky Sour and had smoked half a packet of cigarettes.

'What's up?' I asked with concern.

'Bad news,' she said. 'The worst that could possibly happen.'

'What?'

'Fabian's been transferred.'

'Oh, my God . . . Where?'

'Frankfurt,' she said hollowly.

'When?'

'End of next month.'

'So what does that mean?' I said, with a feeling of dread.

'It means he's moving my whole family there,' she announced, 'and I have to follow.'

'Jeanette, they can't do this to you – or me,' I said, for without her I would be lost. 'They can't force you to spend the rest of your life following him around the world.'

'I've no choice, if I want to be close to the boys.'

'God, I wish you'd found yourself another lawyer,' I said, supporting my head in my hands. 'Then we would have been more prepared.'

'I need another drink.' She beckoned the waiter.

'Order me a double,' I said, taking one of her cigarettes.

'OK, the plan is,' I began, 'we find the best lawyer in town straight away. Forget about the money – I've got some stashed away in England in case of an emergency.'

'No, Emily,' she interrupted. 'I'm not going to take your money, you might need it one day.'

'Jeanette, if I were in the same boat, you'd help out.'

'I know, but it doesn't seem right.'

'Then,' I continued, 'we try to get something on him.'

'What do you mean?' She asked.

'I'm not sure yet, I'm working on it.'

She smiled. 'You're a crackpot, so you are – God, it's a

desperate situation! The boys will be miserable – I'm so worried about them, Emily. I found another bruise on Paul's arm, as if somebody had thumped him. I can't let them go.'

'That's it!' I said excitedly. 'That's the evidence we need to win the case. You don't think "Bony Maloney" might have hit him, do you?'

'More likely Fabian – he's got a rotten temper.'

'I want you to take photos,' I said.

'Of what?'

'The bruise, you idiot, wake up.'

'But it will have faded by now.'

'Then we'll find something else,' I said steadily. 'But first we concentrate on getting the best lawyer in town.'

'That's Fabian's,' she said.

'We'll find an even better one.'

'You've no idea what I went through, Emily. I was fighting a losing battle.'

'Only this time you've got me,' I said.

By the time we left the bar, we were both drunk. We weaved our way along the street, giggling and swaying, finding everything hilariously funny. Jeanette started quoting from *The Lake Isle of Innisfree*, repeating the same lines over and over.

'I will arise and go now, and go to Innisfree,' she chanted.

'And I shall find peace there, for peace comes dropping through the vales of the morning . . .' I added, as we staggered up through the old town, heady with drink and nostalgia for the country that neither of us belonged to.

The last tram had gone, and she was drunk, so I insisted she stay the night. Then when we got back she wanted to open a bottle of whisky and stay up all night drinking it. I persuaded her to have a coffee instead, but we made so much noise making it that Delia came out of her room to see what was going on.

'Everything's under control,' I said, holding onto Jeanette in case she fell flat on her face. 'Go back to bed.' She stared at us curiously, then turned away. I was glad Michel wasn't there.

I made a pot of coffee, found milk and sugar and, putting it on a tray, carried it into the other room – to find Jeanette sitting on the leather sofa, sobbing like a child.

Distressed, I sat down beside her. 'Come on, drink your coffee. We'll win this case, believe me.'

'I don't want to live in Frankfurt,' she kept repeating. 'I don't want to learn German, I'd rather die.'

'You're not going to have to,' I said. 'We're going to find a lawyer.'

She stared at me glassily, and said, 'Tell me, what are you doing with a drunken slob like me?'

'It takes one to know one,' I said, putting my arms around her.

She drank steadily over the weekend, yet remained surprisingly lucid throughout. But she seemed to have lost her fighting spirit. She lay on the leather sofa, flicking aimlessly through magazines, barely talking, eating nothing. She went back to her flat on Sunday evening, not wanting to be with me when Michel returned, assuring me she felt better. 'I've done a lot of thinking,' she said. 'There might be a way after all. I think I'm ready for the bastard this time.'

'Are you sure?' I said worriedly. She seemed to have drunk herself sober, to a state where nothing mattered any more.

'Quite sure – and by the way, thanks . . .'

I smiled. 'It's going to be all right, you'll see.'

We found a Monsieur Le Clerc who specialised in divorce cases, and made an appointment to see him the following week. He listened to the whole story, then asked us to wait in the other room while he made a couple of phone calls. When he came out he informed us that he was unable to take on the case.

'So, that's only one lawyer,' I said as we emerged from his office onto the cold street.

'No one's going to want to take on Fabian's lawyer,' she said despairingly. 'I just know it – there's too much against us.'

'You're wrong,' I said. 'Lawyers have to live, like everybody else.'

We saw two more lawyers that week. One wanted an extortionately high fee; the other informed Jeanette she hadn't a hope of appealing in a case such as this.

By Thursday, we were both beginning to despair.

I made some random calls to lawyers listed in the phone book. One turned out to be a criminal lawyer and two of them wouldn't even come to the phone, then our luck changed. A young Swiss German recently arrived from Berne said he would take on the case.

That evening, Jeanette and I met in the American bar and had a few celebratory drinks.

'This transfer of Fabian's might be your one chance of getting the boys back,' I said. 'But if we win, promise me you won't disappear out of my life for ever?'

'I promise,' she replied. 'You'll have to come and spend the summers in Ireland with me, that's all.'

I thought momentarily of Aunt G, and wondered why she hadn't written for so long. I would ring her this week, I decided, but what with everything that followed, it went clean out of my head.

'. . . anyway, it's hardly a *fait accompli*,' Jeanette was saying.

'No, but I think we're in with a good chance.'

Chapter Twenty-Two

The following week, Jeanette discovered another bruise, this time on Christophe's leg, and I took some of the photographs of it. I put the roll in my bag, meaning to have them developed straight away and deposit them with the lawyer.

We met that evening again in the American bar, and stayed there until closing time.

Neither of us paid much attention to the small curly-haired man at the next table, or considered it odd that he left at exactly the same time as we did and followed us a short distance along the street. I only remembered the flash of a camera afterwards, and dimly registered him behind us as we walked rather tipsily down the street.

Two days later, Fabian announced he was marrying 'Bony Maloney'.

'That was inevitable,' I told a distraught Jeanette. 'The courts are far more likely to favour a married couple than a divorcee with a girlfriend.'

They had decided to get married the next Saturday in Berne, planning the wedding for a weekend when Jeanette had the boys. In the meantime Fabian fired the live-in au pair girl, claiming it was she who had been handling the boys roughly.

He seemed to be always one step ahead of us.

'I'll sabotage their wedding,' Jeanette said, furiously. 'I'll refuse to take the boys – let them ruin their precious ceremony!'

I agreed to be her alibi.

'Just say you haven't seen me. I might go up to the mountains for the weekend, so they can't contact me.'

'It would be my pleasure,' I told her.

Michel warned me to stay out of it, but I took no notice. He was away a lot these days – he'd started playing squash at the tennis club, and never came home before nine. Besides I couldn't discuss Jeanette's problems with him. We were losing track of one other, so when we did talk, his advice had no effect.

I was cooking a solitary dinner on the Friday evening when the phone rang, and I found myself talking for the first time with Fabian Feroux.

'My name is Fabian,' he said in stage English, 'I am looking for Jeanette.'

I felt a flicker of triumph. 'I was under the impression she was spending the weekend in the mountains with the boys,' I said.

'The boys are with me,' he stated. 'We have been waiting for her since noon. We have an important ceremony to attend.'

I kept my tone level, although the urge to be rude was almost overwhelming. 'That's too bad,' I said with false sympathy, remembering he had fired the au pair girl. 'You'll have to take the boys with you, it seems.'

'It is a wedding ceremony,' he said.

'Really?' I replied coldly.

'It's very inconvenient.'

In the silence that followed, a idea came to me from nowhere.

'Why don't you bring them over here,' I suggested. 'I could take care of them until I hear from Jeanette. She's bound to telephone me later,' I added.

A bizarre plan had taken hold. Once the boys were with me, I might be able to get the three of them on a plane and out of the country, to Ireland . . . There would be no way of tracing them there.

But my hopes were dashed. He said, 'Thank you, but there is no need. I will find an alternative plan.'

What on earth had Jeanette in common with this stiff-voiced person? I thought with a sinking heart.

'It wouldn't have been any trouble,' I said, wondering if he had somehow smelt a rat, known he was dealing with the enemy.

'Goodbye,' he said curtly, and was gone.

I dialled Jeanette's number using our special code (which was to ring twice and hang up), but she didn't answer. Either she wasn't taking any chances, or she had already left for the mountains.

I put Jean to bed, wishing suddenly for Michel's company, however remote he was. Coincidentally he had gone to Berne, too. Then I poured myself a drink and sat down to watch a rather violent film on television; went to bed, but couldn't sleep.

I was up early, and drinking a cup of Earl Grey tea when the doorbell rang.

'I'll get it,' I called to Delia, who was feeding Jean. I peered through the spyhole first, and saw a man in a dark coat with a grim expression on his face.

'*Qu'est ce que c'est*?' I inquired, opening the door.

'*Vous êtes Madame Gautier*?' he asked, glancing at the white envelope he was holding.

'*Oui*,' I replied.

'*Je peux entrer*?'

He pulled out a card that read, '*Inspecteur de la Police*', and stepped inside.

'What is it?' I asked fearfully, a chill spreading through me, imagining something must have happened to Michel. But he only handed me the envelope, then stepped back.

They had found Jeanette's body, some hours ago, in the concrete courtyard below her apartment, where the mothers sat on the green benches. Some time in the middle of the night, she had jumped off the balcony. She had left only the one note addressed to me.

I read it with a feeling of icy disbelief.

'Dearest Emily, I have arisen and gone, as I always said I would if things got worse. The lawyer called this morning and basically said we hadn't a hope in hell. Fabian's lawyer produced a series of photos of us coming out of the American Bar – pissed drunk! They searched my apartment over the weekend and found some grass in the fridge – so you see it really was a lost cause.

I once said that you can never cop out when you have children, but I've lost the boys now. I won't live in Germany, and I can't live without them . . .' A tear splashed onto the inky words, blurring them. 'I'll miss you, Emily. Thank you for being such a good friend. Send *The Love Trap* off to a publisher at once, and do me a favour, Emily – don't ever let the walls close around you as they did on me . . . Jeanette.'

The policeman stared at me while I read the note, then looked away. He shifted his weight from one foot to the other and cleared his throat. His English was terrifying – like a Nazi officer in a war film.

'We cannot get hold of Monsieur Feroux,' he began. 'We need someone to identify the . . . body.'

'I can't possibly,' I said. 'Find Fabian, do anything!'

'He is not in his residence.'

'He's gone to Berne,' I told him hysterically, 'to get married.'

'Can you give me an address?'

'Of course not!'

'Please,' he said. 'It won't take longer than one hour.'

I heard Jean crying from the kitchen, and saw Delia's pale face peer round the door to see what was going on. Then I slumped down on the leather sofa, saying, 'I need to call my husband.' I realised then I didn't have an address or phone number for Michel, either. 'I have the baby, you see – I can't leave him.'

'It will only take a short time,' said the inspector, in his cold, authoritative voice 'The girl could take care of him.'

He turned and wandered over to the window, waiting for me to collect myself. I went to the bedroom, swallowing the bile that kept rising in my throat, and pulled on some clothes. Then I cleaned my teeth and brushed my hair, going through the motions like a zombie, while my chest ached from the tears that seemed to be trapped there.

They drove me in a police car to the other side of the lake, where a modern-looking hospital stood, surrounded by plane trees. The inspector helped me out of the car like an invalid, and a hatchet-faced nurse in a white overall appeared. They conversed for a moment, before leading me down some steps, as if into the bowels of the earth.

Inside, everything was gleaming white and reeked of disinfectant. I'd read about the smell of death, but I didn't smell it; just chemicals, overpoweringly strong, as though somebody had spilt a bottle of bleach on the floor.

It was exactly how it is in low budget films. A giant filing cabinet, housing bodies covered in white sheets – only there was no tag hung over the toe in that humiliating last gesture of labelling the dead. I walked with my head bowed, lest I faint, to where a white attendant, who looked as if he were dead too, was dragging out a trolley on which a small body lay under the sheet. On the outside of the drawer they had written, '*Jeanette Joyth, Etrangère*. I moved closer, my hands over my mouth to stop myself screaming and looked.

It was Jeanette, and yet it wasn't. Her face was still beautiful, but so white it looked as if she were wearing make-up. The dusting of freckles showed out starkly against translucent skin. Her expression was completely void, intimating that she wasn't there. They had crossed her hands over her chest like a madonna. The rest of her body, broken by the fall, remained hidden under the sheet.

The tears welled up, and splashed down my face onto the sheet.

'Now you can go wherever you want,' I whispered, choking on the sobs. I turned away, feeling as if I were falling into a deep pit, and would never get out again.

The inspector was watching me intently. 'Is this the ex-wife of Monsieur Fabian Feroux?' he asked.

'Her name is Jeanette Joyce – like James; perhaps you're familiar with his work . . . She's Irish, and a wonderful mother and person . . .' I said hysterically. I turned around to take one last look, but the man with the white face was pushing the tray back, filing her away for ever.

I fainted then, and came round lying on a narrow bed in an adjoining room.

'Are you all right? We are very sorry you had to do this,' said the inspector, 'but the law . . .'

'Don't you talk to me about the law,' I said sitting up and glaring at him. 'It was the laws of this country that killed her.'

The inspector looked away.

I had to sign a sheet of paper then, and it felt unreal – signing an exit visa from this life to the next.

As we came out of the morgue, I fumbled in my bag for a cigarette, my hand knocking against something hard. It was the roll of photographs I had planned to develop and take to the lawyer on Monday.

I got into the car, and as we reached the other side of the lake, said suddenly 'Stop! I want to get out.'

'I can't stop here,' the inspector replied. 'It's illegal.'

I didn't recognise my voice – it was as if I had suddenly become possessed by a devil. 'Stop this car right now!' I said.

He pulled over onto the kerb, and I got out and walked to where the lake lapped against the shore. I crouched on the cold paving stones howling into the wind, calling to Jeanette who could not hear me, before throwing the roll of photographs into the cold grey water.

Chapter Twenty-Three

When Michel returned from Berne later that day, I was lying in bed with the curtains drawn, and Delia had taken Jean out for a walk.

After he had listened to my garbled story, he pulled me into his arms, saying, 'I'm so sorry I wasn't here, if only I'd known!'

You're never here these days, I thought miserably.

'Why don't you go away for a while?' he suggested later. 'Take Jean up to the mountains and get a breath of air?'

'What burns me up,' I sobbed, 'is that despicable Fabian! I could kill him! It's one way to hang onto your kids – put the wife in prison until she dies from unhappiness . . . He should be shot!'

'Em-i-ly, *calme-toi*!' he urged, wiping at my streaming eyes with his handkerchief.

'She might have won, Michel . . . Fabian was hitting the little boy, we had proof – some photographs . . . There's no justice.'

'It's an unjust world,' he said gently. He had run out of comforting words, unable to deal with my pain.

'If only you'd been here,' I said helplessly.

'I'm sorry; more sorry than you'll know.' He rubbed his forehead distractedly. 'Poor girl . . . She seemed to be doomed from the start.'

'Because of the system.'

He squeezed my hand. 'I know, I know. Look, why don't you go away for a few days,' he repeated, 'have a holiday, get some rest?'

I thought of Heronlough, but somehow the idea of going to Ireland was too painful. It was even an effort to get out of bed; the thought of having to make reservations and pack a suitcase was overwhelming.

'Think about it, at least,' Michel said.

Over the days that followed, the weather turned wet and foggy. Heavy grey clouds gathered over the mountains, and the air seemed laden with moisture, a massive weight pressing down on the city. I felt I was existing in a vacuum, and could no longer distinguish night from day.

I begged Michel to come back from the office earlier, but he was caught up in problems of his own, which in my wretched state seemed quite trivial. He was in the midst of moving offices, since the lease on the last premises had expired, and had lost one of his best architects. He rang every so often to check how I was, and kept urging me to drive up to the mountains, saying he would try and join me at the weekend. But I didn't want to go alone.

One wet afternoon, when I had reached my lowest ebb, I called him at the office and begged him to come home.

'I can't, Emily,' he said firmly. 'I'm up to my ears here . . . Look, I'm sorry, but you're going to have to get through this somehow.'

I thought, I'm alienating him by being like this, and wondered miserably if he was putting in all those hours at the office to avoid the misery of being with me.

The following week I wrote to a literary agent in London, enclosing a synopsis and three sample chapters of *The Love Trap*, and received a letter some days later asking to see the manuscript. So I sent it off, as Jeanette had urged me to do, though I didn't harbour many expectations of my own. The story, a poignant portrait of thwarted love, now seemed shallow and trivial in the light of my own loss.

That week, I also decided to redecorate Jean's room, since the wallpaper had started to look childish and dated. Karine, the robot's girlfriend, had told me of a shop in the old town where they sold children's furniture and fittings, so I set off with Jean early one morning towards the *Bourg de Four*, trying not to think of the last time I had walked this way with Jeanette.

The pavements were narrow and uneven, making it difficult to guide the pushchair, so I slowed down, cold numbing my fingers and toes. Jean, dressed in his ski jacket and woolly hat, seemed oblivious to the temperature. He sat up in his pushchair like a little snowman, watching the cars slide by.

By the time we reached the centre, I was frozen and in need of a coffee, so on an impulse decided to go to the Café des Artistes – which, ironically, had become our favourite haunt in the last few months that Jeanette had been alive. The last time we had been there, I remembered, she had talked about 'going out the back door', and I'd laughed it off, claiming she always landed on her feet . . . Well she hadn't this time, I thought, feeling the tears stinging my eyes.

I blinked them back and carried on, bumping over the cobbles until I reached the top of the steep street where the café was. A line of cars was parked outside the buildings, causing drivers to blare their horns, even though there was plenty of room to pass. 'Public policemen,' as Jeanette had called them. I glanced up to the left and saw the shutters of Marguerite's apartment were open, and the window boxes filled with stubby looking shrubs. Then I looked down again, and froze.

There was a green Mercedes parked right outside her building.

I walked towards it with a strange sort of fear; circled it cautiously as if it were primed to explode. It can't be, I said to myself, it just can't be . . . And then I saw the sticker on the back window; 'Let's go sailing'. I stared at it for a moment longer then turned away, feeling as if my world had ended.

So that was why he never came home, I thought, as I made my way back to the apartment, tears scalding my frozen cheeks, that was why he kept urging me to go away . . . What a fool I had been! There had been signs all along – all those late evenings at the office, the trips away – but in my obsessive state, I had taken no notice.

Once back at the apartment, I handed Jean over to Delia, took a bottle of white wine from the fridge, and lay on the bed to drink it. I drank from the bottle like a wino, tears streaming into my hair.

I heard his key in the lock at eight o'clock, earlier than usual, then his footsteps as he came down the corridor.

'Emily, *cherie*, are you all right? What's going on. . . ?'

I sat up and glared at him. 'That's what I want to know,' I said.

He shrugged, as if my behaviour was suddenly more than he could stand.

'I saw your car outside her flat, Michel. What the hell is going on? Is that where you've been every evening – with Marguerite?'

'You are as drunk as a pot,' he said disgustedly.

'Answer the question, Michel!'

'I just dropped off some plans for the new office, that's all.'

'You've asked her to decorate the new office?' I said incredulously, 'I don't believe it . . . And you were just "dropping off" something at her apartment, is that what you're saying?'

198

'Her car is being repaired,' he told me, stony-faced. 'Normally she comes to the office.'

'Oh, that makes me feel one hundred per cent better,' I said sarcastically.

He shrugged and looked away.

'I'm inclined to believe Séverine, this time,' I said.

'That's your choice,' he replied, apparently indifferent.

'Why her, Michel?'

'She's the best.'

I looked around the room – the room that she had decorated, and I had tried to change. In all the time we had been here, I had never mentioned it, but now I felt the sting of injustice, all the stored-up bitterness welling up and spilling over like a dam bursting. 'I don't doubt it,' I said harshly. 'In bed, on the slopes, wherever? Thanks for letting me in on it!'

'Look at you,' he said raising his hands. 'How could I possibly have told you? You're in such a state you can hardly see straight.'

'How long has it been going on?' I demanded.

'*Merde!* Nothing's going on,' he hit back. 'I just went over to drop off some samples.'

'If it's all so innocent, why didn't you mention it?'

'Because I knew you'd react like this – you're so convinced that I still carry the flag for her.'

'The torch,' I corrected automatically.

'Whatever . . . It's your obsession that will drive me away in the end,' he said, 'not Marguerite!' And with that, he stormed out of the room.

'I'm going away for a while,' I told him the following morning, over breakfast.

'I think you should. May I inquire where?'

'To the mountains,' I replied.

'Good idea. Have you decided where to stay?'

'I'll find somewhere.'

'I'll book you a hotel room, if you like?'

'It's quite all right; I have a couple of ideas.'

He nodded, then picked up *La Suisse* and glanced at the headlines.

'I need to think things through,' I said.

'Fine,' he replied with infuriating distance.

'Like whether we're going to make it or not.'

'That depends on you.'

'On you too, Michel.'

'I wasn't considering leaving.'

'It seems to me that you've already left,' I said coldly. When he didn't answer I added, 'I feel betrayed.'

He stared at me with a hard look. 'Get back into the real world, Emily. Nobody has betrayed you. She's designing my office, that's all; she has a life of her own.'

'Almost three years, Michel, and I haven't set eyes on her . . . Why is that?'

'Because she's part of a different circle of people. This is business, she's doing up the offices,' he emphasised, as to a child.

'Get somebody else to do it,' I said.

'Don't ask too much of me,' he said. 'Not now.'

'Why? Is she still that important to you?'

'Oh, for heaven's sake, there's no point trying to explain anything to you, you only see what you want to see.'

'What do you have to do for the special rate?' I asked nastily.

'That was rather cheap,' he answered, 'even for you.'

Chapter Twenty-Four

I set off early the next morning with Jean, soon after Michel had left for work. He left a wad of money beside the bed, and said, 'Take good care of yourself and Jean. Have a rest and come back when you're ready.'

I mumbled something to the effect that I would ring when I arrived, but turned away when he tried to kiss me goodbye.

I put the small bag into the boot of the Volkswagen, lifted Jean into his car seat, then drove slowly towards the French border.

It was a cold, dull day. It still hadn't snowed, and I was impatient to get above the clouds and into the sunshine. We were waved through the border by an official, and headed south along the motorway. It grew brighter as we went; the cloud thinned, and Jean began to sing in the back. Drifts of snow lay on the side of the road, and I moved into the slow lane, allowing the trucks to rumble past.

At last I saw the exit that led up into the mountains. I drove carefully now, for the road was narrow and icy, towards the auberge where Michel and I had come for lunch that first day, which now seemed a lifetime away.

As we emerged through the cloud into the bright sunshine, I felt my spirits lift. The road looked familiar now, as I followed the directions I had been given, past the ski resort – which was empty, the season not yet started – through the valley with its thin crust of snow, until I saw the hotel above and turned off the road into the narrow lane that led to it.

Jean had fallen asleep, so I put him in his pushchair and wheeled him into the hotel reception, towards the fire. The man behind the desk looked up and smiled a welcome. I recognised him as the one who had worn the William Tell breeches, that day when we had eaten lunch on the terrace.

'How long will you be staying with us?' he inquired, handing me a key.

'I'm not sure,' I said. 'Maybe a week.'

'As you like,' he replied. 'We are empty at this time of the year, so you can inform me the day before. I have put a cot for the child in your room, as you requested.'

'Thank you,' I said.

'My name is Guillaume,' he told me. I hid a smile. 'If you require anything, please let me know.'

I filled in the form and handed it back to him.

'Ah, you are English,' he said, immediately switching languages.

'Half English, half Irish,' I told him. 'I'm trying, unsuccessfully, to lose my accent.'

'On the contrary,' he said gallantly, 'it's very charming.' He looked over my shoulder and beckoned a young boy from behind me. '*Marc, s'il vous plait, prenez les valises de Madame, chambre dix-huit.*'

The room was small, with low beams, old-fashioned furniture, and a view across the terrace over the valley. A painting of Mont Blanc had been hung on the wall. There was an ancient wooden cot by the window, which I put Jean into, then I unpacked our few things and crept out of the room and down the stairs.

In the dining room only a few tables had been laid. A young couple sat at one of them, gazing longingly into each other's eyes, and an old lady with a lined and whiskered face sat at another. Suddenly hungry for the first time in ages, I ordered *pâté de campagne*, *steak pommes frîtes*, and a *pichet* of red wine. My mind had gone blissfully blank, all my problems erased or filed away for the time being. I ate slowly, savouring the good food, finished the wine, then lit a cigarette and gazed out of the window across the empty terrace. Then I went upstairs, took off my shoes and crawled into bed, where I fell into an exhausted sleep.

Jean woke me an hour later. I dressed him warmly and we set off for a walk at a snail's pace. A cold wind blew across the valley, but everything still looked lush and green. Soon it would be white with snow, I thought. Winter would come, and the seasons would continue, but what would become of Michel and me?

We returned to the auberge to find the old lady sitting in front of the fire knitting, and Guillaume behind his desk, reading the papers. He stood up and handed me my key. 'Did you have an enjoyable walk?' he inquired.

202

'We didn't get very far,' I told him, 'but the view was spectacular.'

'I will show you some places you can go, which would be more easy for the boy.'

'Thank you,' I said, noticing for the first time that he had extraordinary eyes – almost yellow, like a cat's.

I didn't call Michel that week, and he didn't call me. But as the days passed, it slowly dawned on me that I may have behaved foolishly. I had nothing to go on but my own suspicions, fuelled by Séverine's insinuations. That silent pact never to talk about the past had been a mistake, I thought, causing it to become distorted and shrouded in mystery – a jigsaw with missing pieces. I had tried to do all the piecing together from the bits Séverine had provided and my own fertile imagination, but the picture still wasn't complete. I sat staring across the valley, thinking back to that dreadful argument. Perhaps, as Michel had said, I had been too grief-stricken by Jeanette's death to see straight.

I knew that then I had no choice but to try and put aside my fears and suspicion and carry on. Let Marguerite get on with the office, while I got on with my life. But without Jeanette, it seemed a bleak prospect.

The auberge had become a haven from all the problems I had left behind; the old lady, the loving couple, and Guillaume part of a familiar world I didn't want to leave. Guillaume called me '*mon amie Irlandaise*', and had become besotted with Jean. He showed me a quick way down to the village, from where we could catch a *télécabine* across the valley, organised picnics for us, and greeted me like a long-lost friend every morning.

The daily walks, the fresh air, and the good food were starting to revive me. But at night I cried myself to sleep, thinking about Christophe and Paul, who would never see their mother again. And in those dark hours I longed for Michel; for the way it had been in the early days before we had grown apart, before I had let the ghost of Marguerite come between us.

By the end of the week, I was tanned and rested, and knew it was time to go home. Time to get back to the real world, as Michel had said.

'You must come again,' Guillaume said, 'when the cross-country skiing begins.'

'Maybe I will,' I replied. 'With my husband.'

'I will be expecting you,' he said formally, 'with *le petit*, of course.'

After breakfast I went upstairs to pack, and found a box of hand-made chocolates beside the bed, with a card that read, 'Come back soon, *mon amie Irlandaise* – Guillaume.' I smiled, and put them in my bag to eat on the way home.

The old lady was sitting in her usual place by the fire as we came down the stairs. She seemed to be knitting her whiskers into a long tube that hung from her needles.

'*Vous partez?*' she said in a cracked voice.

'Yes,' I replied in French. 'It's time I went back to my husband.'

'*C'est bien,*' she said, nodding into the fire. '*Ca c'est bien.*'

As we drove down into the clouds it felt as if we were moving into another day, one that was taking place separately under a wet blanket of fog. Suddenly there was no view, just a swirling white mass. I switched on my fog lights and slowed down, afraid to miss the turning that would bring us back onto the motorway, straining my eyes for the sign.

It began to drizzle. The Volkswagen skidded alarmingly on the slushy road, and the visibility grew worse, but at last we reached the motorway that led to the Swiss border. I glanced at Jean in my rear view mirror and saw he was nodding off, mesmerised by the grinding windscreen wipers.

'Papa?' he said sleepily.

'Yes, we're going home to see Papa,' I told him.

The rain became heavier as we approached the border. Cars sped along, showering spray into the air, and trucks fired jets of filthy water over the windscreen. After what seemed an interminable time, I saw the brake lights of cars ahead slowing down, and the grey block of the *Douane* looming, and breathed a sigh of relief.

'We're almost home,' I whispered to the sleeping Jean as I drove slowly towards the lake, wary of the *canari* lurking between the trees. I turned left at the supermarket, past the bakery towards the apartment, and for one illusory moment it seemed we were home.

I looked up as we swung into the building and saw the tip of the pine tree and the plant pots I had never tied down, then noticed a red sportscar parked in the place where the Merc usually sat. Michel's car must be below in the underground car park, I thought uneasily. He had a visitor, it seemed. Cursing the fact that somebody had spoilt our homecoming, I pulled up behind the red sportscar, blocking it in, and got stiffly out of the Volkswagen. Then I unstrapped Jean, grabbed my handbag, and ran across the rainswept courtyard to the entrance door.

The lift seemed to take an age to arrive. I pushed the button impatiently, hearing the echo of voices chattering on the landing above, and at last the doors slid open and I stepped inside, pressing the button to the penthouse flat. There was a strong smell of perfume in the lift – a familiar spicy smell that made me want to sneeze. Sévérine, I thought, with a sudden foreboding. She was back.

The lift reached the sixth floor and we got out. I fumbled with the key in the lock with one hand and pushed the door open, dropping my bag in the hallway, and looked straight across the room. To where Michel and Marguerite sat opposite one another, their heads bent over a large piece of paper.

There were two glasses of what looked like bubbly water on the table beside them, and a cigarette burning in the ashtray. I took a step forward and they both stood up.

'Cherie? You're back,' said Michel awkwardly. He came towards me, but I stared past him at Marguerite.

At last we had come face to face. Gone was the ghostly woman of my imaginings, who had haunted me for so long, and in her place stood this elegant creature. She had dark brown hair tied back in a pony tail, and the same burnished skin as Sévérine; her eyes were the colour of violets, fringed with long black lashes. Her features were not as perfect as her sister's, but that only added to her charm. There was an aura of continental elegance about her that made Sévérine's beauty seem overdone by comparison. She smiled fleetingly, and I noticed her teeth were white and even. I tried to smile back, but my face seemed to have frozen, so it turned into a sort of grimace.

'What's going on?' I asked, in a high, unnatural voice.

I heard Michel say levelly, 'We're going over some plans.'

'I see,' I said, handing Jean to Delia, who had miraculously appeared behind me.

'How was your trip?' inquired Michel. 'I was worried when you didn't ring.'

'I would have thought you were too busy to worry,' I said.

'Come and sit down,' he beckoned, ignoring that remark. 'I'd like you to see the plans we've made for the new office. And Marguerite's found a place where you can buy wallpaper for Jean's room, by the way.

I stared at him, dumbfounded.

'Yes, there is a children's shop on the other side of the lake,' she said equably, her voice an echo of Séverine's.

'Come,' said Michel, trying to take my hand, but I had turned into a pillar of stone.

'I'd prefer to go and unpack my things, if you don't mind. I'm exhausted . . .' I took a step back.

The fury seemed to come from somewhere deep inside me, riveting me to the floor. 'In any case, I've already decided what to do with Jean's room. I'd rather it didn't turn out like the rest of this apartment – I don't want him growing up like a *petit bourgeois* with pine furniture and white curtains, if you don't mind. Do what you like with the office, but stay away from his room.'

I had said what I had tried so hard not to say, right from the beginning. They were both staring at me in shock, as if watching some sort of vulgar and unpredictable show. I noticed Michel flush a deep red, and knew I had embarrassed him. I turned on my heels and stormed along the corridor into the bedroom and fell on the bed, wondering if she had slept in it, then burst into angry tears.

I heard them talking quietly; the front door opened and closed, then Michel strode into the room. 'What the hell has got into you?' he demanded.

'What's got into you, more like it,' I shouted. 'Inviting her here, allowing her to decorate Jean's room – no wonder you were so keen for me to go away! I won't have her touching anything in this apartment again, do you hear me?'

'You've fallen off your rocker,' he fumed. If I hadn't been in such a state, I might have laughed. 'I thought a holiday would bring you back to your senses, make you get over all that, but

206

obviously not. The moment you walked in, I noticed that contaminated look in your eyes.'

'I suppose you didn't expect me back so soon?' I said, knocked back by the force of his words.

'Oh I expected you, all right . . . I just never believed you'd react like this. You're behaving like a lunatic.'

'Why didn't you just book a hotel room?' I stormed. 'Then I would never have known.'

'There's nothing to know, Emily, that's why . . .' He was just about to say something else when the doorbell rang.

I remembered then I had blocked her car in.

He left the room and returned moments later, saying, 'Where are your car keys? she can't get her car out.'

'In my bag,' I said without moving. My whole body had started shaking like a leaf, my teeth chattering from nerves and shock.

I heard him fumble around in my bag for a while, swearing, then in a fury turn the contents onto the floor. Out spilled a jumbled pile of tissues, credit cards, lipstick, keys – and the card Guillaume had left with the chocolates. He picked it up and read the scrawled message, then looked at me coldly.

'You seem to have been pretty tied up yourself,' he said.

'It was nothing, nothing at all; he was just a friend.'

'Just as this was nothing,' he emphasised, slamming out of the room.

Chapter Twenty-Five

He slept on the sofa that night, and for several nights to come, while we remained in a frozen silence during the day. The atmosphere in the apartment was so bad that I asked Delia to leave. She had nothing to do now anyway, since I had turned to Jean for comfort.

Then Michel started staying out the odd night, returning in the morning to shower and change, and it seemed we had reached rock bottom. After he had stayed away three nights in a row, I asked him calmly one morning where he had been, and when he didn't reply, told him we couldn't go on like this.

'What exactly are you trying to say?' he demanded, in a new, hostile voice.

I stared at him, in a turmoil. 'Perhaps we should call it a day,' I said.

I heard the words echo in my head, the words I had never dreamt would be spoken, and it seemed that it was somebody else talking, somebody who was prepared to go much further than I was.

'I see,' he said.

'It's not working, let's be honest.'

'No.' He rubbed his eyes, which looked sore and bloodshot.

'I can't even talk to you any more, you're never here, and even when you are you're like a stranger. Where were you last night?'

'At Gregoire's,' he replied.

'Am I supposed to believe that?'

'Suit yourself,' he said wearily, as if he no longer cared.

'I can't go on like this any more,' I repeated, defeated suddenly.

'You're free to leave, if that's what you want.'

How could this be happening to us? I thought dazedly.

'You've changed, Michel.'

'How easy it is to blame the other,' he replied.

'So you consider yourself blameless?'

'All I know is that I can't seem to make you happy.'

He walked across the room towards the fireplace and stared at a photo of us on the mantelpiece, as though he had a better chance of communicating with the laughing woman there than me.

'You did once,' I said, tears stinging my eyes.

He swung around and seemed to look right inside me. 'What you can't accept, Emily,' he said suddenly, 'is the fact that you've failed!'

I took a step back, afraid now.

'You couldn't make a go of it here, you couldn't integrate . . . I've seen this happen before, but I wrongly imagined you'd cope somehow.' He paused, then added icily: 'So you've rejected my lifestyle, and turned the blame on me for continuing to live it!' Just as Marguerite had failed in London.

His words had turned into a cat of nine tails, cutting deep to the heart. I started to shake uncontrollably. 'How can you say that!' I hit back. 'You're the one who blames me – for not wanting to take over where Marguerite left off . . .'

He folded his arms and stared at me. 'At times, you sound like a neurotic heroine from a second-rate novel,' he said. 'It strikes me that you can no longer discriminate fact from fiction.'

An anti-heroine, more likely, I thought, for I had not triumphed over it all, but opted out, tried to find an alternative lifestyle. There was only the one option left now, as far as I could see, to avoid a crushing defeat – to gather the last shreds of my dignity and walk away.

'I want out of this marriage,' I said, and my voice had turned alien and strange, as if it belonged to somebody else.

'What will you do?' he inquired politely.

'Go back to England, get my job back. Don't worry, I won't try and bleed you dry, like Florence did to Hervé.'

'I'm glad to hear it,' he stated.

'You're as cold as the rest of them,' I told him.

'And what do you think you are, light and sunshine?'

'Sweetness and light,' I corrected.

'I apologise for my bad English,' he snapped. He sat down suddenly and put his head in his hands, as if he, too, were defeated.

'I'll go and see a lawyer in the morning,' I said. It sounded bizarre – saying it as though it were as simple as taking an aspirin for a headache. 'Jean can go to school in England . . . you wanted him to speak perfect English, after all.'

'No,' he said.

'Don't worry, I won't stop him from seeing you – I've learnt that lesson from Jeanette and Fabian.'

'You won't be taking him with you,' he said, without looking at me.

I stood stock still, all senses alert.

'What?' I said.

'Jean stays here with me.'

'Don't be ridiculous, Michel,' I said, trying to remain calm. 'How could you possibly look after him? You spend half your time with your interior decorator, the other half on the lake!'

'I'll get a full-time nanny and give up sailing,' he replied, ignoring the part about Marguerite.

'Forget it,' I said. 'You don't have a chance.'

'I'm afraid you're the one without a chance,' he stated.

My heart was pumping so loudly I wondered if he could hear it. 'What the hell are you talking about?'

'Emily,' he said heavily, 'you haven't the means to support Jean, let's be honest. A struggling writer – with a criminal record! Plus a tendency towards depression!'

'What are you talking about?' I demanded again.

'Hervé showed me the report he made – he prescribed some sort of tranquilliser, it seems.'

'He *what*?' I gasped.

He had the grace to blush.

'That's completely unethical!' I continued, horrified. Hervé, who was bound by a code of ethics, had broken the code? '. . . That's the most outrageous thing I've ever heard!'

'He's my closest friend,' he said defensively. 'He was worried about you . . . He was just trying to help . . .'

'*Help*!' I cut in incredulously. 'By disclosing people's private lives? I could sue him for that . . . it's against the law.' I was gasping like a fish out of water.

'He went through a breakdown after Florence left him,' Michel said, as if that explained it all.

'Christ, he should be struck off – or whatever they do to psychiatrists . . .'

210

'Maybe you should have talked to me?' Michel suggested.

We stared at one another helplessly, then I said, 'Are you threatening me, Michel, with something that happened years ago?'

'I'll use it if I have to,' I heard him say.

It struck me then that normal loving people turned into monsters when threatened. I felt as if I were hovering over the edge of an abyss; any moment I would spin away into oblivion.

'You can't take Jean away from me!' I shouted.

'He's my son too, Emily, or have you forgotten that?'

I stared at him, tears streaming down my face. 'You never even wanted him, Michel,' I said hollowly.

He was walking away from me. I moved towards the mantelpiece and, in a moment of wild and irrational rage, wiped everything off its surface, watching the ornaments, photographs, and other mementoes we had collected over the last three years crash to the floor.

At that moment the doorbell rang, and, wiping my eyes, I went to answer it. It was the woman from the floor below.

'What is it now?' I demanded through clenched teeth.

'Can I talk to you?' she said.

It was the final straw. I looked her straight in the eyes and said, 'I don't give a damn about anything you have to say! Now get away from my door, you miserable, constipated, petty little Calvinist spy, and go jump in the lake!' Then I slammed the door.

Michel had appeared behind me. 'That'll put the fox among the chickens,' he said, but I stormed past him into the bedroom, wishing I could set fire to the whole building and really give her something to complain about.

As I lay alone in bed that night, that dreadful dialogue going round and round in my head, I remembered the first time I'd gone to his Chelsea flat, and how he'd said, 'I find it impossible to let go of anything . . .' My mind flicked to that fateful session with Hervé: 'Michel hangs onto his past like people hang onto old clothes,' he had said. Hervé Dubois, who seduced and betrayed his patients – what sort of friend was he, for God's sake? I knew that Michel would never let go of Jean, just as he had been unable to let go of Marguerite. Soon the walls would close around me as they had for Jeanette. In a bitter turn of events, it seemed that the

211

battle which had started way back, over Jean's birth, was about to become a war.

Chapter Twenty-Six

Michel had left for the office by the time I got up the following morning. I must have dozed off at some stage during the night, but my eyes felt hot and itchy, as if I hadn't slept at all, and my body ached all over.

At nine o'clock I called the office. I had no clear idea of what I was going to say. I would let him speak first.

'He's not here,' his secretary informed me.

'It's important, it's his wife.'

'He's not here,' she repeated in English.

'Please ask him to ring me as soon as he returns,' I said coldly.

I left Jean playing in his room and went to have a bath, listening for the phone. Then I went into Jean's room and started throwing a few of his clothes into a bag. I packed pyjamas, vests, socks, a woolly hat, gloves, some baby aspirin and a few toys, and dragged the bag into the bedroom. I had no definite plan; instinct seemed to have taken over. I found my passport, put it into my handbag, and discovered a wad of notes in my purse – the month's allowance, which I'd barely touched. There were almost three thousand francs, plus my credit cards. I piled my clothes on top of Jean's – jumpers, shirts, underwear, none of the glamorous outfits that hung in the wardrobe, then make-up and sponge bag. I left the emerald ring by the phone, and picked up a pencil to write a note, but nothing came to mind. A farewell note seemed to me the ultimate cliché. Instead I simply grabbed my fur coat and walked towards the front door.

Jean had started crying now, sensing something was in the air – but the phone would ring in a minute, I said to myself, bringing everything back to normal. I dressed Jean in his warmest clothes, strapped him into the pushchair and, grabbing the keys of the Volkswagen, pushed him towards the front door. He started squirming around from the heat, so I opened the door and rolled the pushchair out onto the landing.

I returned to pick up the bag, glancing at the silent phone. Then

I locked the door, and pressed the button for the lift. The doors slid open; I entered with the pushchair and bag and pushed *Rez de Chausée*. The lift descended one floor and stopped, and there was the woman with the scraped-back hair waiting to get in. She shot me a dagger look and moved forward, but I quickly pressed the button and the door closed on her: she started shouting down the lift shaft at me – something about the police. I thought I heard a phone ringing from above then, but it quickly faded away.

Outside it was freezing cold. Small drifts of wet snow were beginning to fall, and the wind stung my face as I crossed the courtyard towards the car. I strapped Jean into his seat, then reversed jerkily out of the car park and away from the building. Instead of turning down to the centre, I drove towards the old town, following the signs that read *Aeroport*.

I cut down a road that ran parallel to Marguerite's street towards the square, over the tram lines to the other side of the city. Tears kept filling my eyes, blurring the way ahead, and twice I nearly drove into the back of another car, but I continued, entering the no-man's land that lay between the city and the airport. I followed an empty bus that swung out on its cable in front of me, then accelerated and passed it illegally on the inside.

I still had no set plan. All I knew was that I had to leave before it was too late, just as Jeanette should have done.

My thoughts returned to Marguerite. How long had she been there, I wondered, hovering on the periphery of our lives like some ignoble siren, threatening to lure Michel away from the wreckage of our marriage onto the rocks? Anger coursed through me as I thought of her sitting in the apartment as though she had never left.

At the airport, I left the car at the back of the parking lot, hoping it would be some time before the police found it, bundled Jean into his pushchair and, hanging the bag over the handles, went towards the departure terminal. What if there were no flight, I thought, terrified now that Michel would guess what I had done and try to stop us.

I made my way to the British Airways desk and stood in a queue for several minutes, glancing around anxiously in case I was being followed. By the time I reached the desk I was in a dreadful state. The woman behind it looked like Amanda Ellis Smith. She stabbed at the computer with sharp nails and said, 'There is a flight about to leave, but it might be too late.'

'Please try and get me on it,' I said. 'It's an emergency.'

'I can't get you on it unless there's a seat,' she pointed out. 'How old is the child?'

'Two,' I said, wondering if I'd have to pay the full fare.

I waited, rocking back and forth with nerves; lit a cigarette. Jean seemed to have gone into a trance. He was watching a woman bundle a tiny dog into her designer bag, as if she were about to smuggle it onto a plane.

'How do you intend to pay?' inquired the woman.

'American Express,' I replied, trying to work out when Michel would receive the bill.

She took ages filling out the tickets, and still hadn't told me if there were any seats on the next flight.

'I need to go to the bank,' I said. 'How much time do I have?'

'Very little,' she replied. 'The flight has already been called. Is that all you have in the way of luggage?'

'Yes,' I told her.

'Then I suggest you carry it on board.'

I breathed a sigh of relief. It seemed we were on the flight.

I made my way swiftly to the bank, hearing the announcement 'Last call for BA125,' as I went.

I handed my bank card to the man behind the *guichet*, then keyed in my private identification number.

'I'd like to know the balance of my account,' I told him.

There was sixty thousand francs in the account. I withdrew fifty-five.

'How would you like the money?' he asked, as I handed over my *carte d'identité*.

'In thousand franc notes, please.' I said.

'Please sign this,' he said, handing me a withdrawal slip with the notes.

I scrawled my signature on the slip and stuffed the notes into the side pocket of my handbag. Then I ran back to the departure lounge. As I passed the British Airways desk, Jean pointed to where a tall-dark haired man stood by the counter firing questions at the Amanda look-alike. He had a broad athletic body, and his hair waved over the back of his collar.

215

'Papa,' Jean said, making me back away. The man turned around suddenly and stared straight at me. It wasn't Michel. With a beating heart, I walked quickly towards passport control and handed over my documents. The official gazed at me, then glanced down at the pushchair suspiciously. He knows, I thought. Michel's already alerted all exits out of the country.

'Have a nice day,' he said, as though I were an American tourist on the second leg of my trip around Europe.

As we took off, Jean fell asleep in my lap. I loosened his jacket, for he seemed slightly flushed, then sat back and tried to relax. Now we were airborne and out of Switzerland, I had to decide what to do next, but the enormity of what I had already done had rendered me incapable of thinking.

By evening, Michel would be on our trail. I would have to continue under an assumed name. I had a vision of Jean and myself lurking in a seedy Earl's Court hotel overnight, and closed my eyes.

Then I remembered Mother saying, 'If ever you need someone to turn to, there's Aunt G . . .', and knew what I was going to do. I would go to Ireland, to Heronlough House.

I wondered briefly if I had left Aunt G's address lying around somewhere – how many Flavells were there in Ireland? Would Michel remember the details? He was bad with names, but it wouldn't take much detective work to find out . . . I would have to start there and move on.

I hadn't heard from Aunt G since early summer, after which I had become so involved with Jeanette's case, I hadn't thought too much about it. But now I realised how odd it was that she hadn't replied to my last two letters. I wondered with a flash of alarm if something had happened to her. I would ring her as soon as we landed at Heathrow. In the meantime there was nothing I could do but sit back and try to relax.

Beggar, then said, shaking hands. a: Manaca sasked. The man turned
around elderly and unsaid to ... upon and its went, and looked. Why
spotting, their shelf a guy towards the short control and
named area, ... about ... at the Then
cloud down slow his pushchair to ... to explains and acknowledge...

Chapter Twenty-Seven

It was drizzling in London, a dull overcast day similar to the day
Michel and I had left, almost three years ago. As I walked down the
drafty corridor towards Customs, Jean woke up and started crying.
His cheeks were unusually flushed, and I wondered uneasily if he
were sickening for something.

As we went, I tried to plan the next step, but by the time we
reached the arrival hall I was in a dither, not knowing where to turn. I
made my way towards the bank first, to change some money, then to
the phone kiosks. I dialled Heronlough House and waited for Aunt
G to answer, but the phone rang and rang. I hung up and re-dialled,
but there was still no answer. I turned away with a sinking heart to
where Jean was now thrashing about in his pushchair, whimpering.

'Don't worry, little fellow, we'll be home soon,' I said trying to
soothe him, though I knew we were still a long way away.

There wasn't an available flight to Dublin until three o'clock in
the afternoon, which was four hours away, so I went and sat in the
departure lounge and waited. I found the baby aspirin in the
depths of my bag and tried to get Jean to swallow some, for he
seemed to have a fever now, but he spat it out, and it ran in a sticky
stream down my coat. Time seemed to grind to a halt as we waited
for the flight to be announced. Every hour I tried calling
Heronlough, but there was no reply; just the sound of a ringing
phone echoing through an empty house.

At one stage I went over to a neon-lit buffet and bought a
sandwich and some fruit juice, but Jean wouldn't touch either. He
lay still now, his eyes glazed and feverish. I remembered the
febrile illnesses he had had as a tiny baby, and suspected that was
all this was, but all the same I was beginning to feel increasingly
worried. I loosened his clothes and tried to rock him to sleep,
longing to close my burning eyes and sleep myself. Why did
nobody answer the phone at Heronlough? Bridget was always
there, even if Aunt G wasn't. Had something happened to her,
and nobody had contacted me?

Jean finally fell asleep, so I turned to the tired-looking woman sitting beside me and said, 'Would you mind keeping an eye on my bag? I need to make a phone call.'

She nodded, then went into a trance again.

I pushed the pushchair over to the phones and dialled the operator.

'Could you put me through to Rathegan, County Wicklow 7986,' I said desperately.

'Hold the line,' was the reply. Moments later, she said, 'Sorry, no answer.'

I was about to ask her to check the number when I spotted a policeman striding towards us. I hung up and pretended to scrabble around in my handbag for something, aware my cheeks were burning. The sight of him brought back the memory of Shariffi's party, when the police had suddenly appeared at the door. We didn't exactly blend into the crowd, I thought – a pale woman with a dark-skinned child. This was the very place they were most likely to pick us up.

'Excuse me,' he said, staring at me then shifting his gaze to Jean.

'Yes?' I said faintly.

'Is that your boy?' I thought he said.

'Yes.' Then I realised he was pointing at my bag, which now lay abandoned beside an empty chair. The sleepy woman had dragged herself away.

'Abandoned luggage will be removed by the police,' he said. 'Please stay with it at all times.'

'Yes, of course, I'm sorry,' I said.

'Good day,' he muttered as he strode away.

At last we were boarding the flight, but Jean was wide awake again and so hot I started to feel frantic. On the plane he writhed around in my arms, thrashing against the safety belt, his cries growing louder by the minute. The air hostess brought damp towels and water and we tried to soothe him, but to no avail. I took off a layer of his clothing, discovering the vest I had put on that morning was soaking wet. Even his stomach was burning hot. As I sponged his body he jerked in a sudden spasm, and clots of milk gushed out of his mouth.

'Christ,' I said, signalling the hostess again. Now I was convinced that something was wrong . . . It's all my fault, I thought hysterically. It seemed in my heightened state that his heart was beating faster and faster, and wouldn't be able to keep up that galloping rhythm for much longer.

By the time we landed at Dublin airport, he had fallen asleep again; a deep feverish sleep, making me afraid he would never wake up.

At the airport, I changed more money then made my way to the phone. There was still no answer. What now? I thought in despair. I walked out of the terminal building in a daze. Pehaps I could take a taxi to Wicklow . . . But at that moment a bus pulled up, and an airport official called out, 'Busaras.'

'Where's that?' I asked a grey-looking man who was standing beside me.

'Centre of Dublin,' he said. 'Where do you want to go?'

'Wicklow,' I told him.

'Then you'll be wanting the train station – that's in the centre . . . Come on, I'll help you with the buggy.'

For lack of any other plan, I followed him. We hoisted the pushchair onto the bus and I sat down, relieved not to have to think for the time being. Jean was still asleep. The bus pulled away from the airport and I closed my eyes, everything temporarily out of my control.

We reached the centre of town, climbed out of the bus, and the grey man pointed me in the direction of the station. 'You'll be able to catch the southbound train to Wicklow from Connolly Station,' he said. 'Will you be all right now?'

'Yes, thank you,' I said, still in a dreamlike state. I picked up the bag and crossed the road towards the station.

Luck was with us: the Wicklow train was already there. I could take a taxi from Wicklow Station, I decided, and if Aunt G wasn't there, ask the driver to take us back to the Grand Hotel in Wicklow. The hotel would be able to call a doctor for Jean.

It was a chill, misty evening, with the smell of woodsmoke in the air, but mild after the biting cold of Switzerland. The train was full of evening commuters – a man with bright orange hair sat opposite us staring into space, and a plump woman in a tight skirt called to her friend across the aisle in a thick Dublin accent. There was a sense of normality about it all that made me momentarily forget the day's dramas.

The train pulled jerkily out of the station, waking Jean with a start to stare around him. He was quiet now, stilled by the fever, two high spots of colour staining his cheeks. 'We're nearly there now,' I whispered, as we crawled past the back yards of semi-detached houses, and out along the sea front. I looked across Dublin Bay and smelt the low-tide smell of salt water; saw two tall chimneys belching smoke into the sky. I could make out the hazy peninsula of Howth Head, and thought of the Howth Oath Jeanette and I had made on that hot July day two years ago. I would go there, when I had found out exactly where Molly Bloom had been deflowered. Aunt G would know, I thought, praying once again that she would be at home.

Now we were racing along towards Dunlaoghaire. We passed the sailing club, where yachts lined the harbour walls, stopping at Toy-town stations on the way. The orange man got out, then the train entered a tunnel and emerged above another wide bay. I saw green fields and hills, and knew we were approaching Bray.

It was growing dark. The sea had turned mauve, and rain clouds gathered over the headland, as the train pulled up with a jerk at Bray station and a few people got out. Jean, still silent, sucked thirstily at the water in his bottle, which seemed a good sign. I hoped that the fever was passing.

It was pitch black by the time we reached Wicklow, and a fine spray blew into the station. I pulled the waterproof cover out of the string bag attached to the pushchair and covered Jean as best I could, then went through the ticket barrier and looked around for a taxi. There was no sign of one. People streamed out of the station and walked towards the town. I turned back into the station and said to the ticket inspector, 'Where can I find a taxi?'

'Ah, there wouldn't be many at this time of an evening,' he replied. 'You might get one in town, but you mightn't . . . 'Tis a bad time now for them. Where're you headin', then?'

'Towards Rathegan,' I said. 'How far is the village from here?'

'Far enough,' he replied. 'You could catch the bus at the crossing, if you happen upon one. They're fairly regular at this hour.' A fine mist blew into the station, and I shivered suddenly.

'I'm trying to get to Heronlough House,' I told him.

'That's the big ould place on the lough?' he said, scratching his head.

'Yes,' I replied. 'Do you happen to know Miss Flavell, who lives there?'

He shook his head and looked vague.

'I've been trying to phone all day,' I told him, 'but nobody answers.'

'The phone lines have been down, what with the rains we've been having,' he told me.

'I have to get there,' I said.

'The bus stop is at the end of the road,' he called after me.

I set off, pushing the heavy load ahead of me, and saw the bus-stop on the corner. Nobody waited there. The rain was coming down horizontally, illuminated by the glow of the street lamp; my fur coat was starting to smell as rank as a wet dog. I began walking away from the town, in the direction I thought Heronlough lay.

We hadn't gone far when I heard the screech of brakes and, turning round, saw a bus pulling up at the stop and a woman getting out. I doubled back, and ran towards it.

'I'm trying to get to a place called Heronlough House,' I said, as the conductor lifted the pushchair inside.

''Tis on the road to Rathegan, near the convent there a few miles up – hop in,' he said. 'Wet ould night.'

As soon as I sat down, Jean started howling, as if he were in pain.

'What's up with you, young fellow?' inquired the conductor jovially.

'He's not very well,' I told him worriedly. 'He has a fever.' I noticed then his bottle was empty, and he still seemed thirsty. 'He'll be all right,' I mumbled, in an effort to convince myself. 'He just needs a drink.'

'God willing,' replied the conductor.

On we went, sloshing along the wet road, until I saw lights twinkling ahead, which ought to be the lights of Rathegan.

'You'll be wanting the next stop,' said the conductor. 'If I'm right, the house is after St Cluny's convent . . .'

The name rang a bell. 'That's it,' I said, pulling my bag off the seat.

'Good luck,' he said, as if he sensed my desperate plight – 'Follow that lane up there on your left – 'twill bring you to the lough.'

'Thank you,' I said, reluctant to leave the warmth and safety of the bus, with only the moonlight to guide me along the dark lane through the bog.

I crossed the road and turned up the mud track. It was so dark, and seemed narrower than I remembered. The trees were overgrown, twisted like gnarled old men, leaning to form a ghostly arch over the driveway, while privet bushes crouched on either side like fat demons. The pushchair squelched through the soft mud, the wheels bumping over the roots of trees, and the night air felt dank on my face. I tripped twice and cursed loudly into the night then carried on, inching my way forwards, terrified that something was about to spring on me from behind.

The driveway curved to the left – in my memory it had curved to the right. I strained ahead through the darkness, searching for a sight of the house, but there was nothing; just the black outline of the trees againt the sky.

In the moonlight I saw the glint of water. We were passing the swamp and I could make out the outline of the bulrushes, standing like pale soldiers at its rim. I thought of Aunt G's story of Mad Maud, who had been found floating through them in a Moses basket, took a deep breath, and forged on, to the sound of water trickling below. Now we were crossing the bridge where Aunt G had played Pooh sticks with the Catholic girl from the village, but there was still no sign of the house. The wind howled through the trees, making me think of banshees sweeping across the bog, and raindrops splattered from the branches.

Please let her be there, I prayed, as I saw a dull yellow light and the black shape of the house ahead. The porch was lit, and light streamed through the fanlight window. Hope surged through me. I quickened my pace, crashing onwards until I reached the carriage sweep, and the wheels of the pushchair ground to a halt in the gravel.

I unstrapped Jean, letting the buggy keel over from the weight of the bag, and stumbled towards the house. Smoke rose from the chimney – somebody was there.

I rang the doorbell, then knocked loudly on the brass knocker, and eventually heard footsteps within. The door opened, and a strange voice said, 'Jesus Mary and Joseph, now who would you be?'

It wasn't Bridget. Aunt G must have died, and this was the new owner. Staring at her, I felt the last of my courage leave me, and slumped down onto the porch, still clutching Jean, and burst into tears.

'Aunt G,' I sobbed. 'She used to live here . . .' Jean started howling too, and the woman stared at us in confusion. Then she moved forward, and plucked him from me like a bird from a nest. She pulled him against the great shelf of her breasts and cooed gently. 'Now, now, what's all this about? Don't be making strange with me.' To my amazement he stopped crying, and stared at her, bewildered.

The woman then turned to me. 'Come in, girl; you look half dead with the cold,' she said kindly.

'Aunt Geraldine?' I said. 'I was looking for my Great Aunt Geraldine . . . Do you know what's become of her? It's Emily, her niece.'

'I thought so,' she replied. 'Your Aunt is resting, so don't be making too much noise – you'll put the fear of God into her.'

The news immediately stemmed the wave of despair that had taken hold of me.

'But where's Bridget?' I asked, following her down the corridor to the kitchen.

'Bridget passed away in June,' she told me.

So that was why I hadn't heard anything, I thought.

I followed her into the kitchen, feeling the warmth from the Aga, and there was Aunt G, fast asleep in her rocking chair, the wireless droning behind her. Her head was at a strange angle – for a minute I thought she was dead, so white was her face. She had aged since I'd last seen her, her hair almost silver, her face creased like an old canvas. She wore the tartan shawl I had given her from The Scotch House all those Christmases ago, and her feet were squashed into orthopaedic shoes.

'Aunt G,' I whispered. She woke up with a jerk and stared at me.

'Peggy,' she said, as if I were the ghost of Mother, then: 'Good gracious me, it's Emily! I don't believe my eyes, come over here to where I can see you, child. You gave me an awful fright; I thought it was your mother and we had met in Heaven!'

Now she was awake she looked alert, almost young again.

'Jacintha, put some milk on the stove to warm, would you dear?

223

emily, this is Jacintha Fahy, a dear friend from long ago. She helps me out now that poor old Bridget is gone.'

It was the Jessie she had played with as a child. I remembered the story of the polishtins.

'Give the young fellow to me, I've been longing to meet him.'

'Aunt G, he's been so ill . . . some kind of fever. He was sick on the plane, and I didn't know if you were here . . .' I burst into tears again.

'Now, one thing at a time. Jacintha, pour us a large sherry, would you, we could both do with one. The phone lines have been down for the last month, that's why you couldn't get through . . . Well, look at you,' she said turning to the startled Jean. 'What a fine young fellow you are – dark and handsome like your Father, I suppose.'

Jacintha handed me a glass of sherry, and I sipped it gratefully. Then she returned with a plate of homemade shortbread.

'Here,' she said kindly, but I couldn't eat a thing.

Aunt G was still holding Jean. 'This boy needs something – warm milk and a bed,' she said.

'I can't get him to drink any milk.'

'Leave it to Jacintha,' said Aunt G, and moments later Jean was sitting in the old woman's lap, sipping milk from a mug. 'If I'd known you were coming, child, I would have arranged for Seamus – Jimmy's boy – to meet you,' Aunt G was saying.

'What's happened to Jimmy?' I asked.

'Nothing but old age like the rest of us. His eyesight is very bad now, so Seamus drives me around – not that I venture far these days.'

'I didn't know I was coming until this morning,' I told her.

'I see,' she replied. There was a silence, then she added, 'I had a feeling this would happen sooner or later.'

I looked away.

'Your letters said it all – you write well, Emily, from the heart. I sensed there was something rotten in the state of Denmark, as they say.'

'Everything was rotten,' I told her. 'Jeanette died – she killed herself – and after that everything fell apart. I was just so lonely. He was never there. He was seeing Marguerite, of course, I know that now . . . Then he threatened to take Jean, it was terrible . . .'

My voice cracked and I wept again – for my lost hopes, for Michel, whom I still loved, and for the failure of our marriage.

'Dear girl,' she said, taking my hand in her stiff one, 'you've had a frightful journey. What you need is a good night's sleep – everything will seem better in the morning.'

'I'm so afraid,' I told her.

'There's nothing to be afraid of,' she said soothingly.

'I'm afraid they'll come and take him in the night.'

'Don't be ridiculous. Nobody is going to come here.'

'For all I know, they're already on our trail – Michel's probably contacted Scotland Yard . . .'

'Enough of this nonsense. You're as bad as your mother. The police have got more important things to do than deal with a domestic squabble – Scotland Yard! Really! No crime has been committed! Besides, nobody's going to come tramping through my house in the dead of night threatening my family. I'll send them away with a flea in their ear.'

'I need a lawyer, Aunt G,' I said, hardly hearing her.

'Well you're not going to find one at nine o'clock on a Friday evening,' she replied. 'On Monday, we'll call the Irish Law Society, but as far as I can make out, you've done nothing wrong.'

'I left without a word,' I said. 'According to the law, I've abducted my child!'

'Nonsense,' she said dismissively. 'And even if he finds out you're here, nothing can be done for at least twenty-four hours, maybe even until Monday.'

'You're dealing with the Swiss. They work on a tight schedule.'

'And they'll be dealing with the Irish,' she said, 'a devious bunch, if ever I knew one!'

'I'll have to move on,' I said, a desperate picture of being on the run for the rest of my days coming to mind. The drama of the last few hours, coupled with fatigue, was catching up with me, and I could no longer think straight.

She looked at me and sighed. 'You remind me so much of your mother. When you walked in like that, it took me right back to the night of the war with the Murphys.' She paused, realising she was digressing. 'Now stop worrying, nothing is going to happen.' There was a slight catch in her voice, causing a violent coughing spasm.

'That cough of yours sounds bad,' I said worriedly. I had been so consumed with my own problems, I'd hardly noticed anything else.

When the spasm was over, she took a sip of sherry and said, 'It's no better and it's no worse. They tried to get me off the cigarettes, but if it's not smoking that gets you in the end, it's something else! I might as well enjoy what's left of my life.'

I stared at her, alarmed.

'Don't look so worried, I'm not ready to fall off my perch just yet – at least, not until we've sorted out this little problem. Now how about getting yourselves off to bed? You both look dead with exhaustion.'

Jean's eyes were drooping, though his fever seemed to have died down a bit. Jacintha had propped him up on the chair while she went upstairs to make the beds. I scooped him up in my arms, and kissed Aunt G goodnight.

'Thanks,' I said inadequately.

'Sleep well, child,' she replied, squeezing my hand. 'You'll see, everything will be better in the morning. Remember there's always a solution.'

Not to this, I thought hopelessly. For no matter what the outcome, one of us was going to lose.

The room at the top of the house was the same as I remembered, only the portrait of Mother had been replaced by 'The Three Old Biddies', and the fading pink wallpaper had starting peeling away from the walls.

I changed Jean and laid him between the cool sheets, then pulled off my own clothes and crawled into the other bed. Staring out of the fanlight window, listening to the wind rattling against it, my thoughts returned to Michel. Tomorrow he would be on to his lawyer, who would start proceedings, if he hadn't already started. How long did we have before they were on our trail?

My visions alternated between Michel arriving at Heronlough, and a plain-clothes policeman banging on the door in the dead of night. It all became hazy and jumbled, as I fell in and out of sleep, until it no longer made any sense.

I slept, and dreamt a fleet of police cars were crawling up the drive to Heronlough. For some bizarre reason a Swiss flag was waving on each vehicle, as if the embassy itself had arrived to reclaim its charges. Then Michel was standing at the front door, holding a purple orchid tied with satin ribbons. A peace offering. He smiled as he handed it to me, then it disintegrated and turned into a piece of paper. I stared at it and saw it was a writ, stating he had filed for custody of Jean.

I woke up with a start, and looked across to where Jean was sleeping soundly, his forehead cooler now, and his breathing more even. Then I slept, and the next thing I heard was a rook cawing above me. It was morning.

Chapter Twenty-Eight

Light was streaming through the fanlight window, and a pale, wintry sun shone from a clear sky. I sat up in bed and gazed out over the lough towards the misty shape of Wicklow Head.

Jean was still fast asleep, his face pale, dark circles under his eyes.

I glanced at my watch. It was eight o'clock – an hour behind Swiss time. Michel would be awake, if he had slept at all, and moving towards the phone. There was, as far as I could see, only the one course of action. I would find a small place to rent close by, somewhere off the beaten track. I had enough money to put down a deposit. Sooner or later I would have to find a job, and somebody to take care of Jean, but for the moment I could manage. These thoughts racing through my mind, I leapt out of bed, pulled on a pair of jeans and crept out of the room.

The smell of bacon wafted from the kitchen. Jacintha was standing over the Aga wearing an ancient cotton apron, cooking breakfast, while Aunt G sat in her rocking chair reading the *Irish Times*.

'Dear girl, how did you sleep, and how's the boy?' she inquired as I went over to hug her. She smelt familiar, of lavender water and soap.

'He's better,' I told her. 'Still asleep. I think the fever has gone, but he still looks a bit off colour.'

'You look a bit peaky yourself! When did you last have a square meal? Let's get a decent breakfast into you.'

'I'm not sure I could manage much,' I said faintly. I couldn't remember when I'd last eaten properly. 'Maybe just some tea and toast.'

'I hope you weren't kept awake by the seagulls? They have a habit of landing on the roof and making a fearful racket. I've got used to them, but the noise can be a bit alarming.'

'I heard something,' I said vaguely. Or was it in my dreams that somebody had been knocking at the door?

Jacintha served fried eggs with crisp bacon, black pudding and some sort of potato mash, then cut up chunks of soda bread which we ate with butter and home-made marmalade. She poured strong black tea into china cups, then sat down herself to eat.

I ate a few mouthfuls, then put down my knife and fork, defeated. Aunt G and I both lit cigarettes, and looked at one another.

'Well?' she said, settling herself comfortably in her rocking chair.

'It's a long story.'

'We have all day,' she replied.

I told her almost everything, beginning with how Michel had never really wanted children and how horrified he had been when I had become pregnant. Of the honeymoon that had turned into a disaster, and of those bleak early days in Switzerland before Jean had been born. I told her about the regattas and the accident that had killed Jean Jacques, and as I spoke it seemed that our chances of ever being happy had been doomed right from the start.

I moved on then to Jeanette, the friendship that had changed everything until she had made that fatal decision, and how everything had fallen apart soon afterwards. Of how Marguerite had re-entered our lives, (if indeed she had ever left) culminating in that final bitter scene.

I heard Michel's words echoing in my head as I spoke.

'. . .what you can't admit in your heart, Emily, is that you've failed.'

'He said some terrible things,' I told her. 'We both did. Then he suddenly announced he wanted custody of Jean.'

Aunt G listened without interrupting, and when I had finished said, 'So nothing has been done?'

'No, I left before he had time to take out a court order preventing me bringing Jean out of Switzerland.'

She frowned. 'Do you really think he would have done that?'

I stared across the room. 'If you'd asked me that question six months ago, I would have said no, of course not. Now I'm not sure. He won't let go of Jean – he never lets go of anything. He'll fight to the bitter end . . . and I haven't a hope in hell against the Swiss judicial system.'

Aunt G looked sceptical.

'You should have seen what they did to Jeanette,' I said. 'We couldn't even get a lawyer to take on the case!'

'Somehow I can't see Michel going that far,' she said after some consideration. 'I've never met the man, but all the same, it doesn't ring true, Emily. It doesn't go along with everything else you've told me about him.'

'People change under pressure,' I said, quoting Jeanette.

'So what do you intend to do?' she asked finally.

'Aunt G, I can't stay here. I'm thinking of finding somewhere around here to live. Nothing grand – a couple of rooms would do. But it would have to be off the beaten track.'

She smiled. 'Hide yourself away in the bogs of Ireland for the rest of your life? And what about the boy?'

'Well, he could go to school here – you always said Ireland's a wonderful place to bring up children! And I'll get a job.' I paused. 'And write novels in my spare time. Maybe eventually I'll get one published.'

'What happened with the novel you were writing?' she inquired.

'Nothing – I sent it to an agent, but it's probably on the slush pile of some editor's office somewhere! I should write this story,' I said wryly. 'I just wish I had some control over the ending!'

'It's the most hare-brained idea I've ever heard in my life,' she said.

'I don't have a choice.'

'How about going back to that husband of yours and trying to work something out?' she suggested.

I blinked back impending tears as this hopeless vision rose, then faded away.

'It's too late for that,' I said. 'Too many things were said.'

At that moment, I heard a plaintive cry from above. Jean had woken up. I ran up the stairs and heard him call, 'Papa?' I took him in my arms and whispered, 'Maman and Papa aren't going to live together any more. Later, when you're older, you can decide where you want to go, but for now I'd be honoured if you'd stay with me.'

He grinned, as if he had understood. 'I love you,' I said, swallowing the lump in my throat.

Later that afternoon, when Jean had fallen asleep, Aunt G suggested we go for a walk.

'Put some colour into those cheeks of yours,' she said, producing an old windcheater and some wellington boots from a cubby hole in the hall. So we set off slowly across the damp lawn towards the lough, Aunt G huddled in a grey shawl like one of the 'Three Old Biddies', a scarf tied under her chin.

The garden looked bare and drab now, the flower beds empty except for a few late chrysanthemums and michaelmas daisies, and I noticed the rowan tree was dropping its leaves. But I was glad to get out of the house. The wind banging against the windows was making me uneasy, and I kept imagining the sound of a car on the driveway.

We reached the lough, and I saw that the old rowing boat was rotting away – the swans now used it to nest in the spring, said Aunt G. I thought of the Murphy boy with the beautiful face that sunny day years ago, when my dreams had still been intact, before the marriage had run aground like *Running Tide* on the Barrier Reef.

'Do the Murphys still trespass on the lough?' I asked, as we followed a muddy path down to the beach.

'The youth are too busy making money these days,' she replied. 'The old man is riddled with gout – props up the bar most of the time. Not that I ever darken his doors; I hear all this from Jacintha.'

The chicken farm had gone now, she told me, and the county council planned to build ten houses in the field where it had been.

'Perhaps that was what was wrong between Michel and me,' I said, as we reached the beach. 'Just too different, when all was said and done.'

'Your mother and father were very different too,' she replied. 'He was sailing mad, she was afraid of the water. Yet they had some very happy years.'

'Maybe she would have been happier with the "rough diamond",' I said.

'I doubt it. In any case, you can't rewrite history.'

We walked for a while in silence along the stony beach. The sea looked grey and storm-tossed. In the distance, a ferry boat ploughed through the waves on its way to England. To the left of us the salt marshes stretched away towards the hills.

'This coastline is very beautiful,' I said, gazing across the bay.

231

'It's still mild now, but it can be very bleak in the heart of winter,' she replied. We must have walked a couple of miles – I noticed she was slightly out of breath.

'Why don't we go up the beach a bit?' I suggested. 'It's tiring walking on these stones.'

We followed a deserted railway track, where brambles and weeds straggled over the line.

'Where did the trains go?' I inquired.

'They moved the line further inland, which is a blessing for the people who live in those cottages. This part of the coastline is eroding.'

We continued until we reached a grey stone cottage with a tiled roof, standing behind the deserted track. A couple of tiles were broken and the windows were low and narrow, picked out in red brick. There was something so familiar about it that I stopped and stared.

'The Railway Cottage!' I exclaimed. 'This is it!'

'Yes,' replied Aunt G. 'Have you never been this far down the beach?'

'No. What an incredible likeness, it's exactly as you painted it.'

'The interior has been done up since,' she told me. 'It used to be a waiting room before the trains were diverted; you can see the remains of the platform. Then it was converted into a cottage, but nobody rents it out any more. The owner's a Wicklow man, who's been trying to sell it for donkey's years, but it's too far from the village, and the road that leads to it is in a dreadful state.'

I approached and looked through the grimy window. The drawing room was tiny, with a blackened stone fire-place and a battered collection of furniture – wooden chairs, and a shaky looking table. Tattered rugs covered the stone floor.

'What a view!' I exclaimed, undeterred by the shabby interior.

'In the summer, it's glorious here,' she said, 'when the gorse is out, and the heather blooms. But now it's very bleak. Although it's a different place from what it once was.'

'Have you been inside?' I asked, walking around to peer into the kitchen. The paintwork was peeling and the stove rusting away, yet it was cosy in a decrepit sort of way.

'Yes,' she replied. 'I know it very well.'

'Who used to live here?' I inquired.

'I didn't know the last tenants, or the people before them. I knew the place before it was done up. It was a shambles then, with mice, and as damp as the grave.'

'Is that when you painted it?'

'Yes,' she replied.

'Who was the shadowy woman inside?' I asked with interest.

She looked away towards the sea. 'That was Peg,' she replied, after a silence. 'Your mother lived here for almost a year.'

I stared at her, dumbfounded. 'Here? Why?'

'After the family turfed her out, she had nowhere to go.'

'Because of Tom Murphy?'

'Yes . . .' Aunt G hesitated, then said, 'Healy and Nugent from Wicklow had already bought it by then, and were trying to rake up the money to do it up. They let her live here for next to nothing, but it was a miserable place. There was hardly a stick of furniture.'

'Why didn't she go to England straight away?' I asked.

'For a start, she didn't have the fare to cross the water. She was cut off without a penny.'

'How did she manage to rake it up in the end?'

'We sold some of my paintings without the family knowing. I knew some wealthy people from the city, through the Kildare Club. But for some reason "The Railway Cottage" never went. Too bleak, perhaps. I only painted it to keep her company.'

'God, poor Mother,' I said, thinking of her orderly ways, and how desperate she must have been to live here.

Aunt G leant against the windowsill with a distant look in her eyes, struggling with some painful memory of her own.

'The worst part was when she left,' she said. 'I remember seeing her off on the mail boat. It was as if only her body was getting on, and she was leaving her soul behind.'

'I thought she felt nothing for this country,' I said, 'from the way she became so English.'

'She started a new life in England – it was the only way for her to escape the memories,' said Aunt G.

'I wish I could go in,' I said then. I felt suddenly closer to Mother than I had ever been when she was alive. I circled the cottage, peering curiously through the windows. Around the back was a small shed, furnished with rotting shelves, thick with mould, and a few ancient rusty tools. I stumbled through the tangled bracken, the idea coming to me like a bolt from the blue.

Aunt G was still leaning against the windowsill, gazing out across the sea.

'Do you think it's still for rent?' I asked, excited now.

'Probably, but I doubt they'll find anybody to rent it to.'

'Aunt G, it's perfect,' I said.

'Oh, no, it's not! It's lonely and isolated and a good three-mile walk to the village.'

'It could be made cosy, with a few things.'

'That boy is used to central heating; he'd catch his death.'

'He'll adjust to the climate.'

'You'd need a car.'

'I'll catch the bus. I'll buy a second-hand car – an old banger. I've some money stashed away in England.'

'If you intend staying, why don't you live with me at Heronlough? I could do with the company.'

'Because one day the doorbell will ring, and it'll be Michel looking for Jean . . . I can't Aunt G.'

'You know that if he really wants to find you, he will.'

'Yes . . . But by then I'll be more prepared. I'm buying time, I realise that.' I stared at her wildly. 'But it's all I have left.'

She looked away. ' "Time spent in reconnaissance is time well spent" – but I doubt you'll last a week here.' She shook her head, impatient now, and said, 'We'd better be heading back, before we both catch double pneumonia.'

We walked slowly, picking our way along the broken railway tracks.

'I have to see if I can survive alone, Aunt G. If I can't, there's no hope for me. I should have stayed in Switzerland.'

'You won't sleep at night,' she said. 'You'll be scared out of your wits.'

'I'm already scared out of my wits,' I replied. 'I won't sleep wherever I am.'

The evening was closing in, the sky darkening as the sun went down behind the hills. And suddenly, all my resolve was sinking with it. It wasn't fair on Jean, she was right – living like some sort of criminal, hiding away from the rest of the world. The more I thought about it, the madder it seemed.

We rounded the gorse bushes and started across the fields towards Heronlough, and as we approached I heard the sound of car wheels scrunching against gravel.

I looked towards the drive and stiffened. There was a Gardai car pulling up in front of the house.

A policeman was getting out and walking towards the porch. Jean would be waking up, crying for me. I was caught between running towards the house to silence him, and running away.

Aunt G had spotted the Garda too. 'Why don't you wait here,' she said calmly, 'and I'll go and see what it's all about.'

I crouched down in the thicket, my heart hammering, and found a squashed packet of cigarettes in my pocket. The last Barclay. I lit it, cupping my hand against the wind, and inhaled deeply. They were standing in front of the house and Aunt G was smiling and shaking her head, as if trying to send him off our track. It seemed an eternity before he turned on his heel and strode back to the car.

I walked across the lawn, shivering now, and into the house. 'What was it all about?' I asked.

'A local boy was drowned off this coast last week,' she told me. 'It was all over the papers. The police were just doing a routine check to see if I'd heard anything. It was one of the Murphy clan,' she added with a frown. 'That family have had their fair share of tragedy, so they have.'

I followed her into the kitchen, longing for a stiff drink but resisting. I was going to need my wits about me from now on.

'I thought he'd come for Jean,' I said.

'There are more serious things going on out there than domestic quarrels,' she said crossly.

'I know, but as long as I'm afraid, it makes no difference! I'm going to try and rent the cottage,' I told her. 'I can't live like this.'

She looked at me sternly, settling herself in the rocking chair. Then she picked up her newspaper, as though the issue were closed.

'I'll have Seamus drive us into Wicklow on Monday,' she replied some moments later, 'but don't hold out too many hopes of moving in straight away. For all we know there mightn't be water or electricity. Nugent may even have decided to put it on the market again, who knows?'

She saw my worried face and said, 'Don't worry, child, if the worst comes to the worst, we'll furnish it ourselves. Lord knows I've more furniture here than I can use.'

'Thanks Aunt G,' I said, hugging her. 'What would I do without you?'

'You'd manage,' she replied briskly. 'Now stop worrying – we'll sort something out in the morning.'

For her, there would always be a solution in the morning – when the darkness had faded, and the dawn had broken, heralding a new day.

But morning was only a matter of hours away, I thought fearfully, and by then another twenty-four hours would have gone by. In that darkest hour before dawn, I was still wide awake, praying that Michel wouldn't find us in the meantime.

PART THREE

Chapter Twenty-Nine

Ireland, the winter of 1985

I am writing this by the fire in the Railway Cottage. 'All's quiet on the Western Front,' as Father used to say, although there have been a couple of incidents.

I moved in three days after the Garda came to Heronlough looking for information about Eamonn Murphy's death. Seamus drove us into Wicklow to Healy and Nugent estate agents, and Aunt G introduced me to Aidan Nugent, a dapper little man who oozed charm and told me exactly what I wanted to hear. Sure the cottage was for rent, he said. (He would have sold it to me, given half the chance.) There was electricity, and plenty of hot water – it was just a matter of connecting a few wires. The heating worked, although we might have to bleed the radiators, and the kitchen was stocked, give or take the odd item. He wanted a deposit, which Aunt G dismissed, saying he was to take care of those details first, and promises and assurances were made that all would be dealt with in the morning. But I have since learnt that in this part of the world, where time is allowed to drift away unaccounted for, tomorrow can take for ever.

The weather has turned wet and foggy over the last few days. Veils of misty rain sweep along the coast, making the cottage very cold and damp inside. The roof has sprung a leak, and the walls are soaking to the touch. I've been burning turf, as it's less expensive than wood, in an effort to keep the main room warm, but sometimes – sitting by the fire with Jean in the early evenings, the heat warming my face and a cold draught at my back – I feel as if I'm fighting a losing battle. Aidan Nugent promised to send somebody over to clean the chimney, which is clogged with birds' nests, but we're still waiting. It is one of the few things that makes me long for the quiet efficiency I took for granted in Switzerland.

The cottage is cosier now, however, than when I first moved in, although there is still that pervading brackish smell of damp which no amount of airing seems to dispel. Aunt G gave me some

*furniture from Heronlough that she no longer has any use for – a
couple of armchairs that need re-upholstering, a coffee table, some
hand-made rugs woven by locals on the Aran Islands to cover the
stone floors, an old wireless to keep me company in the evenings,
and extra blankets for the cold nights. I have moved Jean's bed into
the main room close to the fireplace, since he seems to have a
permanently runny nose and chesty cough. I only hope he'll
eventually adjust to this dramatic change in lifestyle.*

*Aunt G was right, of course. I'm scared out of my wits. There are
times when I'd give anything to turn the clock back, and have
Michel lying beside me as though nothing had changed. In those
moments, I feel a deep regret for having stolen away like a criminal
from the failure of our marriage. At other times I feel anger and
resentment against Michel, for not being able to let go of Marguerite
and the past, and for those threats he made. But most of the time, I
feel incapacitated – as if I've hacked off both my legs and can't move
about freely any more.*

The day we moved in, Jacintha and I cleaned and swept the rooms
while Aunt G kept an eye on Jean. Then Jacintha took him for a
walk on the beach, and I made a pot of tea, and we sat down at the
rickety kitchen table to drink it. That was when Aunt G fixed me
with her steely blue gaze and said, 'It's time you and I had a little
chat.'

'What about?' I asked warily.

'You must write a letter to that husband of yours, Emily,' she
said firmly, causing me to tense all over.

I stared at her. 'I can't possibly. It would put him straight on our
track.'

'I'm not suggesting you tell him where you are,' she cut in, 'but I
do think he has a right to know that you're both still in the land of
the living!'

'I don't know,' I said uneasily.

'Look at it this way – if you were in his shoes and he upped and
left with the child, how would you feel? What would you do?'

I shrugged. 'Send out a search party, I suppose?'

'Exactly. But if you received a letter saying they were both safe
and well, and needed some time to think things through, for
instance? I think it might well buy you the time you need.'

'How would we do it?' I asked.

'That's the easy part – we could give the letter to May O'Connor. She owns a boutique in Wicklow and flies to London regularly on buying trips. She could post it from there.'

It took me a whole morning to write the letter. The words poured into my head – all the things I had been unable to say. I told him how lonely I'd been after Jeanette had died, and how I felt he hadn't been there. How I had been forced to live a lifestyle he had chosen, in a country which had seemed alien, among people who were worlds apart from me, forever in the shadow of Marguerite. If anybody had failed, I concluded, it had been him for not being able to understand any of this. I re-read the letter and tore it to shreds, picked up my pen again, and wrote instead:

Dear Michel, I just wanted you to know that Jean and I are safe and well and that there is no need to worry. Please don't attempt to find us, as I need time to think things through.
Yours, Emily.

Aunt G gave it to May O'Connor the following day, who promised to post it from London. Now I'm begining to worry that Michel has somehow seen through the subterfuge, and is already on our track.

They found Eamonn Murphy's body swept up on the beach between the Railway Cottage and Heronlough House.

Aunt G said, 'That family have been marked by the devil, so they have.'

Her feelings towards the Murphys veer from sympathy to the solid conviction that they've always had it coming to them. Afterwards the police roamed the coast, knocking on doors to try and establish if anybody saw anything that night, which made me realise that you can't live an anonymous life like I'd imagined, nor erase the tracks behind you. Deep down, I knew Aunt G was right. If Michel wanted to find us, he would.

Then there was the incident in the middle of the night. I was half asleep, with one ear listening out for any strange noises. The cottage, such a haven during the day because of its remoteness, became frightening at night for the same reasons. Exposed to all the elements, accessible from land and sea, every noise seemed like a threat. Sometimes the wind sounded like a wild animal howling outside the window.

But that particular night there was no wind, for once. Nothing stirred, and through the almost unnatural silence I heard something moving above. It sounded as if somebody were scrabbling across the tiles, attempting to get into the cottage from the roof.

I sat bolt upright in bed, my chest tight with fear, my heart hammering. Through my fear, I registered the multiple thumps of more than one person moving, followed by the sliding sound of a dislodged tile falling to the ground. I leapt out of bed, afraid to turn on the light, and tiptoed swiftly into the living room, where Jean was fast asleep, curled up in a tight ball. I stood beside him, afraid he'd wake up and alert the intruders, then went into the kitchen, picked up a sharp knife, and crept determinedly towards the door. I pulled up the catch, flung the door open so it swung on its hinges, and looked wildly around.

It was a cold, clear night. The moon cast a bright passage across the sea; nothing stirred. I looked along the railway track towards a clump of bushes, and thought I saw the distorted shadow of somebody crouched there.

'Who's there?' I called, my voice wavering from fear. In reply there was a sudden screech that chilled me to the bone, and a frantic whirring sound as three white gulls took off from the roof across the moonlit sea.

'Christ!' I muttered, feeling foolish now, and backed into the cottage, my heart still racing. Of course, Aunt G had warned me about the seagulls.

Shivering, I went back to bed and tossed and turned for hours. I finally dozed off at dawn, and had one of those vivid morning dreams in which everything shrank to minuscule proportions, including Jean, who became the size of a tadpole. I searched the tiny cottage for him, shaking out the sheets and looking through the dust under the bed, then in the most unlikely places – the bath and sink, fearing he had been swept down the plughole, or been swallowed up by the lavatory cistern. I went outside and searched through the brambles, then looked up and saw him – a tiny bundle wrapped in a white sheet, held in the beak of a giant bird that soared away from me. I woke up frantically calling his name.

Later that morning, we crossed the railway track and followed the muddy path down to the beach, where I sat on a rock, watching Jean throw pebbles into the sea. It was mild and misty, and I felt too warm in the windcheater Aunt G had lent me. I moved further down the beach to the water's edge, that horrible dream still with me, and saw the ferry setting off for Holyhead. My thoughts returned to Mother and the lonely days and nights she must have spent in the cottage before leaving for England. I thought of Aunt G saying, 'It was as if she was leaving her soul behind . . .'

Jean interrupted my drifting thoughts. He had found something on the beach, a whitish object, which he waved at me before running over and throwing it in my lap. It was an empty Barclay cigarette packet.

I stared at it, puzzled. I hadn't smoked a Barclay for a while; the last time had been the day the Garda had come to Heronlough. I thought I had thrown the empty packet away then, but this one was fresh, and a good three miles away from where I had crouched behind the gorse bushes. I was filled with a sudden unease. Now I was sure I'd heard another noise in the night, one that could not be attributed to the seagulls. Somebody on our trail? My letter would have arrived weeks ago. Had Michel seen through the phoney postmark and sent somebody to search the Irish coast for us?

Aunt G dismissed it immediately. 'You must have had another packet all along,' she said. But still the fear lingered like a sea mist, obscuring the way ahead.

I was changing Jean out of his wet clothes after one of our walks along the beach when a sudden unbidden memory of Bertrand 'the robot', with his flashing camera, came to mind. I often thought back to that first skiing season in Mégève, imprinted on my memory like a dark stain, although the days were clear and sunny. Bertrand smoked Barclay cigarettes. Yet the idea of him snooping around here, squelching through the mud in his Bally shoes, was simply too bizarre to contemplate.

The thought that somebody might have been spying on us, however, forced me out of the cottage each day, along the muddy lane to the village, Jean trotting behind me.

The buses were unpredictable in these parts. Sometimes one didn't come at all, in which case I strapped Jean into his pushchair and walked the two and a half miles to the village. I intended

243

buying a second-hand car, which would make life a lot easier, although Aunt G insisted I could borrow the Daimler. Seamus drove her into Wicklow twice a week to buy groceries, and she urged me to accompany her. The alternative was to shop at Murphy's Food Store in the village, which I knew she disapproved of, but for the time being I felt I had no choice.

Two girls worked behind the tills at Murphy's Food Store. One of them was beautiful, with a mane of black curly hair and dark blue eyes, but one of her front teeth was missing, and she never smiled because of it. Her name was Geraldine, like Aunt G, but her friend called her Ger; I wondered if she had sprung from the 'rough diamond'. The other girl looked completely anaemic beside her, with her dull brown hair and matching eyes, and skin so freckled it looked as if she had contracted some rare disease. She must have been hired from the village, since she didn't fit the Murphy mould – although according to Aunt G, Tom had bred far and wide.

I still hadn't set eyes on Tom Murphy. On one of those forays into the village, I paused outside Murphy's Lounge Bar and looked inside. It took a few moments for my eyes to adjust to the darkness within; then I saw through the gloom a long L-shaped bar lined with stools, and low tables covered in battered beer mats. A few solitary drinkers sat around the room, and in one corner a television flickered, but there was a dullness about the place, an air of hopelessness about the people who drank there at such an early hour.

Everything appeared functional, geared towards the business of drinking, the television the main focus of the room. I noticed the dark shape of a piano mounted on a platform in the corner, but it too had the dusty air of abandon, as if it stood there only as a reminder of happier times.

Behind the bar a black-haired man pulled pints of Guinness. The lights from above shone down on his tousled hair, but his face was in shadow, until he moved out from behind the bar and stared across the room, straight at me.

I stared back. He was beautiful, there was no other way to describe him, his features chiselled as if from marble. It took me only a moment to recognise the boy who had come trespassing on the lough all those years ago. The intervening years hadn't changed him much. I felt my heart constrict and quickly withdrew, aware of an odd foreboding, as if I were slowly being drawn into the same dark trap that Mother had spoken of.

But as I walked away the feeling was replaced by an almost overwhelming curiosity, a sudden longing for a glimpse of the man who had had such an enormous effect on Mother's life.

Chapter Thirty

It continued to rain over the week leading up to Christmas, a steady drizzle that seeped into the cottage until even our clothes felt damp, and we steamed in front of the fire. Condensation streamed down the windows, and puddles of rainwater from the leaking roof collected on the floor. The rugs became caked with mud from our sorties to the beach, so I rolled them up and put them away. If it didn't stop raining soon, the cottage would become waterlogged and float away like Noah's ark.

Aunt G insisted that we spend Christmas at Heronlough, and sent Seamus over the day before to drive us to the house. Normally I would have walked the short distance, but the heavy rain had turned the roads to rivers, and the swollen lough flooded the surrounding fields. The Daimler almost got stuck in the mud-clogged lane down to the main road.

Arriving at Heronlough was like coming home. The fire was lit, a Christmas tree sparkled in the hallway, and the house smelt of spiced fruit and woodsmoke. The first thing I did was run a hot bath and lie in it for ages, for although there was plenty of water at the cottage it was peat brown, and there is something slightly offputting about bathing in water that looks dirtier than you are. I thought of Michel then, and wondered if he was spending Christmas in Mégève, under a burnished blue sky above the clouds, with Gregoire and his minions, and Marguerite back in the fold.

I had bought a few small things for Jean's Christmas stocking, a glossy book about art for Aunt G, and some talcum powder and soap for Jacintha. As soon as I'd wrapped them up and put Jean to bed, I went and sat in the kitchen and helped Jacintha stuff the turkey. Aunt G was sitting in her rocking chair, in front of the Aga. She appeared to be reading, but from time to time I caught her glancing at me over her newspaper.

'You look pale, child,' she said, putting it down.

'I've had a couple of bad nights, that's all.' (I'd already told her about the seagulls landing on the roof.)

246

'I still think it's the daftest idea,' she said. 'I wish you'd come and live here, where I can keep an eye on you.'

'I have to give it a couple of months, Aunt G – if I have that much time,' I trailed off.

'You have time,' she said reassuringly.

Sometimes it seemed Aunt G had the ability to see what lay around the next corner. For her the future was like a summer's dawn, bright with promise.

When I didn't answer, she said, 'He would have come by now.'

'I suppose,' I said, wondering if Michel had decided to wait until the new year, when all the festivities would have died down, and the system be working properly . . . Or maybe he had changed his mind, and never wanted to see either of us again.

I heard Jacintha mutter behind us. ' 'Tisn't natural, so it isn't. The boy needs his father . . . and that's as much as I'll say about it.'

Aunt G and I exchanged glances. I often felt uncomfortable in Jacintha's presence. There was something vaguely disapproving in her attitude towards me. In her book married people stayed together for better or for worse. Her own husband had died five years ago from the drink, according to Aunt G, but Jacintha stuck by him until the bitter end. She seemed fond of the 'odd jar', as they say, herself; one of her close friends owned O'Brien's, the pub outside Rathegan, and Jacintha disappeared on a Saturday evening, returning on Monday somewhat the worse for wear. It was through her that Aunt G learned all the village gossip and snippets about the Murphys, since Jacintha knew the family and was friendly with Tom's wife Moira. I heard her mutter something else, and changed the subject.

But on Christmas Day, I began to wonder if she was right. It began badly, with Jean waking up and crying out for me. I sat up and saw he had fallen out of bed and was lying on the floor, the contents of his Christmas stocking all around him. When I tried to pick him up, he screamed louder and flung one of his new toys at me, a fluffy clockwork rabbit that waggled its ears and tail.

Aunt G came bustling into the room with a cup of tea to wish me a happy Christmas. 'What sort of a way is this to greet the birth of the Lord?' she inquired with a frown.

'I don't know what's got into him,' I said. 'He won't let me touch him. It's very odd – he normally loves opening presents.'

'All this has been a big upheaval for him,' she answered soothingly. 'Give him time to adjust.'

I wondered if he was angry at me for having taken him away from his father.

'He must miss Michel,' I said.

'Of course he does.' Aunt G never beat around the bush.

'Sometimes, I find the responsibility of what I've done overwhelming. If anything should happen to him . . .'

She looked at me with one of her wise expressions. 'Having a child is having a hostage to fortune,' she said. 'You can't live your life worrying about what might or mightn't happen.'

'You're right,' I replied, thinking that we were all hostages to fortune, at the end of the day.

Aunt G had invited some of her rather ancient tweedy friends over for drinks before lunch, and we all sat sipping sherry in the drawing room in front of a smoking wood fire, everybody talking at once. The most ancient of them all, a frail and bent old woman with only one eye who had known Mother, quizzed me for ages, wanting to know why I wasn't spending Christmas with my husband. We were separated, I told her – trying to come to terms with this as I spoke, for eventually we would be divorced, and custody set one way or the other. The thought hit me with a jolt, causing me to look away, but the old woman must have sensed my distress. She seemed to look right inside me to where the turmoil lay, like a cyclops, all expression directed like a beam from that one cold eye.

'Don't let the sun go down on your wrath,' she said, grasping my hand in her bony fingers. 'Work it out, child, before it's too late.'

She must have heard about it from Aunt G, who still believed that the marriage could be salvaged, although I kept telling her it was over. Soon the time would come to make it official – 'sort out the wheat from husk', as Michel would say. No doubt he would make the first move, guided by some rigid principle of his own. A principle that would lead him to fight tooth and nail for Jean, the child he never really wanted. Although the latter part was no longer valid, I reminded myself. He loved Jean as much as I did, and felt perhaps rightly, that he was better equipped to look after him. He was always a very contradictory person, a conformist who broke the rules – steadfast and morally sound, but like Fabian Feroux; once challenged, playing the same dirty game.

248

The sun had already gone down on our wrath, I concluded, as the old lady clasped my hand in hers, eclipsing those bright days once and for all . . .

It was a relief when, with sudden unspoken accord, the guests finally got up and gathered raincoats, galoshes, umbrellas, and hats, and took themselves off down the rainswept drive to the next gathering. Seamus then left in the Daimler to collect the elderly cousins, Lilly and Louise Flavell, and we sat down at one o'clock to eat, a motley group all talking at cross purposes. Everybody except myself became quite light-headed from the wine, and Louise, who had been so unpleasant all those Christmases ago, suddenly got it into her head that I was Mother.

'Come back to put the world to rights, then, have you Peg? Well he's a changed man, pickled from the drink so he is.'

'Emily is Peg's daughter,' Aunt G kept trying to tell her.

'You should have followed your head not your heart,' continued the old woman spitefully.

Aunt G shot me a sympathetic glance, intimating that Louise was no longer *compos mentis*. The woman suddenly digressed, in the way of the very old, and started talking about Sheelagh de Courcy Evans, who had done an even more unspeakable thing (although she had every intention of speaking about it), and she forgot about me after that.

When they had left, I put Jean to bed and sat down by the fire with Aunt G.

'Louise is quite dotty, you realise that?' she said, imagining the gloom that had descended on me was something to do with the old woman.

'Yes,' I replied. 'Poor Mother, no wonder she left like that!'

'Things were very different in those days,' Aunt G told me. 'The family were much more of a unit, always poking their noses into each other's business. It's too late for those two to change now, of course.'

'I'm surprised they didn't turn against you for supporting Mother,' I said.

'Oh, they did,' replied Aunt G wearily. Her eyelids were drooping; I could tell she was about to fall asleep. She looked so old suddenly, and I realised with a stab of alarm that she wouldn't always be here for me. 'But they got over it – water under the bridge now.'

I sat there for a while longer, watching the flames die down, and listening to the rain beating against the windows, wishing I could fall asleep too.

At around four o'clock, I left Aunt G dozing and, taking an old Barbour from the hall, walked down the long drive towards the village.

It had stopped raining at last, but the clouds hung grey over the hills and raindrops fell from the trees. I hoped a walk would ease the aching depression that had descended on me.

The village was deserted. The houses were lit up with Christmas lights, wreaths of holly hung on the doors, but everything was closed and unnaturally quiet – not a car passed by as I walked. The people must have been inside – 'jollificating', as Jimmy would say.

I reached the main street, passed the Food Store noticing the petrol pumps were covered, then crossed the road towards Murphy's Lounge Bar. The pub was closed but lights blazed from the windows. I wondered if it was a family gathering, and drew closer. Then I heard a solitary voice rising from the general chatter within, accompanied by the hollow chords of a piano. It was a strong baritone, hitting the high notes of a haunting love song. I stood in the yellow glow from the window, listening.

> And fare the well, my own true love,
> And fare thee well a while,
> And I will come again my love,
> Though it were ten thousand mile . . .

It was Tom Murphy, I knew it instinctively. My eyes filled with tears. The song had struck a lonely chord inside, like the nostalgic wail of a violin, gripping me with an aching sadness.

I turned away then, wiping my eyes, not sure whether it was for Mother I wept, or for myself.

Chapter Thirty-One

It was hard to return to the Railway Cottage after the warmth and companionship of Heronlough. But the time had come to plan the future and stop dwelling on the past. I transferred money from my savings account in England and opened a bank account here; I also spoke to Aunt G's solicitor, who said my situation was somewhat precarious. The only way I could gain legal custody of Jean was through the Swiss courts, and that would mean returning to Switzerland and filing for a divorce. By leaving as I had, I would have strengthened Michel's case, he warned. It was an added irony that I had landed in the one country that does not recognise divorce.

The days started to follow a pattern. It was still mild for winter, with dry mornings and damp afternoons. We spent a lot of time on the beach. Jean never seemed to tire of running along the water's edge, shrieking at the waves, while I sat and watched the ferry setting off for England.

Jean didn't mention Michel again after Christmas Day. He seemed to be gradually adapting to his new life. He slept in the afternoons, giving me some time to myself. In those quiet hours, I sat by the window, until the daylight faded and my hand grew stiff from writing. Putting it all down on paper was like unburdening myself of a heavy load. For a while, there was a sense of release.

Things couldn't continue like this indefinitely, however. Sooner or later I was going to have to get a job, try and carve out some sort of life for us here. Jacintha offered to 'mind' Jean for me whenever I wanted, but she was already busy up at the big house, tending to Aunt G's needs – besides, they'd both done so much already.

I started by looking for a second-hand car. I was walking through the village, with Jean in the pushchair, when I saw a notice in the window of Murphy's Food Store for Cahill and Ryan Car Dealers. I jotted down the phone number, and went into the pub to use the phone.

I glanced along the bar, wondering if I might catch a glimpse of the 'rough diamond' propped up there, but it was empty; nor did there seem to be anybody serving behind it. Then, as I looked around for a phone, I saw the man with the chiselled face come out of a side door and stopped in my tracks, as I had all those years ago when he had come trespassing on the lough. He watched me curiously, almost challenging me to approach.

I moved forwards. 'I need some change for the phone, please,' I said briskly, 'and a packet of cigarettes.'

'Which brand?' he inquired, still staring at me.

'Major,' I replied, picking a local brand. He handed me a pack, then opened the till and counted out the change.

'The phone's on the left – out that door,' he told me. 'Give it a kick if the money sticks, or give me a shout.'

'Thanks,' I replied, suddenly all of a dither.

He was still staring, as if trying to place me. 'I seen you before,' he said disconcertingly. The years hadn't improved his grammar much, it seemed.

'Probably in the village,' I replied, 'shopping or something.'

''Twas a while back,' he frowned. I wondered then if he too remembered that meeting on the lough. 'I never forget a good-looking woman,' he added with a grin.

I found myself smiling back. He was heart-stoppingly handsome, I thought, in an unruly way. His voice was deep and heavily accented – all traces of girlishness disappeared when he spoke. I wondered if Tom Murphy had been equally handsome.

'It's a small village . . .'

'Damien Murphy,' he said, still grinning at me.

'Emily, er – Emily Gautier,' I added, after some hesitation.

'What sort of a name is that?' he inquired.

'My husband is Swiss,' I told him, thinking he was not backward at coming forward.

'Ah.' He looked at me closely before glancing across at the pushchair, to where Jean had fallen asleep.

'We're separated,' I added, wondering why I felt the need to explain.

'Where are you from then?'

'England originally, although I have some family here. But I've been living in Switzerland for the last three years.'

'Switzerland,' he repeated, as if it were the back end of

beyond. 'Banks and cuckoo clocks.'

I laughed. 'And a whole lot more.'

'How about a jar?' he suggested, gesturing towards the bar.

'Oh, no thanks,' I said hurriedly. 'I just need to use the phone.'

I moved to go, but as I did so another man appeared beside him and said, 'Starting early this morning Damien, chatting up the women?'

Damien didn't look in the least put out. He grinned and said, 'This is my brother Sean – he's just jealous. Emily's from Switzerland,' he added briefly.

Sean was taller and bulkier, his features less defined, but he had the same mop of wild curly hair. 'Are you here on your holidays?' he asked, as I tried to back away.

'No – I'm staying for a while.'

They were both watching me with interest, causing me to step back in confusion and almost trip over the pushchair.

'Come down and have a drink one of these nights,' said Damien. 'Tomorrow's a good night,' he added. 'There's a session on.'

'I might do that.' I glanced across the room towards the piano. 'I thought I heard somebody singing on Christmas Day?'

'That was the boss man,' Sean said grimly. 'Our ould man! He used to sing every night – now he's jarred out of his mind most of the time, so it's only once in a while.'

'What a waste . . . of talent, I mean,' I said cautiously.

'The only talent he has nowadays is for talking crap,' Sean mumbled.

There was an awkward silence. What had persuaded him to sing that lonely love song on Christmas Day, I wondered?

'Well, I must be off,' I said, heading blindly towards where I imagined the phone to be.

'It's the other side,' Damien called after me. 'That's the Jacks!'

Two doors faced me, with the signs *Fir* and *Mna* – Men and Ladies, although I still wasn't sure which was which. Blushing, I crossed the room, aware he was still watching me with amusement.

I telephoned the number of Cahill and Ryan and was told they were a couple of miles out of the village on the Wexford Road, and to come over any time and ask for Christie or Kevin.

The next day I borrowed the Daimler, and set off with Jean for the garage. The sky was pale and clear, everything green and lush after the rain.

I saw the sign 'Cahill and Ryan' on the left, slowed down, and turned into the forecourt. I lifted Jean out of the car and went towards a ramshackle office. Pushing open the door, I saw a dark-haired man sitting behind the desk, writing something in a ledger.

'Well hello there,' he greeted me. 'What can I do for you?'

His voice was pleasantly soft, his accent a mixture of Irish and American.

'I spoke to somebody earlier about a second-hand car, and was told to ask for Christie or Kevin.'

'I am neither, but look no further, because I'm your man,' he said.

He grinned loftily and I noticed his eyes were almost navy blue, etched with deep lines.

'I need something reliable,' I told him, 'that's not too heavy on petrol – just for getting to Wicklow and back.'

I was about to tell him how much I wanted to spend, when he said, 'I have the very thing. Follow me.'

He patted Jean on the head, saying, 'Hello there, young fellow, what's your name?' as he led us out of the office.

'Jean, or John,' I answered. I often anglicised his name these days.

'French name?'

'Yes – in fact he's half Swiss, half Irish,' I told him. I also claimed my Irish nationality, having discovered I could hardly go anywhere without divulging who I was or where I'd come from. People were naturally curious in this part of the world.

'Used to speak a bit of French myself,' he told me. 'Travelled through France when I was a young lad, although that's going back a while.'

I guessed he was in his late thirties, and somewhat weathered by the years.

I followed him around the back, to where a number of cars in various stages of rusty decay were parked. It looked more like a scrapyard than a car showroom, I thought, my heart sinking.

'She's had a few owners,' he was saying, 'but she's in grand shape. Worn better than most of us, I'd say!'

He stopped short and pointed to the left, causing me to bump into him. I smelt the oiled-wool smell of his thick jumper, mixed with tobacco, and stepped back in confusion. But he didn't seem to notice my clumsiness.

'There you go,' he was saying, pointing to a bright turquoise Fiat. 'You can take her for a spin if you like.'

I went closer and glanced inside. It looked as if it had been resprayed several times, for it didn't have a natural sheen, but there was no sign of any rust or damage. In fact it appeared almost new, compared to some of the wrecks around it.

'I'll move the van out of your way and you can give her a test drive,' he said.

'Thanks. I'd like to try it out.'

He handed me the keys, saying, 'I'll go with you, if you like – keep an eye on the young fellow.' Before I could answer, he'd scooped Jean up and was walking towards the car.

We might have been old acquaintances, I thought, watching him settle himself in the back with Jean.

I climbed into the driver's seat, switched on the ignition, and drove across the forecourt towards the main road.

'So what brings you and your mother to these parts?' I heard him ask Jean.

'I've come here to write a novel,' I answered on the spur of the moment.

'What about?' he asked.

'I suppose it's a kind of child-tug-of-war story,' I replied diffidently.

'Ah ha . . . and who wins in the end?'

'The ending is still not clear,' I told him, after a pause. 'What about you? You don't sound as if you're from these parts.'

'I come and go,' he told me. 'Like a lot of Irish folk, I took off for the States at the first God-given opportunity.'

'I thought so from your accent,' I said, shifting the Fiat into fourth as we gathered speed, so it sounded less like a racing car in distress.

'And what brought you back?'

'I ran out of luck,' he told me.

255

'A girl?' I asked, since the conversation had taken such an informal turn.

'That and my job, so I decided to pack it in . . . Turn right here,' he instructed, 'to get back to the garage.'

'What were you doing over there?' I asked, turning the windscreen wipers on instead of the indicator.

'Anything and everything! I worked on a building site for a while, washed dishes, whatever I could get, really . . . Smoke?' he inquired, pulling out a crumpled packet of Carrolls and handing me one.

'Thanks.' I took it from him. 'And now you're a car salesman?'

'For the moment.'

'Well you've just made a sale,' I said, pulling into the garage again.

'I'm pleased you like it. Engine's built like a tank. She won't let you down, Mrs er . . . ?'

'Just Emily,' I said.

He grinned. 'And I'm just TJ. If you'd like to accompany me into the office, Just Emily, I'll sort out the details.'

He climbed out of the car, trying to lift Jean at the same time, but Jean started shrieking indignantly and wouldn't budge. Instead he pushed his way between the seats, in an effort to get behind the wheel.

'Come on,' I said irritably. 'We've got to buy it first.'

But he had positioned himself behind the steering wheel, and was turning it in both directions.

'Drive car,' he said determinedly.

I took the key out of the ignition, and said, 'OK, have it your way! You can stay here, but you won't get very far. He'll be all right for a moment,' I told TJ.

'It won't take a minute,' he assured me, as we made our way towards the office.

He sat down behind the desk, lit another cigarette and flicked through a pile of papers, searching for the car registration and driver's manual. He seemed to work in a state of total chaos; I was amazed when he produced the relevant documents.

'I suggest you let us get her cleaned up a bit, oil changed and all that, and I could bring her over in the morning,' he said after I had written out a cheque.

'That would be fine,' I replied, then tried to explain how to get to the Railway Cottage.

'I think I know where you are,' he said, after listening to my vague directions. 'I used to play on the strand down there, when I was a young fellow – where the old chicken farm used to be.'

'That's it,' I said.

'I've flown over it a few times – I'm a hang-gliding fanatic,' he explained.

Michel had loved hang-gliding, but seldom found the conditions right.

'I could bring her over about lunch time tomorrow?'

'That would be great,' I said, wondering if he really meant tomorrow.

He handed me the documents, and I was about to ask him for a business card when I heard a horn blaring outside. I turned to look out of the window to where Jean was still sitting in the Fiat, and did a double take. He was stretched across the steering wheel, his body against the horn, and as I watched it seemed for one hallucinatory moment that the Fiat was moving.

Then, with a jolt of fear, I saw that it wasn't a trick of the eye at all. The small car was rolling forward towards the main road, into the path of the oncoming traffic.

'My God!' I shouted. 'Jean! The car's rolling away!'

'Holy shit!' exclaimed TJ, and leapt up from his seat.

We both ran out of the office across the forecourt. The car was gathering momentum now, heading down the incline towards the busy road, where cars sped along like bullets.

TJ flew past me. He was running like the wind, his long legs flying across the forecourt. He reached the car within seconds and flung himself against it, as if he had the power to stop it, then somehow managed to get the door open and grabbed the wheel.

I watched with relief as he steered the car into the side of road. 'The keys,' he shouted, and I realised I was still clutching them. I threw them to him, and he reversed the car up the slope, back into the forecourt. He climbed out and handed a stunned Jean to me, and we stared at one another speechlessly.

I hugged Jean's small body to me, my heart still pounding, then I noticed TJ's head. A trickle of blood ran down his cheek from a cut high on his temple.

'You're hurt,' I said in alarm.

He pulled out an oily handkerchief that looked like an old rag, and wiped at his head.

'It's nothing, just a scratch.' But I saw it was a wide gash, rapidly filling with blood.

'There are some bandages inside,' he said, turning stiffly towards the office.

I followed with Jean, feeling as if my legs were about to buckle under me.

TJ fumbled around under the desk for a moment, but instead of producing a first aid box, found a bottle of Paddy's Whiskey, took two chipped mugs from a shelf behind him, and poured a hefty measure into each of them.

'Best first aid I can think of,' he said.

I took the mug and gulped back the whiskey, saying, 'We must do something about that cut.'

He lit two cigarettes and handed one to me, all barriers between us broken down by the narrow escape, and said, 'You haven't a mirror in that bag of yours, by any chance? I'll take a look.'

I handed him my pocket mirror, and he glanced at the wound then held the handkerchief against it to try and staunch the flow. I spotted the first aid box on a shelf above and climbed onto a chair to reach it. Inside were surgical spirit, cotton wool, bandages and scissors.

I took out the spirit and the bandages, and cut off a long piece.

'That stuff'll sting the hell out of it,' he complained.

'We'll have to clean it somehow, that handkerchief of yours is filthy.'

'It's clean dirt,' he argued, wincing as I placed the spirit-soaked lint against the gash.

As soon as I had the bandage in place I sat down again, one eye on Jean, who was now playing with a rusty nail he had found on the floor.

I took it from him, and said to TJ, 'I'm so sorry, it was my fault entirely. I must have left the handbrake off.'

'I'll take a look at that handbrake,' he said. 'Might need tightening.'

I looked away, overcome by his generosity. It hadn't occurred to him that it was all my fault; instead, he had blamed the handbrake. Relief and inadequacy caused my throat to thicken. What sort of a mother was I, rushing off into the unknown, imagining I could cope alone? It was all too much all of a sudden. I leant forwards, put my head in my hands, and burst into tears.

I didn't see him get up, just felt the coldness of his hand on the back of my neck. It was rough and heavy, and sent a shiver up my spine. I tried to sit up, but felt his other hand rub my shoulder gently. There was something unreal about the whole thing – for a moment, I lost all sense of time and place.

I sat up, and saw he was watching me. Close to, his eyes were a deep indigo, the same shade as Jean's.

It was Jean who broke the spell, by crying out suddenly, causing us to move apart.

'I'd better be going,' I said with a dry mouth.

'I'll walk you to the car.'

He held open the door of the Daimler, and waited while I strapped Jean in beside me. 'No more driving jaunts for you, young fellow,' he said as he closed the door.

'Your head?' I inquired, before driving away.

He grinned. 'I've felt worse with a hangover.'

'Yes, but this time you didn't even have the pleasure of getting drunk!'

'No, but I had the pleasure of meeting you,' he replied. 'Here's my card, by the way. I'll be over around noon tomorrow, if that's all right?'

'That would be fine. And thanks again.'

'Don't mention it,' he replied with a wave.

I drove back to Heronlough to return the Daimler, my mind still on that narrow escape. Aunt G had gone to have tea with one of her bridge-playing friends, and Jacintha was in the kitchen making pastry.

'Will you be staying for tea?' she inquired, wiping her floury hands on her apron. (By tea she meant supper.) There was a slightly wild look about her. Her hair fell across her forehead, and she leant against the table for support. I noticed an open bottle of brandy beside her.

'Mince pies,' she said, pointing vaguely at a bowl full of raisins and chopped fruit. I wondered how much brandy had gone into the mixture and how much into her.

I hesitated. 'I think I'd better get back and put Jean to bed,' I said finally. 'We've had a rather fraught day.'

She scattered flour on the table with abandon, so it rose in a dusty cloud around her.

'What have ye been up to then?' she asked suspiciously.

'I bought a car,' I told her, then briefly explained what had happened, ashamed once again of my carelessness. 'If it hadn't been for that guy . . .' I fumbled in my bag for the card he had given me.

'So you'll be staying for a while, then?' she said tightly.

'Yes.' I sensed she was about to make one of her disparaging remarks, and tried to change the subject.

'Worrying your aunt like that – 'tisn't right, so it isn't.'

'I know, Jacintha. I've no intention of being a burden. That's one of the reasons I bought a car – so I could be more independent.'

She pursed her lips, reminding me of Mother suddenly.

I glanced at the card as I spoke, and read *Thomas John Murphy, Salesman, Cahill and Ryan Motors*.

''Tisn't natural, so it isn't . . .' Jacintha was saying as I stared at the card.

So he was a Murphy too. Probably from another branch, for although he had the typical dark Murphy looks, he had seemed a different breed from Damien and Sean – more refined somehow. The name was common enough in these parts, after all. But all the same, I quickly put the card back into my bag, without mentioning it to Jacintha. Then I made my excuses and left her, still muttering crossly to herself.

When I related the story to Aunt G the following day, I left out that small detail once again, knowing she wouldn't like the fact that I had bought a car from a Murphy, however distant the connection.

Chapter Thirty-Two

He arrived at the cottage with the Fiat at around one o'clock the following day, when Jean was asleep. I heard the sound of the car and, glancing through the kitchen window, saw the dark shape of TJ at the wheel. He was wearing faded, oily jeans and a denim jacket over the same rough wool jumper he had worn the day before. A cigarette was planted in the corner of his mouth.

'Where's the young fellow?' were his first words.

'He's asleep,' I answered. 'How's your head?' I noticed he hadn't removed the bandage, though it had partly come away, exposing the raw purplish graze beneath.

'Sure, it was only a graze.'

'Why don't you come in for a moment, and I'll put another dressing on it,' I said, surprising myself. I had never been the fussing motherly type.

'OK,' he said, and followed me through the back door into the cottage.

I went into the bathroom, found some plasters, then returned to find him over by the window, gazing across the sea.

'Here,' I said, pulling off the old one. 'A clean dressing.'

'You're taking good care of me,' he said with a slow smile.

'If it wasn't for me, it wouldn't have happened,' I pointed out.

He shrugged, dismissing it. 'Don't know how you managed without wheels,' he said. 'Must have been a headache?'

'My aunt lent me the Daimler a lot of the time,' I told him, 'but it wasn't ideal.'

'Young Fernando here will make life a lot easier,' he said, gesturing outside to where the Fiat was parked.

I laughed. 'Fernando the Fiat – it's a good name. Would you like a drink of something, by the way? Tea? Coffee?'

'Haven't you anything stronger?'

'I don't have any spirits. I'm trying to keep off them myself, but there's wine, and some lager in the fridge.' I had recently taken to drinking the local brand.

'I could murder a pint,' he said.

I went into the kitchen, took two cans of Harp from the fridge, found some glasses and carried the drinks in on a tray. He was crouching down by the fireplace, rubbing his hands.

'You could put a match to it,' I said. 'It's cold in here. Only one of those radiators works.'

He took the can off the tray, ignoring the glass. 'I'll bring you over some turf,' he said, looking at my meagre supply. 'I can get a load of it from the guy who supplies the pub.'

'The pub?' I repeated.

'My old man owns the pub in the village – or Lounge Bar, as he prefers to call it.' There was a slight edge to his voice.

I felt my heart quicken. So he was one of *the* Murphys, after all.

'Then Damien and Sean must be your brothers?' I asked, surprised.

'You've met Damien and Sean, have you?' he said, his face brightening. 'Trust Damien! He's a terrible man with the women!'

'I met them for the first time the other day,' I told him. 'I went into the pub to call the garage, in fact.'

I remembered then that I had got the number from Murphy's Food Store. They were obviously all tied in together.

'Damien and Sean are my half brothers,' he told me, taking a long draught of beer.

'Oh,' I said, understanding the differences between them better now.

He lit a cigarette, handed me the packet, then stretched his legs out in front of him.

'Are you the eldest, then?' I inquired.

He nodded. 'The "boss man", as he's known by all and sundry, married twice. I'm the result of the first marriage. Then he married Moira and had Sean, Damien, Conrad, Kathleen, Ger and Sinead, in that order.'

'That's quite a family!' I thought of Eamonn Murphy, who had drowned so tragically, and wondered if he had been a cousin.

'My real mother was a tinker,' he told me after a pause. 'A raving beauty, so they say – wild, wild woman! My old man lured her away from her caravan, married her, then broke her heart. She died giving birth to me.' He stopped and looked away, adding bitterly, 'And my father has never let me forget it.'

262

'That's awful,' I said, fascinated now. So Mother was not the only one to be affected by the lure of Tom Murphy. 'He sounds quite a character,' I said diffidently.

His face clouded over. 'Ah, he's a real piss artist! An aggressive bastard, if truth be known. That's why I left when I was seventeen. We never got on. I don't know how Damien and Sean can work for him,' he continued moodily. 'They're more tolerant than me, I suppose.'

'What about your stepmother? Do you get on with her?'

He shook his head. 'Nope. She never accepted me – bloody snobbish woman, so she is. Didn't like the fact that my mother was one of the "travelling people"!' He put on a posh accent for the words, then added in his normal voice, 'Reckons she's above all that! Before my old man made his money, we used to live in one of them terraced houses in the village.'

I had noticed them as I passed by – a row of council-type houses with grey net curtains and rather squalid back yards.

'. . . but that wasn't good enough for Moira O'Farrell! She had delusions of grandeur. Wanted to live on one of the new housing estates. Well she got what she wanted in the end – a brand-new Merc, the lot!'

He glared out of the window. 'Poor Mam; she's better off where she is, that's for sure . . .' He was talking about his real mother again, it seemed. I imagined a dark sultry girl with wild gypsy hair and his sea blue eyes. 'My old man took her to hell and back – married her when she was already expecting me, then had it off with half the village, including the local gentry!'

Shock made me drop my glass, so it crashed to the floor and shattered, the contents splattering over the hand-woven rug Aunt G had given me.

I stood up in confusion, muttering something about a cloth, but he was kneeling down and picking up the broken pieces of glass, saying, 'You should drink out of the can, like myself. Saves a fortune on glasses.'

I went into the kitchen to try and get a hold of myself, found a cloth, and brought it back into the living room. We wiped up the mess between us, then I fetched another two cans of beer and sat down again, but the mood was broken. He had moved on.

'And you,' he said, 'what are you running away from?'

I smiled. 'A failed marriage, and the law.'

'Ah, you're having me on.'

'No I'm not,' I teased, watching his reaction.

'What did you do, rob one of them Swiss banks?'

'You could say that,' I laughed, remembering how I had emptied our joint account. 'It's a long story.'

He settled himself more comfortably. 'This I have to hear.'

I talked until it started to grow dark outside, stopping once to get Jean up and feed him, then continued while he played on the rug in front of the fire, until I reached the part where I had left Switzerland that freezing morning, without a word. In the course of this lengthy explanation I mentioned Aunt G twice, wondering as I did so if he knew about the feud between the families, and that Mother had been one of the 'local gentry' his father had chased. But if he did, he said nothing.

When I had finished, he let out a great sigh of incredulity. 'That's amazing,' he said. 'I can't believe they could take the kid away from you. I mean you are the mother, aren't you?'

'And Michel's the father,' I reminded him.

He considered this for a minute, then said, 'Ah, that's different. Anyone can be a father!'

'Unfortunately, it's the father who pays most of the bills,' I said.

He glanced around the room. 'You don't seem to be doing too badly on your own.'

'No, but eventually I'm going to have to get a job – and that will mean finding somebody to look after Jean.'

'You could ask Mad Molly from the village,' he suggested. 'She looked after my younger sister, when my stepmother was sick. Don't worry,' he added, seeing my face, 'she's only slightly mad. The kids love her! She runs the playschool behind the old knacker's yard. D'you know where I mean?'

'Not exactly.'

'Down there behind Meany's, the newsagent . . . come to think of it, my sister Sinead will mind him for you. She babysits to make a bit of pocket-money. What sort of job are you looking for?'

'I used to write for a living,' I told him. 'Then I went to live in Switzerland, and wrote a novel which never got anywhere. Now I'm writing another one, but to be honest, I can't see it supporting us in the long run. I need a proper job.'

'The story that hasn't ended?' he said. 'The child-tug-of-war?' He glanced at Jean, who was chasing a rubber ball across the floor. 'I hope the mother wins in the end.'

'Nobody really wins, in those situations,' I said. There was a short silence. 'I'd like to try and get in with some of the local newspapers, or magazines,' I digressed. 'The trouble is you need connections, and I'm not a local.'

'What about Great Aunt Matilda?' he inquired. 'She must know a good few people.'

'Geraldine,' I said with a laugh. 'Yes, she did introduce me to a reporter who works for the *Irish Times*, but I need to approach some editors myself.'

'I know the very man,' he said suddenly. 'Michael Dunne, he runs the *Wicklow Herald*. You could tell him you're a friend of TJ Murphy. He'll give you a job – might not pay a lot, but it would be fun . . .' He glanced at his watch. 'Jasus, is that the time? I was meant to meet somebody at three-thirty.'

It was almost five o'clock.

'I'm sorry,' I said, 'I've been talking too much.'

'Ah, he'll wait.' He picked up his jacket and cigarettes.

'I'll drive you,' I offered. 'Give me a moment to get Jean ready.'

He stood up. 'You know you've got a leaking roof? I could stop by next week and fix it for you, if you like?'

'Thanks,' I called from the other room, thinking that events were running out of control. I could hardly believe I had spent the whole afternoon talking to him. I pulled on Aunt G's windcheater, resolving once again not to mention it to her.

He climbed into the back with Jean, and I negotiated my way through the dark puddles along the lane in silence. But as I reached the main road, I said, 'Did you know that there's been a feud between my aunt and your family for years?'

'Doesn't surprise me,' he said moodily. 'The boss man is famous for his tribal wars.'

'Aunt G won't shop in the village to this day.'

I glanced at him in the rear view mirror. His face was expressionless, as if he neither knew nor particularly cared about the details. Petty battles of this nature were of no interest to him, it seemed. He lived in a larger world, where cats were cats and dogs were dogs, their differences part of the natural order of things, their fights of no consequence.

'Doesn't surprise me,' he repeated. 'I rarely go near the place myself!' This time he changed the subject. 'Would you like to join us at the weekend? There's a whole gang of us meeting up at O'Brien's. If the weather's in any way decent we go hang-gliding off the Sugar Loaf. If not, we stay in the pub till closing time.'

'It must be a bit cold – hang-gliding at this time of the year?' I said evasively.

'Ah, you don't notice the cold once you're up there,' he said. 'I fly in all weathers. It's mild at the moment.'

'It's almost tropical, compared to Switzerland,' I said, 'but slightly wetter!'

'Do you know Paddy O'Brien's?' he asked. 'It's just beyond the garage on the left there. Damien and Sean will be there, with their mots – girlfriends,' he translated, 'and my sister Ger and her boyfriend.'

I remembered O'Brien's was Jacintha's local pub. 'I'll have to see,' I said guardedly. 'It's difficult with Jean.'

'Sinead will mind him for you,' he said. 'Give her a ring.' Before I could reply, he had scribbled a number on a piece of paper and handed it to me.

'We meet up on Sunday afternoons, too.'

'I'll think about it,' I promised, pulling into the garage.

'See you, then. Cheerio, young fellow, try and persuade your Mother to come, will you?' Then he was gone.

Although tempted, I wouldn't go, I decided. Things had gone far enough already. Aunt G's request that I stay away from the Murphys, the only thing she had ever asked of me, was one reason, but there was also something else that I couldn't quite put my finger on. I had no intention of letting history repeat itself.

But though I was unwilling to go against Aunt G's wishes, nor could I be expected to continue with a feud that had nothing to do with either TJ or me. I felt my resolve weaken, as I drove back to the Railway Cottage. I remembered that windy day when Mother, Charlotte and I had walked back from the village to Heronlough, and how she had started to tell us about Tom Murphy. 'We were worlds apart, that was the trouble, but by the time I realised that, it was too late . . .' I knew now that Tom Murphy had been the one great love of her life. But he had married somebody else – a woman more suitably matched, like Marguerite perhaps, who had waited confidently on the sidelines to make her move.

The woman he was destined for all along, perhaps?

Chapter Thirty-Three

That week Aunt G took to her bed with a bad chest, making me forget all about TJ and his invitation.

She stayed in bed for several days, overcome by coughing fits. I drove over to Heronlough in Fernando every afternoon to sit with her. By the end of the week she was sitting up again, wearing a pink bedjacket trimmed with silk ribbons, her face pale and dusty with powder. I kissed her soft cheek, smelling the familiar lavender scent, relieved that she seemed slightly better. That was the day I learnt she had emphysema.

Jacintha let it slip by mistake. Aunt G had always said Jacintha had 'a hotline to Scotland Yard', and could never keep anything to herself.

'How is she?' I asked, letting myself in through the back door.

'She had a good night,' she informed me, 'but 'tis a terrible effort for her, with them stairs. We might have to move her bed down here, before the emphysemia robs the breath from her body.'

She had added another syllable to the lung disease, but I knew immediately what she was talking about. Lungs that had lost their elasticity, causing shortness of breath.

'Oh God,' I said, sitting down. 'She's going to have to stop smoking.'

'And pigs might fly,' answered Jacintha gloomily. 'She was exactly the same when she was younger, stubborn as the Divil himself – wouldn't listen to a soul.'

I went upstairs with a heavy heart, only to find Aunt G looking marginally better.

'Emily dear, come over here where I can see you. And pass me that ashtray, would you? I could do with a cigarette.'

'You mustn't smoke,' I said. 'Doctor's orders.'

'Nonsense, I feel as fit as a fiddle.'

'Maybe because you haven't had a cigarette for a while?'

'There's nothing wrong with me,' she argued, then she saw my face.

'I've known people die of emphysema who've never smoked in their lives,' she said stubbornly. 'Now give me a cigarette, or I'll get up and find one myself.'

I sighed, and handed her one of my own. Major were far too strong for her, but Jacintha must have confiscated her usual Silk Cut, for there were no packets lying around. Then I sat down on the bed and took her stiff hand in mine.

'Emily, I'm worried about you,' she said, surprising me. It was typical of her to turn the worry around, and focus it on the other person. 'You've been withdrawn lately.'

I looked at her guiltily. Whereas once I had confided everything, now I had started omitting the odd detail. Like the afternoon TJ had come to the Railway Cottage.

'There's nothing wrong, is there?'

'No,' I lied. 'Everything's fine.' I studied my nails with great concentration.

'Are you still worrying about that husband of yours?' she inquired.

'He's taking his time,' I admitted, 'which is alarming. Like waiting for an animal to spring – you don't know when it'll happen. I've been here over a month now.'

She glanced at me sharply. 'Sometimes I don't know what's upsetting you most – the fear of him arriving out of the blue, or the fact that he's decided to stay away.'

I looked away in confusion. She was right. I was still afraid that I'd open the door and find Michel standing there, yet at the same time I could not reconcile myself to the idea that the chapter was closed – that he had turned the page, and decided to carry on without us. The thought of him cutting us out of his life was as painful as the other. Had he decided to let go of Jean after all, realising he was not equipped to bring up a child alone? I remembered how he had said once, 'I don't have to live with my possessions, I just have to know they are there.' Did he consider the marriage unsalvageable as I did? I couldn't believe he had simply failed to track us down. Each scenario went through my mind regularly, but as the days passed the cold realisation that it was over was beginning to settle on me. Now he'd had a taste of his former freedom, he no longer needed us. Perhaps he'd gone back to Marguerite, as Sévérine had always predicted.

I turned back to Aunt G, at a loss.

'I need to get myself a job – something to keep my mind occupied. . . .' I was about to tell her my plan of contacting the editor of the *Wicklow Herald*, but was afraid she might ask how it had come about. So I said instead, 'I'm going to get in touch with a few editors – I'll try the local newspapers first.'

'As soon as I'm up and about, I'll give Jack Harcourt a ring,' she said. 'He knows all sorts of people in literary circles; he . . .' She was caught up short by another coughing spasm.

I handed her a glass of water, and watched her worriedly. 'How long have you known about the emphysema?'

'I've known for a good while,' she answered. 'I can live with it.'

'This weather probably doesn't help,' I said, looking out across the green lawns of Heronlough. Another sea mist was rolling in from the channel, yet it remained mild for the time of year.

'Besides, there are worse things than this,' she said vaguely.

I looked at her stiff hand lying uselessly by her side – the hand that had painted all those beautiful scenes – and my heart ached for her.

'I know,' I said finally. 'Souvenirs aren't always enough.'

The following day, I rang the *Wicklow Herald* and asked to speak to Michael Dunne, saying I was a journalist, and a friend of TJ Murphy. The receptionist put the call straight through to his office.

'Hello, friend of TJ Murphy,' said a loud booming voice.

Taken aback, I said, 'Hello . . . My name is Emily Summers.' (This was to be my *nom de plume*, I'd decided.) 'I was wondering if I could pop in and see you – I used to write for a number of magazines in London, I've done several interviews, and have a bit of reporting experience.'

'English, are you? ' he inquired brusquely.

'Half English, half Irish, but I'm living here permanently now.'

There was a short silence, then he said, 'Come in and see me tomorrow. I've meetings all day today, but I'm free in the morning. This is only a small paper,' he added, 'with a modest circulation. I presume you have other freelance work?'

'I'm working on it,' I replied.

'I'll try and fix you up,' he said genially.

I left Jean with Jacintha, briefly explaining I had an interview, and drove towards Wicklow to the address he had given me. The mist had lifted, and a wintry sun shone through the clouds. The Alps would be white with snow, I thought as I drove, the lake steel grey . . . I was back in Switzerland suddenly, remembering those still winter days, the morning fog on the lake, the biting frost . . . And then cars were flashing their headlights, and I realised I was on the wrong side of the road. I swerved into the left-hand lane and slowed down, shocked back to the present.

The offices of the *Wicklow Herald* overlooked the harbour. A container ship was being unloaded and another pulling away from the quay. I parked Fernando in the carpark, and made my way towards the building.

Michael Dunne was a huge hunk of a man, with a beer belly and the high colour of the heavy drinker. His office was shabby and cluttered, with cuttings strewn all over the desk.

'So how do you know TJ?' he inquired, shaking my hand painfully.

'I haven't known him long,' I admitted. 'I bought a car from him a few weeks ago.'

'Ah, he used to be a wild man,' he told me, sinking down behind his desk. 'We were great drinkin' partners . . . Then he started that parachutin' lark, and quietened down a lot.'

'I suppose you can't do both,' I said, a vision of TJ crashing drunkenly into the side of the Sugar Loaf mountain coming to mind.

The interview centred more around TJ and their friendship than my writing abilities, as it turned out. He didn't ask many questions, which was a relief as I had little to show him, only verbal assurances of past liaisons with magazines such as *Healthy Lifestyle* and *Woman*, and the novel that had never been published. But he said, 'You could look into this for me, for starters,' and handed me a sheet of paper on which was written, 'check out lifeboat story – hoax callers'.

'The lads who work on the lifeboat have had a bit of trouble recently – eejits sending them off on wild goose chases, so when there's a real tragedy like poor Eamonn Murphy drowning, they don't know whether it's for real or not . . . Have a word with them, would you, and turn it into a good story. I might use it on the front page. I pay after publication, at the end of the month.'

Half an hour later I was standing outside his office clutching the piece of paper, not knowing where to start.

That same day, I went out and bought myself a typewriter, and after several afternoons spent tracking down the lifeboat team, I interviewed a couple of them, who told me a colourful story about the recent hoaxes. Then I sat down and wrote the article, heading it 'Hoax Callers send Lifeboat on Wild Goose Chase, by Emily Summers'.

Michael Dunne seemed pleased, and put it on the front page. 'I like your style,' he said, 'although you'd be better cutting out some of those old-fashioned words like "whilst" and "unbeknownst" . . .' He put it on his desk, saying, 'How about discussing your next assignment over a jar?'

We went to the pub across the road, where Michael claimed they served the best pint of Guinness in town, and sat in the lounge over our drinks. 'So tell us, how did you get into this game?' he demanded. 'And how far do you want to go with it?'

I sipped a coke and lit a cigarette. 'I've always wanted to write,' I told him. 'And like most writers, I suppose the ultimate dream is the novel . . .'

'Why?' he inquired.

I was getting used to his direct approach.

I shrugged. 'It's a form of escapism, I suppose,' I said finally. 'Creating a world that's preferable to the one you're living in.'

'You have a point there,' he said with a grin. 'Tell you what, I'll put you in touch with some publishers if you like; I know a good few people in this game. Now get your mind off fiction, and take a look at this – something to whet your imagination . . .'

I read the notes with mounting curiosity: 'Mystery of missing baby Declan Ferns'. A young couple from a small village in County Wexford claimed their child had been snatched from its cot in the middle of the night, a fortnight ago, since when there had been no trace of it.

'I want you to interview them for a centre page spread,' Michael was saying. 'You've got a week.'

I couldn't help but be fascinated by the story. I arranged to meet the couple the following Friday, and since I was early spent an hour wandering around the village – a village similar to Rathegan, with a small Catholic community, a convent and a couple of pubs.

272

I went into the larger pub and asked one of the locals, a toothless old man, if he knew anything about the missing child.

He shook his head and muttered something about 'strange goings-on in the village'.

'What sort of strange things?' I inquired. He said something about 'a circle of evil' – of gambling and drinking, and debts that were never paid, but wouldn't go into detail.

The young couple lived in a small semi-detached house on the main street. The husband was about my own age, with closely cropped hair and a blemished pasty skin. His wife, who was fat and equally unhealthy looking, sat slumped in grief on a broken armchair, staring into space. There were statues of the Virgin Mary all over the room, and pictures of the baby Jesus in his mother's arms on the walls. On the mantelpiece was a photograph of a chubby smiling baby – the missing Declan – in his mother's lap, emulating the ones above.

The husband said, 'Can I get you a cup of tea or something?'

'Tea would be lovely, thank you,' I said, sitting down.

He left the room, leaving me alone with the silent girl. There was a smell of Brussels sprouts wafting from the kitchen. I cleared my throat, wondering how to begin. I had left my note pad behind, figuring it would seem tactless under the circumstances. Michael had insisted on sending a photographer over later on, which I considered equally callous.

'Look, I'm so sorry about Declan,' I began. 'I know what you must be going through . . .'

The girl continued staring into space. 'You couldn't know,' she said hollowly, as the husband reappeared with a mug of tea.

'Do you have any idea what might have happened?' I ventured, addressing him.

He shook his head.

'Did you hear anything that night?'

'Not a thing,' he replied. He muttered something about 'God's will' without meeting my eyes.

Realising I wasn't getting very far, I said, 'Would you allow me to have a look at Declan's room, perhaps?' It wasn't my style to play detective, but I was not prepared to accept the theory of divine intervention.

The room was decorated in baby-blue wallpaper covered with

teddy bears and balloons. In one corner was a drop-side cot over which a mobile hung. The windows were shut, but they were flimsy and one of the frames was bent; it would have been easy enough to open from the outside, and smuggle the baby out that way. It struck me that this was a simple kidnapping case – a woman who could not bear children of her own, perhaps.

The empty cot, the silent room, caused my heart to constrict, and I felt tears sting my eyes. Was this what greeted Michel every morning?

Both parents were watching me. I said with difficulty, 'Do you know of anybody who might have wanted Declan for their own?'

The girl shot her husband a strange look, and suddenly said, 'It's your fault, Matt and you know it.' She turned to me. 'He never paid up, so they took our child . . .'

'Shh, Patricia, you're getting hysterical again.' He said to me, 'She's not well, keeps imagining things.' There was a warning edge to his voice.

'It must be hard for her,' I said, backing away. The walls were beginning to close in on me, the smell from the kitchen making me feel nauseous.

The girl started crying quietly. I felt out of my depth, and, not wanting to intrude a moment longer, I turned to leave the room, squeezing her hand briefly as I went.

'I'm so sorry,' I said, as we filed back into the sitting room.

The phone rang, and the husband left the room again. It was then that the girl told me how he had lost his money gambling with his two brothers, Mick and Pat, who were powerful influences in the village. Then Mick had suddenly left the country, without a word. His wife had disappeared too – a woman who, apparently, had been unable to bear a child. I listened to this story in amazement, my heart aching for her. She was completely bereft, cut in half, her child gone, stolen from her – just as I had taken Jean from Michel.

I left the house before the photographer arrived, thinking of that blue room, with the empty cot.

I called the article 'Without a Trace', and spent a whole day working on it. I hadn't enough evidence to support the gambling debt theory, and knew better than to delve into the hostile territory of a family feud. In the end I could only describe that desolate scene – the empty room, the mother's grief. It was the most difficult article I'd ever had to write.

Chapter Thirty-Four

I was sitting at my typewriter finishing the article when I heard the sound of a vehicle outside.

I rose swiftly and went to the kitchen window. I wasn't expecting anybody. I knew it couldn't be Seamus, since Thursday was Aunt G's bridge day, and now that she was up and about he would be driving her into town. There was no one else it could be, unless it was somebody looking for us . . . My heart started thumping.

I peered out of the kitchen window and saw a blue van bumping along the rutted lane towards the cottage. As it drew closer, I recognised TJ at the wheel, and beside him a man of about the same age with carrot-coloured hair. I went and opened the back door.

'Hello there, stranger,' TJ greeted me. 'I have a load of turf for you in the back, and as we were passing, I thought I'd drop by and check you were still alive. This is Kevin Ryan, by the way.'

'That's very good of you, but you shouldn't have,' I said awkwardly. 'Can I give you some money for it?'

'Not at all, I took it from the pub. We missed you the other week,' he digressed. 'We were in O'Brien's for a good while, having a few jars.'

'My aunt wasn't very well,' I told him.

'Is she better now?'

'Yes, thank goodness.'

'Kevin's my hang-gliding partner and workmate,' he said by way of introduction. He grinned. 'In fact we get on better in the air than on the ground – no need for conversation up there in the clouds, right Kev?'

Kevin shifted from one foot to the other and grunted. He was speckled like a hen, with orange eyebrows and eyelashes. He looked completely washed-out beside TJ.

I was wondering if I should invite them in, when TJ said, 'Go inside for a moment, Kev, while I unload the turf.'

'Yes, please come in,' I said and he followed me wordlessly into the cottage.

'Would you like a drink?' I offered.

'A pint,' he replied, sitting down on the most comfortable chair and yawning widely.

I had bought more lager the day before. I took three cans out of the fridge and put them on a tray, without bothering to add glasses, then went back into the sitting room.

When I returned, Kevin was leaning over the table, reading the finished article 'Without a Trace', that I'd left lying there.

'Is that your name then? Emily Summers?'

'That's my pen name,' I answered stiffly.

He sat down again, and stared around the room, squinting slightly as though he didn't like what he saw.

There was an awkward silence, and I understood TJ's comment: Kevin didn't seem to have much to say for himself. He rolled himself a cigarette, lit it, then said, 'You look familiar. What's your real name?'

Irritated, I said, 'Why do you ask?'

'You remind me of somebody, that's all.'

'I don't think we've met before,' I replied.

'What are you doing in Ireland, anyway?'

'I'm a journalist,' I answered defensively. 'And what do you do?'

'My old man owns the garage,' he answered, still staring at me.

Luckily TJ appeared then, and took over. 'Emily's an aspiring novelist! She has quite a story to tell.' He winked, as if we had known one another for years.

'Aspiring is the right word,' I replied, handing him a can of lager. 'By the way, I wanted to thank you. I went to see your editor friend, Michael Dunne, and he gave me a job with the *Herald*.'

'I know,' he answered. 'He hasn't stopped talking about you since.'

'He's quite a character.'

'Michael's a good man,' he said, sitting down and knocking back half the contents of his can. 'He could even drink my ould man under the table.'

'He told me you used to be great drinking partners,' I said.

'Did he now? Sure, I couldn't keep up with him.'

'He's given me some interesting articles to research – I didn't realise so much went on in these small villages.'

'You could write a book about life in rural Ireland,' said TJ. 'By the way,' he digressed, 'there's a session on in O'Brien's next weekend – Kevin here plays in a band . . . Would you like to come along?'

'So you're a musician as well,' I said, turning to the silent Kevin.

'He plays the tin whistle,' said TJ with a grin.

Kevin shot him an angry look. 'I'm a guitarist,' he said flatly. He didn't like TJ's jokes, it seemed. 'Do you fly?' he inquired suddenly, as if puzzled by TJ's interest in me.

'No,' I said, realising he was talking about hang-gliding. 'I'd be scared out of my wits.'

'No you wouldn't, you'd love it,' said TJ. 'We go to some beautiful places. Last summer we went to Achill for a fortnight. It's the best way to forget your problems – fly above them.'

'Perhaps I should learn, then,' I grinned back at him. There was a feeling of intimacy between us, as if we had become conspirators since exchanging our life stories.

'That reminds me, I brought this for the young fellow. Still asleep, is he?'

He handed me a hastily wrapped package containing a small bulky object. I opened it, and pulled out a model of a hang-glider made from wood and cloth. A little wooden man was attached to the kite by a tiny leather thong.

'It's fantastic, a real work of art!' I said. 'Where did you get it?'

'I made it,' he told me, 'from a piece of old wood.'

'It's too good for a toy,' I said admiringly. 'I'd hate Jean to break it.'

'If he breaks it, I'll make him another one,' said TJ airily.

'Thank you,' I said, placing it on the mantelpiece.

'I'll do something about that roof of yours, the next time,' he promised, lighting a cigarette.

We chatted easily for a few minutes, while Kevin stared from one of us to the other, seeming puzzled by our friendship. He was beginning to make me feel uneasy.

By the time they were ready to leave, TJ had extracted a promise from me that I would meet them in O'Brien's pub the following Saturday around noon.

'Thanks for the drink, Emily Summers,' said Kevin as he got up.

'You're welcome,' I said formally. He seemed to be insinuating that I was some kind of impostor, living in hiding under a false identity.

TJ winked and squeezed my hand.

'Thanks again for the turf,' I called after him as he climbed into the van.

'You can buy me a drink on Saturday,' he replied with a wave. Then they were gone.

It was all fairly harmless, I thought, as I went back into the cottage. Aunt G didn't have to know. I would buy him a drink, that was all. It was the very least I could do.

But it was with some trepidation that I entered O'Brien's pub the following Saturday, having left Jean with Jacintha, claiming I had an article to write.

The pub was dark and smoky, with connecting public and lounge bars. I walked into the public first, where solitary old men sat drinking pints of Guinness, and the air smelt of sour beer and cigarettes. One man turned around and glared at me as I entered, as if women were not welcome, and the barman gestured towards the lounge to confirm this.

TJ's crowd were huddled in one corner, around two tables covered in half-empty pint glasses. There were only about nine of them, but they were making the noise of twenty-nine. TJ stood up immediately he saw me and beckoned me over.

Sean and Damien were there, with two pale girls who looked like twins; then there were Kevin Ryan, a thin lanky boy, and a couple who sat holding hands without speaking. TJ appeared to have a girlfriend with him, a beautiful black-haired girl with a sulky face, until I realised it was his sister Ger, who worked in the Food Store. She looked different all made up, her missing tooth emphasised by a mouth shiny with lipstick. She sat wedged between TJ and Kevin, while the lanky boy opposite kept reaching over and patting her knee.

Damien said with a wink, 'I heard you got conned into buying one of TJ's wrecks. Could he not find you a decent car?!'

'Don't insult Fernando,' TJ retorted, 'he's very sensitive.'

I smiled, taken aback once again by Damien's beauty. He was

wearing a red checked shirt and corduroy trousers, and had managed to tame the tangle of curls into a more controlled style. The two pale girls couldn't keep their eyes off him.

'Fernando's behaved perfectly well so far,' I told him.

TJ briefly introduced me to the others, then asked what I was drinking.

'No, this one is on me – I insist.'

'It'll mean buying a round,' he said. 'That's the way it's done around here.'

'Then I'll buy a round.'

I was aware of Kevin's pale eyes on me again as I searched for my purse. TJ beckoned the barman, saying, 'Give us another round there, Jimmy, and an extra for the lady here.' The pints were brought over, and TJ swiftly handed him a note.

'Wait a minute,' I said, still digging around in the depths of my bag.

'Are you fumbling, or do you intend to pay?' inquired TJ with a grin.

I laughed, uplifted by his good humour. 'Well the next one's definitely on me,' I said.

More pints were drunk, and the conversation grew even louder. TJ had told them I was writing a bestseller, and Sean and Damien wanted to know what it was about. We talked about books for a while – they all seemed extremely well read, discussing authors I'd never made the effort to read. Ger didn't join in but, like Kevin, stared at me suspiciously from time to time, as though I had blown in from another planet. For a brief moment she reminded me of Séverine. I noticed her lean against Kevin, causing him to flush with pleasure, and the lanky boy to glare and place his hand firmly on her leg. Each time the attention shifted to me, she yawned and looked around boredly, until Damien said, 'Are we keeping you up Ger?' making everybody laugh.

The conversation moved on to hang-gliding, wind directions and equipment, and somebody called Piggy O'Dwyer, who had recently landed in Farmer Doherty's field, incensing his prize bull. There were other anecdotes that made everybody laugh, then Kevin produced a tin whistle and played a tune that had us all clapping.

'Diddly ido, diddly ido, diddly ido day . . .' sang TJ tunelessly.

So it went on until Holy Hour, when the barman rapped on the counter to tell us it was time for last orders. I looked at my watch, amazed at how the time had flown. Just for a while, I'd managed to forget everything else.

'Same time, same place, tomorrow?' TJ said, as we left the pub.

'I'll have to see,' I replied. 'I usually have lunch with my aunt. Sunday's Jacintha's day off, and I keep her company.'

'I told Sinead you were looking for a babysitter, by the way. She's going to drop by one evening, to meet Jean.'

'Thanks,' I said, wondering how I'd ever managed without him – first a job, and now a babysitter.

'So now you haven't any excuse,' he said.

Chapter Thirty-Five

It was a few weeks before I saw TJ again, however. The days were growing longer and milder as spring approached. Time was rushing by now, gathering momentum as Jean and I began to adjust to our new lives. Michel would be growing restless, I thought, in that nothing time between seasons when the snow was melting and the season ending.

One evening there was a knock on the door, and I opened it to find a young girl standing there.

'TJ said you needed a baby minder,' she said.

'You must be Sinead. Please come in,' I replied, looking at her curiously. She was a pale version of a Murphy, with thick brown hair and eyes of an indeterminate colour. I thought briefly of the tinker woman who had given birth to TJ, and wondered if Sinead too had sprung from a different source. She had a shy, rather more genteel manner than her sister Ger, and was noticeably friendlier.

'Did you have any problem finding the cottage?' I asked.

She shook her head. 'TJ told me where it was. I came on my bike.'

I had gathered the Murphys lived on the wealthy housing estate the other side of the village. Within minutes she had settled Jean in front of the fire and they were playing together happily, forgetting all about me.

She started coming to the Railway Cottage regularly to babysit. She often brought something for Jean – a toy, a bag of sweets, some crayons – and they would play together for hours. She was quiet and gentle, and far more patient than I ever was. Jean called her Snade, and would run to the door to greet her, shrieking with delight.

I told Jacintha I had found a young girl to babysit, without mentioning her name, and she didn't ask for details. Instead, she said rather indignantly, 'I don't know why you bothered – I would have minded him for you any time.'

But this way fewer questions would be asked, I thought; questions I did not want to answer.

Michael Dunne put me in touch with another editor, as he had promised, opening yet another door, and I contacted the *Irish Times*, submitting a piece about Switzerland, which to my delight they agreed to publish in the summer.

So the days continued uneventfully, and with the passage of time came the knowledge that Michel would not come now. The anger and bitterness I had felt had been replaced by a sense of bewilderment and loss. It seemed now that I had never really known him. We had gone through the motions together, got married, had a child, loved one another and fought bitterly, but that was all it had been – a ritual coupling that had ended as quickly as it had begun. Michel had belonged to a different world, after all. Was it pride that had stopped him coming after us, or the fact that I had not been able to follow the rules? Perhaps he had simply woken up to the fact that we weren't compatible after all. Yet it still didn't add up. Michel loved Jean, even if he had stopped loving me, but had apparently decided to live without either of us.

I remembered that idyllic weekend we had spent together in Paris, before Jean was born, and the artist who had portrayed us ten years down the road. Michel had laughed it off saying, 'So what, we'll grow old together . . .' Tears burnt my eyes, and I blinked them back angrily. 'For God's sake stop dwelling on it,' I said out loud. Then I had a fleeting vision of him the day his Mother died. '*C'est fini*,' he'd said, in that awful dead tone of voice that made everything seem so final. 'It's over.'

It was a pale March day, with a touch of spring in the air. I was sweeping the kitchen floor when I heard the sound of a vehicle.

I went outside, and watched it pull to a halt. The chatter of voices sounded from inside, then TJ got out and came over to me.

'We're going hang-gliding off Devil Hill in the next county. If you've nothing better to do, come with us,' he said.

I wasn't doing anything at all.

'Give me a few minutes,' I replied, 'I'll get Jean ready.'

I decided to follow in Fernando, so I'd be free to leave when I wanted, and set off after them, turning right along the coast road.

The sea looked icy blue in the pale sunshine. I saw a few sailing boats in the distance, and realised the season would be starting soon. We followed the coast for some miles, past long shingle beaches and small villages, then wound up a steep hill into a lush wooded area, where we pulled off the main road. TJ rolled down the window and called out. 'We're going to drive up further, but you'd be better off parking here and coming with us; it's a bit rough for Fernando.'

'I'll walk up,' I called back. 'I'd like the exercise.'

'Right you are.' He waved and drove on.

I got Jean out of the car, and we followed a path through the woods, then up some steps cut into the side of the hill. A cold breeze blew in from the sea, and the sun slanted through high racing clouds; below stretched the long sweep of coastline. I carried Jean up the last bit, spotting the others as the trees thinned. They had parked the van some way below, and were carrying the equipment up to the ridge.

Ger had a different boy with her this time. He had a mop of blond hair and dark brooding eyes, and like the lanky boy, he couldn't keep his hands off her. They snuggled up together and nibbled each other's ears. This time she paid no attention to Kevin, nor did he seem aware of her, setting up his equipment for flight. The mood was serious now, as they prepared to take off into the wide blue vista beyond.

TJ was pulling on a blue quilted suit, and adjusting the emergency parachute on his chest. 'If you get cold, go and sit in the van with the heater on,' he said. 'But I'm sure the young fellow would like to see us take off.'

Jean was staring in amazement at the proceedings. 'Birdie,' he said, pointing up. Above us, a hang-glider already circled.

'He's right,' said TJ. 'It's the nearest man's got to what a bird can do . . .' He picked up a piece of grass and let the breeze take it, so he could gauge the wind direction. 'It's a good day for flying,' he said. 'It can be bloody dangerous up here if the wind isn't right. That's why we call it Devil Hill – it's a devil of a place to land. Today, we might have to land on the beach below.'

I looked down across the wide curving bay and long stone beach.

'Be careful,' I said.

He shrugged. 'I've known a guy land in the sea. He managed to break free of the harness, and was picked up by a passing trawler. I've also known one poor bastard who drowned in six feet of water. Storm clouds are the worst, cumulus nimbus – they can suck you up and spit you out . . .'

I looked up anxiously at the gathering clouds. TJ followed my gaze. 'It's a grand day for it,' he assured me, adjusting his helmet.

I turned around to look for Jean. There was no sign of him.

Alarmed, I followed the ridge around to the other side, and found him playing in a small outcrop of rocks. From this side, there was a view across Dunlaoghaire harbour, beyond Howth Head. I stood there thinking of Jeanette and our plans to spend the summers in Ireland together, and felt the familiar ache inside. Then I beckoned Jean and went back towards the others.

TJ was the last to take off. I watched him run a few steps, to where the hill swept down to the sea, then he was running on air, before rising into the sky. He hovered for a second, the orange kite poised like an exotic bird, then began to swoop in wide circles above us. I followed his progress, wishing suddenly I was up there with him. The wind seemed stronger suddenly, and I pulled the windcheater around me, thinking longingly of my mink coat. Jean seemed oblivious to the cold, running hither and thither along the ridge, shouting into the wind.

I was so lost in my thoughts I jumped at the sound of a voice, then looked up and saw Ger standing behind me, a strange expression on her face. The wind lifted her dark curls, and her mouth was parted slightly, revealing the dark hole of her missing tooth. Her boyfriend stood some feet behind her, smoking a cigarette.

'Cold wind,' I said, but she was not one for small talk.

'What are you doing here?' she demanded abruptly. It seemed like the start of an inquisition. I had felt the same antipathy from some of the locals when we had first moved to the Isle of Wight, but there seemed to be something personal in her dislike of me.

'Do you mean what am I doing standing on this hill in a freezing cold wind, or what am I doing in Ireland in general?' I replied.

She shrugged, as if waiting for an answer to both questions.

'I came to Ireland because I have family here, among other things,' I said, 'and I came today because your brother invited me.'

Her face seemed to cloud over. I sensed she was possessively jealous when it came to TJ, and felt her dislike like the cold blast of the wind.

'I know your aunt's cook, Jacintha Fahy,' she said then. (She pronounced it Jacinta.) 'She's a friend of my Mam's . . . told my Mam you ran away from your husband with the child.'

I looked at her warily. Jacintha must have been gossiping again. 'Really?' I said, wondering if she knew about the feud between the two families.

'Why did you come here?' she demanded again.

'I have family here,' I repeated, meeting her gaze with a hard look. 'I don't know what you've heard,' I said, 'but remember there are always two sides to every story. Unless you have the whole picture, it's difficult to judge.' I paused, remembering Michel had said something similar when I had tried to explain Jeanette's story. It seemed I had lost Ger's full attention, though. She looked at me as if all her suspicions were confirmed, and I was indeed an alien, then went back to her boyfriend. She whispered something in his ear, and they both stood there smoking and talking, their eyes on me, then turned and headed back to the van.

Jean's lips were starting to turn blue with cold, and I was shivering. I looked up at the swirling clouds, searching for the three kites, then walked to the edge of the hill and saw two specks hovering over the beach below. There was no sign of the third.

I turned away and went towards the van, deciding I would leave a message with Ger.

They were sitting in front, and must have turned the heater on, as the windows were all steamed up. Then I saw they were kissing, devouring one another hungrily: I hesitated before knocking on the window.

Ger pulled herself free of the boy's long arms and glared at me, then rolled down the window.

'Could you tell TJ we were getting cold,' I said, in as friendly a voice as I could muster, 'and that I'll be in touch?'

She stared at me darkly. 'Keep away from TJ,' she said ominously, and rolled up the window again.

I made my way down the steep path, uneasy now, wondering what else Jacintha had said to make her so hostile.

I drove back to the Railway Cottage deep in thought. She was the second person to warn me to keep away from the Murphys. The feud lingered on, it seemed, like a hereditary disease, affecting some while others remained oblivious.

For me, the whole thing held a sort of compelling fascination. I knew I couldn't keep away.

Chapter Thirty-Six

Aunt G had given Jacintha the afternoon off, and we were sitting in the kitchen, drinking tea and eating home-made scones. She looked better, although she had made no attempt to stop smoking, and I knew she never would. I still hadn't told her about the job with the *Wicklow Herald*, but now I produced the article about the lifeboat, and waited while she read it.

'Very impressive,' she said, glancing at me over her reading glasses. 'One might have thought you were a local, to write about it like that.'

'It's my nautical background! I spent ages down there, talking to the lads,' I said.

'You're even beginning to sound like a local,' she said, but she didn't smile.

'So what do you think?'

'I wish you'd told me beforehand,' she answered.

'I did mention I was going to contact some editors of local newspapers. Why?'

'The *Wicklow Herald* . . . Well to be honest, it's a bit of a rag. Don't get me wrong, I take my hat off to you for going out and getting yourself some work, but I would have preferred it if you'd found a less biased newspaper.'

I knew immediately what she was hinting at. The paper had a Republican slant.

I was about to tell her about the *Irish Times*, but she spoke first.

'How did you find out about it?' she inquired – the question I had known would follow, and didn't know how to answer.

'Through the guy who sold me the car,' I told her briefly.

But she was immediately alert. 'That car salesman turned out to be quite a hero,' she said, 'what with his rescue operation, and now finding you a job! Who is he, anyway?'

I felt the awkwardness between us, and made an instant decision. She deserved the truth.

'Of all the coincidences, he turned out to be one of the

Murphys,' I said casually. 'I presumed he was from another branch.'

Her expression altered. 'Emily, I haven't asked much of you – your happiness is more important to me than anything. But I did ask you to stay clear of that family, for reasons I thought were patently clear!'

'I tried, Aunt G – I had no idea they were in the second-hand car business as well.'

'If it was advertised in the supermarket, I would have thought it was obvious – they're all in cahoots, the whole lot of them, which is why I keep away from Rathegan. I know it was difficult for you at first, but now you have a car there's no reason to go near the village.'

'He didn't even know about the feud, Aunt G. It's us who are keeping it going!'

'That family destroyed your mother's life, Emily. She sounded breathless. 'It goes way back, before my time even. The Flavells have their own good reasons to keep clear, and certainly not to do business with them!'

'I had no intention of getting involved . . . I'm not involved,' I amended hastily. 'Although I have to admit I'm curious about the whole thing.'

'About what? There's nothing in the slightest bit mysterious about any of it! It's the oldest story in the world. Peg fell in love with a man from the other side of the fence, and lost her family in the process. They threw her out of her own house because of it – while Murphy just walked away without a backward glance, wrecking her life completely. The Murphys have brought nothing but ill on everybody around them.'

She was panting now, like a dog on a hot day. I stared at her, alarmed.

'I'm sorry,' I said.

'You'll never change history, Emily.'

'Only in fiction,' I said, with a strained laugh.

'Then I suggest you stick to that.'

Michel Dunne liked my article about the missing baby Declan. He called it 'an emotive piece', and said I had written it with rare insight and feeling.

288

'Now I want you to go off and research the history of Rathegan,' he said, handing me some scrawled notes.

I hesitated. 'Does Rathegan have much history?' I inquired.

'It's an old village, it must have something to say for itself. The Catholic church there is several hundred years old.'

'Is it really?' I answered, feeling a flicker of interest at this new assignment. 'What about the Protestant church?'

'That was sold and turned into a private house.'

'The Murphys seem to have the village pretty well tied up,' I said, 'what with both pubs and the grocery store.'

'Use the family as your central theme,' he suggested. 'Find out about the old days, the sessions in the pub before the old man hit the bottle.'

'Michael, I . . . er.'

'What is it?'

'I just wondered, if you had another assignment . . . I was thinking about covering the Red Cross story. They've moved their unit into the centre of town, according to the evening papers.'

'Sounds fascinating!' he said sarcastically. 'What's wrong with what I offered you? It's going to be a centre page spread. Just make it good, and by the way I need it by the end of the month.'

'Fine,' I said, backing away.

I went and had a look at the church first. It was very beautiful, with stained glass windows and the original stone and timberwork. Behind the church, the graveyard looked over the sea. I walked along a row of headstones, where people had placed flowers in plastic crosses and dried bunches on the tombstones. RIP, I read, and wondered fleetingly if Jeanette was resting in peace.

A Tom Murphy had died in 1897, beside him his wife Mary and his son Christie, and there were several others nearby. I carried on along the row of them, thinking, as I often did these days, of the futility of life's petty feuds, and of Michel, from whom my life had already become separated, and wondered what it was all about. The 'rough diamond' would be buried here too, one day, amidst the rest of his clan, which was more than mother had been allowed. I think I understood then, what Aunt G felt, and yet to carry on the feud seemed so pointless.

I wrote in my notebook, 'The ancient Catholic church, where

generations of Murphys have come to rest, has its original stonework and has been carefully preserved.'

Then I went to the town hall and found out about the general activities that went on in the village, noting them down on my pad. The village was twinned with one in Brittany; there was a flower show once in a blue moon; it had never won a Best Kept Village competition; in August a carnival passed through it. Reading my notes, I realised that without people there would be no life to the article. It was time to pay a visit to Murphy's Lounge Bar, and seek out the 'rough diamond'. It was work, I convinced myself, trying to clear my conscience. Aunt G was going to have to understand. Besides, there was no guarantee of getting an interview with Tom Murphy. He was by all accounts an elusive, difficult man, who seldom talked to anybody. But curiosity burnt like a flame inside me, and it seemed as if fate were leading me to him.

After some thought, I decided to approach TJ first.

I stopped by the garage two days later, and found Kevin pottering around the office, trying to put some order to the place.

'How's it going?' he inquired gruffly.

'Fine. I was looking for TJ.'

He stared as if still trying to place me. 'He's round the back, on a job.'

'Thanks,' I said, retreating hastily.

TJ was jacking up one of the wrecked cars to change the tyre. He wore a pair of dirty white overalls, and a cigarette dangled from his mouth.

'Well if it isn't the elusive woman herself,' he said, wiping his hands on his overalls, 'still doing her disappearing act.'

'I'm sorry I left before you landed, that day,' I said. 'Jean was getting cold, but we enjoyed it very much.'

'You still haven't bought me that jar,' he said huffily.

'How about now?' I offered.

'I can't, I have to see a man about a car . . . This evening would suit me, though.'

'The problem is Jean,' I said. 'It's rather late to ask Sinead.'

'You could ring her,' he said, pointing towards the office.

'All right.'

To my relief, Kevin was just coming out of the office, with an older man with the same carrot-coloured hair – presumably his father, who owned the garage. Neither of them paid any attention to me as I passed. I picked up the phone and dialled Sinead's number.

A woman with a cold voice – the snobbish stepmother perhaps – answered the phone.

'I'm looking for Sinead – she babysits for me. It's Emily.'

'I'll see if she's in,' she said shortly.

Sinead told me she had planned to drop by later in any case, and agreed to be at the cottage by six o'clock that evening.

'So where are you taking me?' TJ inquired, when I told him the news.

'How about dinner? I've just received my first pay cheque.'

'You're on,' he replied. 'You'll have to come and collect me, though, as the van's laid up. I live the other side of Wicklow – a mile along the coast road, up near Dartry's pub. The house is called Gort na Mara – it means Sea Fields in English.'

'I'll find it,' I said.

The house was large and dilapidated, with pebble-dashed walls and wide bay windows, and set amid green fields that stretched down to the sea. It reminded me of the house on the Isle of Wight. Inside the rooms had the same damp and musty air, but unlike Sea View, they were cluttered with what seemed to be a lifetime's worth of bric-à-brac. A film of dust lay over the furniture, and the floors were covered in wood shavings from carvings he hadn't finished. The house belonged to a friend of his who had gone to live in America, he explained; he was 'minding' it for him. TJ lived through contacts alone, it seemed.

'Good God, I thought I was messy,' I said, glancing into the kitchen and backing out again. The sink was filled with unwashed dishes, and there was a smell of rotting food in the air.

'Ger stays here when things get too bad at home,' he told me. 'She cleans up the place, but she hasn't stopped by for a while.'

'I see,' I said wryly. 'You wait for your younger sister to do the dirty work?'

'I'm not too good on the domestic front,' he answered, amused by my reaction.

'Or is it that you consider it a woman's job?' Michel had, but he'd always been prepared to pay for it.

TJ looked sheepish. 'I've not been properly house trained, that's my problem.'

'Well it's never too late! I tell you what – if you clean up, I'll cook you dinner here one night. But the kitchen has to be impeccable.'

'Jasus, woman, you strike a hard bargain,' he said, 'but you're on. Give me a couple of days, and you won't recognise the place.'

I smiled, wondering if he'd ask his sister to do it.

We went to O'Brien's for a drink and after three pints of Guinness TJ said he wasn't hungry, so we stayed there until closing time, eating Tayto crisps and talking. I sipped a glass of Guinness, trying to acquire a taste for it, but I had recently lost the desire for alcohol. Michel could no longer accuse me of being a heavy drinker, I thought with irony.

We chatted easily at first. TJ was telling me of his years in America, and of the girl who had broken his heart.

'She was another independent type,' he said. 'Started her own business, in fact. I thought I was going to be able to retire and live happily ever after . . . turned out she had some rich guy paying the bills all along.' He shrugged. 'Never trusted a woman since . . . until I met you, of course.'

It was hard to know when he was being serious and when he was joking.

'I can't think why you should trust me,' I replied.

'I like you,' he said disarmingly. 'You're the genuine ticket' – he touched a strand of my hair – 'Just Emily.'

I shifted on the hard bench and lit a cigarette.

'How complicated it all is,' I said finally.

'What? Friendships, relationships?'

I hesitated. 'It's just that for the first time in ages, things seem to be running relatively smoothly.'

He stared at me for a minute and said, 'What is it, Emily? Are you still besotted with Mr Perfect?'

'I don't know,' I replied, confused. I hadn't stopped loving Michel, but some self-protective instinct had dulled the longing. Contrary to what he thought, I was back in the real world. 'I just don't dare get involved again.' I said. 'And risk failing again, I suppose.'

'Everything has its risks,' he argued. 'It's like hang-gliding –

once you've taken that first step it's irreversible, there's no turning back . . . You've got to fly.'

I smiled at his analogy. He became quite eloquent after a few drinks.

I thought of that first step I had taken into the unknown, with Michel. We had flown high for while, before coming down to earth with a bump.

But then, as he himself had once said, 'You can't live on cloud ten all the time.' Perhaps I had expected too much.

TJ edged closer and put his arm around me. Then he tried to kiss me.

I pushed him away, playfully. 'TJ, be serious, I need your help. Michael wants me to write an article about Rathegan, using the Murphys as the central theme . . . Do you think your father would talk to me about the old singing days?'

His expression immediately hardened, and he drew away from me.

'I don't know, I haven't spoken to him in a while. Damien and Sean have more to do with him than me.'

'Do you remember the old singing days?' I asked, with some trepidation, for his good mood seemed to have evaporated.

'I left when I was a kid,' he replied. 'Ran away, like you – I know all about running away from the bad stuff.'

'I'm sorry,' I said. 'I didn't mean to upset you.'

'Is that why you lured me out? To find out about my old man?'

'Not exactly,' I lied.

'Could have fooled me.'

'TJ,' I said in despair, 'please.'

'Just one thing, Emily – don't bullshit me, OK? Don't ever bullshit me . . .' His voice had gone hard suddenly, with a guttural Dublin edge.

'I'm sorry,' I said. 'I'm really sorry you took it that way. I had hoped we could be friends – that's all I'm capable of at the moment . . .' To my embarrassment, my voice wavered.

He looked at me, and said in a softer tone, 'I'm sorry too. It's just you don't get offers like mine every day of the week, that's all.'

'I know that,' I replied, attempting to smile. 'I know a good thing when I see it.'

We sat in silence for a while, then he said, 'I'll settle for a drink on Saturday night?'

'OK,' I said with relief. 'But this time, it really is my treat.'

I had been so caught up in our conversation that I hadn't noticed the group of women sitting at the next table – three oldish country women wearing headscarves, like 'The Three Old Biddies'. As we got up to leave, however, I saw that one of them was Jacintha. I remembered that O'Brien's was her local, and she was friendly with Paddy, the owner. She was staring at me with a glazed look, as if she'd had one too many.

I smiled awkwardly and raised a hand in greeting.

She nodded back, then said something to one of the other women. All three of them turned and stared at us as we left the pub.

'Oh, hell,' I said to TJ, as we emerged into the cold night.

'What is it?' he inquired.

'That was my aunt's housekeeper. She must have been watching us all along.'

'So?'

'Oh, it's just she's a terrible gossip.' I also remembered Ger mentioning that Jacintha was friendly with TJ's stepmother.

'So you're ashamed of being seen with me?' he said.

'No, TJ,' I said firmly, 'it's not that at all.'

'What, then?'

'It's just too complicated to explain.'

'Why is everything so bloody complicated with you?' he demanded, climbing awkwardly into the Fiat and slamming the door.

I got in the other side and we set off, an angry silence between us.

As I pulled up opposite his house, I said, 'Look, I'm sorry, TJ. It's just my aunt . . .'

'I'll see you around, Emily,' he interrupted, jerking at the handle of the door, 'when it's not too complicated!'

I can explain, I was about to say, then I realised he didn't want explanations. He slammed the door again as he got out, and strode away towards the dark shape of the house, leaving me staring miserably after him.

Chapter Thirty-Seven

Damien was serving when I arrived at Murphy's Lounge Bar the following evening. 'It's the woman herself!' he exclaimed. 'So you've come back to me after all. I knew you'd see sense in the end!' He had a wild, sleepy look about him, as if he'd spent the previous night tumbling around in the hay.

I smiled back; it was impossible not to be affected by him. 'I actually wanted to ask you something.' I hoped he wouldn't react as TJ had, and turn cold on me. I was still upset about the way TJ and I had parted the evening before.

'Yes, you can have my body, but my mind's spoken for,' he said.

'Damien, be serious! I'm writing an article about Rathegan for the *Wicklow Herald*. I need to find out about the old singing days, when the "boss man" used to perform . . .' (I had learnt that he had even released a couple of albums in the early days.) 'Do you think he'd talk to me?'

'I doubt it,' he replied. 'That is, he might talk to you, but not about the old days. He's an unpredictable ould bastard – you never know what mood you'll find him in!'

'When does he usually come down to the pub?' I inquired.

'Used to come every night, but he hasn't showed up for a while – thanks be to God,' he added. 'It's always a quiet night without him. If he comes, 'twould be around six, before his tea.'

'Do you think he'd talk to me?'

'He might or he mightn't – could even throw you out on your ear, on a bad day!'

'It's a risk I'll have to take,' I replied. 'I'll come back tomorrow at six – without Jean.'

'How about a drink on the house?' he offered in an effort to waylay me.

I smiled. 'No thanks, I've got to get a tired boy to bed.'

'I'm pretty tired myself,' he said, yawning widely. 'Does that count?'

'You never stop, do you?'

'No,' he admitted, 'I've the energy to go on all night!'

'I'll bear that in mind,' I said, waving goodbye.

I made my way to the phone and dialled Sinead's number before I left. This time she answered; she said she was free every evening for the next week, and would be over by six.

As soon as she arrived the next day, and Jean was playing happily with some toys she had brought, I drove into Rathegan to wait and see if Tom Murphy would show up.

I passed the empty terraced houses that skirted the village, where TJ had grown up, glancing at the last in the row – a large semi-detached Victorian house, run down and apparently empty. The windows had been boarded up to keep out squatters, and somebody had erected a barbed wire fence in front. There was something slightly hostile about it, I thought. It was hard to reconcile Mother with that other life, when she had fallen in love with the young Tom Murphy who had lived here. Had he been like Damien, I wondered, irresistible to the naïve Protestant girl who had grown up knowing 'nothing of the ways of the world'?

The 'rough diamond' didn't appear that night, or for the next few. Some evenings, both Sean and Damien were behind the bar, and I would sit on a stool listening to their banter.

I learnt more about the family over those days. How TJ had become estranged from his father after a drunken row one evening in the pub – it was Sean's opinion that the 'boss man' was still suffering from the rift, for he kept asking for news of his eldest son, but TJ had no intention of making it up. I got to know Damien and Sean better, too and concluded that if once they had been 'malodorous malingerers', then they were so no longer. Or perhaps, as Mother had been by Tom Murphy's, I was being taken in by their charm. How easy it would be to succumb, I thought, watching Damien make eye contact with a beautiful chesnut-haired girl across the room. If I had been that much younger, perhaps; if I had not known Michel . . . I noticed there was always a different girl hanging around the bar, waiting for Damien to sweep her away into the night at closing time. Like his father, he seemed to leave a string of broken hearts behind him.

Night after night I waited for the 'rough diamond' to stagger in on his gout-thickened legs, but I waited in vain. I rang Michael

Dunne towards the end of that week, and asked for more time to complete the article.

'You can have another week,' he said, 'but no more.'

On the Saturday, when I'd almost given up hope of ever setting eyes on Tom Murphy, Damien announced that he was on his way over. 'Sean just spoke to him,' he told me. I felt a sudden prickle of fear and wondered if I were making a terrible mistake. Who was it who had said 'curiosity killed the cat'? Jeddi, the night of Shariffi's party! A warning that had been a prelude to disaster . . . But there was no time to backtrack now.

There were a number of people in the pub that evening – some loud youths over in one corner, while scattered couples sat talking more quietly over their drinks. The serious drinkers – a few solitary old men – were in the adjoining public bar, which was visible from where I sat.

A bank of cigarette smoke hung in the air, and the noise level increased as the pub filled up. Damien's mood had altered. He pulled pints of Guinness with great concentration, and kept glancing agitatedly towards the door.

I saw the large frame blocking the entrance of the pub first, and noticed Sean and Damien stiffen.

'Looks like it's himself,' said Damien under his breath.

I stared with mounting curiosity at Tom Murphy as he walked painfully towards the bar. He was enormous, bloated from the beer, his skin blotchy with purplish overtones, his hair a wild shock of grey curls. I could see that he must once have been handsome, before the drink had got to him, turning his eyes bloodshot and puffy. He hadn't shaved, and the stubble of his grey beard gave him a desperate, wayward appearance. I stood up involuntarily to make way for him, aware of the sudden hush as he approached.

'Pour us a pint there, Damien,' he called, his voice reverberating around the room. He drew closer without looking at me, coughed loudly, and plonked himself down on a bar stool. Then he folded his arms and rocked backwards, as if on the verge of sleep. I wondered if he was already drunk.

I couldn't drag my eyes away. My mind seemed to travel back through the years, until at last I was seeing him as Mother must have seen him.

I wanted to speak, but could only sit and watch as Damien topped up a pint of Guinness, set it in front of him, then poured a measure of whiskey. Damien didn't speak either. He seemed distant and sullen; there was no communication between them at all. I edged closer, my legs trembling, hoping Damien would introduce us, but the silence continued. I took a shaky breath and said, 'Excuse me, Mr Murphy?'

Tom Murphy opened one eye and squinted at me. Then he opened the other and stared, as if he had seen a ghost.

'Who are you?' he demanded – quite rudely, I thought.

'My name is Emily Summers,' I said, using my *nom de plume*.

'And what do you want?'

'I'm doing some research into the history of the village,' I explained with a dry mouth, 'and your family have been here the longest. I was wondering about the singing sessions in the pub?'

'Oh yes?' he said in a milder tone.

Then I made a fatal mistake. 'It's for the *Wicklow Herald*,' I said helpfully.

'Then Miss . . .'

'Emily,' I said pleasantly.

'Emily, I suggest you go back to the *Wicklow Herald* and tell them to write their filthy slander about somebody else!'

I flushed and backed away. I noticed Damien recoil too, as if the attack were directed at him, while Sean had retreated to the other side of the bar. What a dreadful man, I thought. No wonder TJ was so bitter.

I stood up, flashing him what I hoped was an angry look, and he startled me by smiling brilliantly. 'Come on, take it easy, have a drink on the house instead! Damien, pour the young girl a dacent drink! – Sit down, sit down,' he ordered, causing me to stumble against the bar stool, almost knocking it over.

'I'll have a Coke,' I said to Damien, whose face remained expressionless.

'Have a dacent drink,' repeated Tom Murphy boorishly. 'When I say a drink, I mean a drink . . .' He rocked backwards again, and lit a fat cigar. 'For a moment, you reminded me of somebody.'

Mother, I thought, my heart lurching.

'It's the voice,' he said. 'English, are you?'

'Half,' I said, then, terrified of the direction the conversation

298

was going, added impulsively, 'I heard you singing on Christmas Day.'

He frowned at me. 'So it's a song you're after now, is it?'

'It was very beautiful,' I said, my face burning. 'I'd love to get hold of one of your albums.'

'If it's a song you want, then I'll give you a song,' he said, and stood up.

Damien stared at him in amazement. 'Blow me down,' I heard him say under his breath, as we both turned and watched Tom Murphy lumber towards the piano.

There was dead silence in the pub, everybody watching the old man. He stood there swaying slightly, opened the piano lid, then sat heavily on the stool. Damien had placed a whiskey in front of me. I took a sip, thinking that the whole thing had taken on a dreamlike quality – the sudden hush, the smoke, and the hollow notes of the piano, transporting us back to the past.

Tom Murphy struck a few chords then opened his mouth and sang, in an extraordinary clear voice redolent with nostalgia.

'The violets were scenting the woods, Maggie, displaying their charms to the bees, when I first said I loved only you, Maggie, and you said you loved only me . . .'

A lump rose in my throat.

'. . . the birds in the trees sang a song, Maggie, the robin sang loud on the breeze, when I first said I loved only you Maggie, and you said you loved only me . . .'

Nobody moved. Everybody seemed to have stopped what they were doing, frozen in mid-sentence, as they waited for the next verse.

'Our hopes they were never fulfilled, Maggie, our dreams were never to be . . .'

I blinked back the tears that had filled my eyes. The song seemed to encompass all the lost opportunities of the world.

'. . . when I first said I loved only you, Peggy, and you said you loved only me . . .'

Or had I imagined it? Peggy? Maggie? The names were so similar.

I wiped my eyes as he snapped the piano lid shut, and heard him say, 'That was for young Emily from across the water.'

He walked towards me, picked up his glass, and knocked back

the rest of his pint in a series of swallows, then did the same with the whiskey, before heading for the door.

'Well . . .' I said, completely at a loss.

'Holy Mary Mother of God,' said Damien. 'I can't believe he did that!'

I stared after him. 'Perhaps I reminded him of somebody,' I said.

'I couldn't get much information out of Tom Murphy,' I told Dunne the following Monday. 'I don't know what the *Herald*'s done to make him so defensive.'

Michael frowned. 'We ran something on the pub and its liberal licensing laws a while back,' he replied, 'but I'd hoped you'd be able to use your charm.'

'I'm not the right person,' I replied. 'I tried to tell you that when you asked me to write the article.'

'Of course you are,' he said. 'I thought a complete stranger would do the trick.'

'Well I'm not . . .' I began.

'Not what?' he demanded.

'I mean, I'm not very good at getting information out of people, that's all.'

'I thought you'd done interviews?' he stated.

'My subject normally wants to be interviewed,' I emphasised.

'It's part of the job. Either you're a journalist or you're not. I was beginning to think that you were! Write something,' he ordered. 'I need to fill those pages.'

I went back to the cottage and, after sitting over a blank piece of paper most of the morning, finally wrote about the close village community of Rathegan, with its powerful family in the centre, and hinted at halcyon days gone by.

'The Murphys speak for themselves,' I wrote, 'with the owner of the pub a living legacy of the old days, when people used to come from all over to listen to his haunting melodies. But his voice is still the same, echoing yesteryear perhaps, with the resonant nostalgia of lost hopes and broken dreams . . . It is a rare pleasure to hear Tom Murphy sing.'

Michael somewhat grudgingly agreed to use it for the centre page spread.

Chapter Thirty-Eight

Two days after the article was published, something odd happened.

Fernando wouldn't start, so I had no alternative but to walk to the village and phone the garage, in the hope that somebody other than TJ would be able to help out. I had planned to drive to Wicklow with Jean and buy some groceries, but now I'd have to go to Murphy's Food Store, as I had no idea how long I'd be without a car. I got the pushchair out, strapped Jean in, and started walking down the lane towards the village. It was a mild, pleasant morning. I heard a lark singing above, and felt my spirits rise.

I stopped at Murphy's Food Store first, and made my way down the aisles picking up bread, milk, fruit juice, some yogurts and a few other items, then went towards the cash register to pay.

The speckled girl was at the till that day. She stared at me with her dead brown eyes, and mumbled something incoherent, ignoring the items in front of her.

'What's the problem?' I inquired, counting out the exact change.

'I can't be serving you,' she said helplessly. 'I'll have to speak to Ger.'

'What are you talking about? You are open, aren't you?'

'Yes, but . . .'

At that moment Ger appeared behind her. Her hair was tied back in a ponytail, and once again, I was struck by her beauty. Until she opened her mouth.

'Hello there,' I said with an amiable smile, but she looked at me coldly, as if she no longer knew me.

'What's going on?' I inquired. 'She won't serve me.'

'We can't serve you,' she stated flatly.

'For what reason?'

'I've been told not to be serving them lying snoops who come spying on us,' she replied, as if quoting from somebody else.

'What?' I said incredulously. 'What are you talking about?'

Jean had started crying, sensing the tension in the air. But she ignored him.

I was about to ask to see the manager, then remembered she was the manageress. 'Now listen here,' I said. 'I'm not a snoop or a spy, I'm a journalist – I haven't written any lies or anything to offend anyone. I don't know what you're talking about. I suggest you add these things up for me straight away.'

'Can't,' she said immediately.

'Fine,' I said trying to sound unfazed, above it all. 'I'll take my patronage elsewhere, like I should have done right from the beginning.' Then I walked swiftly out of the shop.

I crossed the street and entered the pub. Sean was behind the bar, while Damien was dragging a crate of mixers across the floor. I strode up to the bar and noticed the change in Sean's face immediately. He looked faintly embarrassed.

'Sean, what's going on? Your sister wouldn't serve me in the shop!'

Damien came over and joined us. 'The boss man has got it into his head that you're a spy,' he said under his breath, as if his father was lurking in some dark corner. 'We can't serve you.'

'I don't want a drink,' I said. 'I just want to use the phone.'

'He hates anybody bringing up the old days,' Damien said. 'I did warn you.'

'He's showing all the signs of a bad conscience,' I retorted.

They both shrugged.

'What exactly was it that offended him?'

'Not sure – something about broken dreams.'

'It happens to the best of us,' I said bitterly.

They both looked away. 'Could I have some change for the phone?' I asked them, 'or is that out of bounds too?'

Sean opened the till and handed me some coins.

'I'm sorry if I've offended anybody,' I said in the silence, 'but believe me, that wasn't the intention.'

'I told you he was an unpredictable ould bastard,' Damien said.

'Yes, you did,' I replied. 'I should have listened.'

TJ answered the phone at Cahill and Ryan – sounding his normal self, to my relief. I explained what had happened with the car and he said, 'I can get over around lunch time, not before.'

'Thanks. I think the starter motor might have gone.'

'I'll take a look at it for you.' There was a silence, then he said, 'Look, I'm sorry if I went a bit overboard the other night. You have that effect on me.'

'That's all right,' I replied, relieved that he at least hadn't gone cold on me. 'I haven't forgotten I owe you that drink, by the way.'

'Nor have I! Talk to you later on today.' And he was gone.

I walked slowly back through the village deep in thought, and it seemed to me that people recoiled from me as I went. An old man crossed the road as I approached, and two women standing in a doorway fell silent as I passed. Had Tom Murphy somehow managed to turn the whole village against me? Had he recognised me and imagined I had come back to settle an old score? Damien had referred to that bit about broken dreams – had the old man read it as a double entendre, and guessed I was on the trail of the past? I thought again of the song 'Maggie', and how he had seemed to be singing about Mother.

Yet there had to be more to it than that. The whole business was a mystery, as it always had been. Aunt G was right, I concluded uneasily; I should have stayed away.

TJ arrived at lunch time, with a tow van to take Fernando back to the garage.

'Would you like to eat before you leave?' I offered. 'It's the least I can do.'

'Thanks,' he answered formally, and followed me into the cottage. He had brought another present for Jean, this time a model of a sailing boat. He had varnished the deck and painted the hull a creamy white. It reminded me of *Jolie Brise*.

'A memento,' he said, handing it to me.

'Thank you,' I said, wondering miserably if this was some kind of parting present.

He seemed removed from me too, a barrier between us. I busied myself in the kitchen with a plate of sandwiches, then brought them in on a tray with a can of beer and a Coke.

'I've had a bad morning, what with one thing and another,' I told him. 'First the car wouldn't start, then Ger wouldn't serve me in the shop.'

'I heard about it,' he said, without much interest. 'I spoke to Sean this morning.'

'I didn't write anything bad,' I said, sipping my Coke, 'that's what puzzles me. I know he doesn't think much of the *Wicklow Herald*, but . . .'

'He found out about Great Aunt Matilda,' he cut in. 'That you were her niece.'

So that was it! I hadn't even considered that possibility. Ger must have told him.

'God, I don't believe it . . . All because of an old feud that started ages ago, that has nothing to do with me! No wonder there are so many problems in this country! People just can't forget the past!'

'Let them get on with it,' TJ said irritably. 'It's all a load of bullshit anyway.'

He shifted in his chair as if eager to change the subject.

'There's a nice breeze out there – I feel like taking the rest of the afternoon off and going up the Sugar Loaf to fly. Come with me,' he suggested. 'It'll do you good to get some fresh air.'

'Maybe I shouldn't be seen with you, either,' I said gloomily.

'I don't give a flying feck what people think,' he said, getting up. 'Come on, you can be my noseman.'

I smiled. The way he spoke, his expressions and devil-may-care attitude, reminded me of Jeanette. 'What about Fernando?'

'We'll bring him to the garage on the way, and pick up the van and the gear,' he replied. He was back to his old self again. The barrier between us had gone.

'Jean's still asleep,' I told him.

'Then we'll wake him up.'

'You have a solution for everything, don't you?' I joked.

'You're the one finding all the problems!'

We picked up the van and the equipment and set off for the mountain, with Jean wedged between us.

'Take these broken wings and learn to fly . . .' TJ sang, in the wrong key, making Jean laugh delightedly. I smiled, thinking he hadn't inherited his father's extraordinary singing voice. His talent lay with his hands.

We turned off the main road, and followed a steep winding lane, jagged rocks poised above us.

'This is Rocky Valley,' said TJ, and as the road levelled I saw the purple edge of the hills in the distance. We drove parallel to the mountain for a few miles, passing a scattered group of tinker caravans where freckled children with pale red hair played in the fields, and a woman with a distended stomach stared as we passed by. In the same field, a few ragged horses were tied to a fence.

'My roots,' said TJ cynically. 'Tinkers – or travelling people, as they're now called.'

'You don't look like immediate family,' I told him, trying to lighten the moment.

'I've inherited my father's looks, for my sins,' he said briefly.

He pulled into a gravelled car park, opened the gate, then drove along a rocky path up the mountain. The track grew steeper as we went, and stones thumped the van beneath us.

TJ pulled to a halt saying, 'Can't go any further – we'll destroy the sump. 'Fraid we'll have to carry the gear from here.'

I climbed out of the van, lifting Jean, and stared around in awe. The view was spectacular. To the right stretched the glittering sea, a ferry moving like a phantom on the horizon; to the left, a tapestry of undulating fields in different shades of green; in front of us stood the Sugar Loaf, as Aunt G had painted it, with its sprinkling of white rocks. I felt the pull of the wind, and wondered if TJ would be able to fly, for it seemed to be gusting from the east.

TJ unstrapped the equipment from the roof rack and laid it on the ground.

'It's a bit of a sweat, but it's worth it,' he said. He picked up the long canvas bag and hoisted it effortlessly on one shoulder. I took the other end, while Jean ran alongside us, shouting into the wind. Groups of sheep parted and scampered away over the rocks as we approached. The kite grew heavier as we went, my shoulder beginning to ache from the weight of it.

'Nearly there,' said TJ encouragingly. Now I knew why he was so fit – I was gasping for breath by the time we reached the ridge. The wind was stronger up here; I drew my windcheater closer round me, and crammed my hands into the pockets.

TJ laid the equipment on the ground, unzipping the canvas bag. He tested the wind direction using the grass trick, then spread the sails. 'Hold the control bar for me, would you, while I set it up?' he said.

It took a while. I watched him put in the battens to stiffen the kite, and then he was strapping himself into his harness and tying on the knee hangers, explaining what everything was as he went along.

'This is my favourite launching spot,' he was saying. 'I used to come up here when things got really bad at home.'

'When was that?' I inquired.

'After I came back from the States, and the ould man and I were fighting like cats and dogs. 'He grinned. 'Bastard couldn't get me up here!'

I had planned to tell him about the night in the pub when his father had sung that haunting love song, but something stopped me.

'How long did you live at home?' I asked instead.

'Oh, about twenty-four hours! Then he fired me from the pub. He was pissed out of his mind, one night, and took a swing at me. Said I was a layabout and that nobody would ever employ me. I went and lived in County Cork then, with some friends of mine who have a farm. Good guys – grow their own grass and live off the land – but I got restless after a while. I came back and met Kevin hang-gliding one weekend. He asked me to come and work in the garage for his old man. It's worked out well so far. I manage to avoid the boss man – and see the family . . .' He pulled on his quilted flying suit, disgressing suddenly. 'There's a red flag in the last field just before the tinkers' caravans – you can see it from here.' He pointed somewhere to the left of him. 'That's where I intend to land, with a bit of luck . . . If not, come and pick me up – here.' He threw me the keys of the van, then hooked the harness to the kite.

The wind seemed to be buffeting me from behind now, as I held onto the nose. TJ lay horizontal on his harness to test his position, then said, 'OK, you'd better keep clear now.' I let go of the nose and moved aside. He took a couple of steps, then rose and sped like an arrow across the green fields.

I held Jean's hand as we made our way down the steep path towards the van, watching TJ circling above us.

I thought, we're both rootless, directionless, drifting with the wind . . . Was that what drew me to him? Or was it the fact that he made few demands? There was something so relaxing about his company, I felt as if I had known him for years.

He missed the field with the red flag, and came down in a patch of scratchy gorse beyond it. Jean and I ran towards him, and helped him pull the kite free of the bushes.

'Overshot that time,' he said with a grin. He unhooked himself and took off his helmet. Jean immediately climbed under the kite as if it were a tent, and TJ turned to me and smiled.

We stared at one another without speaking. This time we both moved towards each other at once, as if we'd suddenly heard the boom of a distant gun and must set off on that unknown course together . . .

The kiss was like a betrayal. I felt my body straining forwards, and closed my eyes. The wind was whipping around us, but I was no longer aware of the cold. I smelt the rough wool smell of him, and my senses reeled.

Then he let go, causing me to stumble back in confusion. He lit a cigarette, cupping his hand against the wind. The breeze blew his dark curls back from his face, making him look younger; almost boyish. I wondered if it was some belated sense of exhilaration that had prompted that sudden kiss, then I heard him say, 'I love you, Emily. You know that, don't you?'

A number of different emotions whirled around in my head. For a moment I couldn't speak.

'It's OK,' he said finally. 'No conditions attached. You can just be my nosewoman for the moment.'

I smiled, my heart still pounding. 'I'd be mad to turn down an offer like that,' I replied.

It was only when he had packed up the equipment, and TJ had hoisted Jean onto his shoulders and was carrying him towards the van, that I thought again of that kiss and realised how easy it would be to let things take their course. He loved Jean . . . he would take care of both of us, there would be no more lonely nights . . . But TJ was a Murphy – from a family which had, according to Aunt G, 'brought nothing but ill on everyone around them'.

It was growing dark now, and as he drove back through Rocky Valley towards the village, I realised it was the first evening in ages that I hadn't thought about Michel. It was as if the more painful memories had been swept away by TJ's kiss . . .

As we approached the Railway Cottage, I looked up and spotted a shooting star, travelling away from me at great speed across the darkening sky.

Chapter Thirty-Nine

Our meetings became more frequent. I would watch him take off from Devil Hill, or if the wind was blowing in the wrong direction we'd climb the Sugar Loaf, hoisting the equipment between us up to the ridge.

When the weather was wrong for hang-gliding, we'd go for long walks on the beach, ending up in O'Brien's, or sometimes we just stayed in the cottage and talked while Jean played on the rug in front of the fireplace. I looked forward to his visits more and more, but I didn't want to think of the future, nor could I bring myself to consider the past. For the first time in my life, I lived totally in the present.

He lived the kind of bohemian lifestyle where time meant nothing. He ate when he was hungry, rather than at mealtimes; slept irregular hours, or sometimes didn't go to bed at all. Once he left for five days without a word – afterwards, I learnt he'd been to visit his friends in County Cork. I sometimes had the feeling that he might disappear out of my life for ever.

He was astute and charming, romantic and unpredictable, but oddly naïve in some ways. On the surface, our relationship was friendly and light-hearted, as if we'd known one another all our lives, but I knew he was waiting for some kind of commitment from me.

He finally cleaned the kitchen, and I cooked dinner for him one evening – an evening that was perhaps a turning point.

I had planned to make him a cheese fondue.

'A what do?' he inquired when I told him so.

'TJ, don't tell me you've never eaten a cheese fondue?'

'Is it one of those melted jobs? I'd hardly call that proper food,' he joked.

'You'll see,' I said, wondering if I'd ever be able to buy the right cheeses in Wicklow.

I drove into town the following day and found a store that sold kitchen equipment. There was a dusty fondue set at the back of the shop they had abandoned all hope of selling, which I bought, then crossed the road and walked down the main street, looking in shop windows as I went. I paused at the butcher's, wondering if I should buy some meat instead, and saw a row of pigs' trotters lined up against the window. Underneath, was a notice reading PIGS FEET – VERY LOW MILEAGE. I smiled and wandered on, past the Bank of Ireland and the betting office, then spotted a delicatessen on the right and went in, racking my brains in an effort to remember Michel's recipe.

I bought a selection of imported cheeses and some bread that was close enough to a French baguette, then went into the supermarket further down and bought a bag of new potatoes, garlic, mustard, cornflour, cayenne, salad things and two bottles of dry white wine. For dessert, I got a fresh cream cake from the cake shop. Pleased with my purchases, I set off for TJ's house.

He had laid the table and placed a red rose in the centre. He wore a white tee-shirt and clean jeans for once, and had smoothed his hair back from his face: I stared at him, aware of an odd twinge inside.

I grated the cheese and put the potatoes on to boil, then went into the sitting room and sat down beside him. He had put on some rather dated rock music and switched off the main light.

We had drunk half a bottle of wine by the time the fondue was ready. Our mood was giddy, but there was an underlying tension in the air.

He put his arm around me then, and said, 'Stay with me tonight, Emily?'

'There's Jean . . .'

'We'll bring him over.'

I hesitated.

He pulled me into his arms and kissed my neck, his hands moving slowly down the length of my body. He smelt of soap and turf fires. I heard the splash of water coming from the kitchen – the potatoes boiling over – and gently extricated myself.

'Wait a minute,' I said breathlessly.

He followed me into the kitchen.

Once again, doubts assailed me. I thought of taking Jean out of his bed, and bringing him into another strange house – then I thought fleetingly of Michel. 'Maybe another night,' I said finally.

He shrugged, as if puzzled by my reaction, and poured himself another glass of wine.

I set the pot of melted cheese on the burner and we both sat down.

'It's bloody good wine,' he said, 'but I think I'll have a beer all the same.'

'They say wine goes better with it, makes it easier to digest.'

'Who are "they", anyway?' he inquired, heading for the fridge and coming back with a can of Smithwicks.

'I don't know – the experts.' TJ always made his own rules. I remembered Aunt G talking of Murphy's Law all those years ago, and smiled.

'Where did you learn to cook this, anyway?' he inquired.

'From watching Michel.'

'Ahh . . . Mr Perfect could cook too?'

I nodded.

'I still don't understand it,' he said, taking a large swig from his can, and sitting back.

'What?'

'Why he didn't come chasing after you. I would never have let you go.'

I concentrated on stirring the fondue with the bread, as Michel had taught me, to stop it from burning.

'I suppose he must have accepted it as well,' I said finally.

'Accepted what?'

'That we were too different . . .' I paused. 'Mother was always warning Charlotte and me not to fall in love with a foreigner, but neither of us listened.'

He considered this for a moment, then said, 'You don't choose who you fall in love with. It just happens.'

I nodded. 'She knew that better than anybody else . . .' I paused again, not sure if I should go on.

'You still love him, don't you?' he said, looking at me intently.

I fished out a piece of bread that had fallen into the pot.

'It's over,' I replied.

'Is it?'

I nodded.

'I'm not so sure,' he said.

He got up, then, and walked around to the back of my chair; put his hand on my neck as he had that first time in the garage. I remained motionless. 'It's OK,' he whispered. 'I'll wait.'

I said nothing to Aunt G. I seldom went near the village now, but drove into Wicklow to shop and kept away from Murphy's Lounge Bar. TJ and I continued to meet up with the others in O'Brien's – Damien and Sean seemed to forget about the business with the *Wicklow Herald*, and the boss man's antipathy towards me. Ger remained hostile, but I rarely met her now, as she was seeing a boy from Wexford and spent most of her time with him.

When Sinead didn't come to the cottage one evening as arranged, I didn't think anything of it. But when there was still no sign of her after a week, I rang her at home, and her mother informed me coldly that she wouldn't be babysitting for me any longer.

'Could I speak to her at least?' I asked, taken aback. Jean was constantly asking for 'Snade', and I too missed her quiet company.

'She's not here,' replied the woman firmly. I wondered then if it was something to do with TJ and me, and Ger had been talking.

'Then perhaps you could tell her Emily called,' I said.

'She's very busy studying for her inter,' replied the cold voice. (The inter were the school exams that took place in the summer.)

I put down the receiver, frustrated. 'What's going on?' I said out loud for the umpteenth time.

The following week I hired a young girl from the village to take her place, but I never felt quite as comfortable leaving Jean with her as I had with Sinead.

Spring was drifting into summer, the days lengthening. The weather was warmer now; honeysuckle grew around the door of the Railway Cottage and the surrounding fields turned yellow with gorse.

TJ and I had taken to walking along the beach in the opposite direction from Heronlough, to a sandy stretch where Jean could paddle in the shallow water. One afternoon we got caught in a heavy shower, so we made a dash for the cottage. TJ scooped Jean up in his arms and ran along the railway track, his feet pounding against the broken sleepers, while I followed some paces behind.

By the time we reached the cottage we were all soaked to the skin. I changed Jean out of his wet clothes and saw he was rubbing his eyes tiredly, so put him into my bed and went back into the main room, where TJ was building a fire – it was always cold in the cottage, even when the sun was shining outside. TJ had taken off his wet shirt, and wore nothing underneath it. The muscles stood out on his arms, and his chest was covered in fine dark hairs. An involuntary shiver ran down my spine, and he said, 'Come over here, and let me warm you.'

I moved across the room, no longer in control of my senses, and the next moment he had pulled me roughly against him and we were kissing. He took off my cardigan and traced his fingers down my neck. 'God, you're a beauty,' he whispered, then scooped me up in his arms and carried me over to the sofa.

My heart was beating erratically; every nerve seemed to be on edge. I felt the weight of his body on top of me, and strained upwards to meet it. Behind us, I heard the muted sound of a love song on the radio, and felt his warm breath at my neck. He was kissing me all over, and I wound my arms tighter around him, not wanting to let go, knowing there was no turning back now . . .

The sound of a car coming up the lane, and the screech of brakes as it drew to a halt, recalled me with a start.

'TJ,' I whispered, 'did you hear something?'

'Shit,' he said, sitting up. He rolled off me, and looked around for something to cover him.

I quickly pulled my clothes together and smoothed my hair as the visitor started banging on the door. I heard a woman's voice call, 'Anybody at home?' and watched helplessly as Jacintha walked into the room.

There was a dreadful silence. Then she said, 'God bless us and save us!' staring at TJ in horror. She made the sign of the cross and looked away, as if the sight of him had deeply offended her.

'What is it, Jacintha?' I said, my face burning. She must consider this the ultimate sin, I thought uncomfortably, for in her eyes I was married and always would be.

'What sort of carry-on is this?' she demanded harshly. 'And you a married woman and all!' She glared at TJ again. 'I tried to turn a blind eye, that time there in the pub, hoping 'twas nothing . . . But now I find yous together like this – may God forgive the two of ye!'

'Jacintha, please,' I said, trying to soothe her.

'Don't mind her,' said TJ. 'You should keep your nose out of other people's affairs,' he said loudly, as if she were deaf.

But Jacintha was retreating, backing away from us.

I went after her. 'What was it you wanted, Jacintha?' I asked gently, trying to hold her back, stem the shock in her eyes.

''Twas your aunt who wanted you to come over this afternoon and help her with some messages . . .' (Messages meant chores.) Her eyes didn't meet mine. 'I'm after doing the shopping with Seamus, and thought I'd drop by and see the young fellow – you never bring him over nowadays,' she added accusingly. 'Corrupting a poor wee child like that, God forgive the two of ye!'

I stared at her, speechless. Why was she reacting so violently, I wondered? Because I had in her eyes committed the fatal sin of adultery?

When she had gone, I sat down weakly on the sofa. 'That was awful!'

'Oh don't mind her,' TJ replied, lighting a cigarette, but I could tell he was shaken too. 'They're like that around here – living in the fear of God.'

'I've never seen her like that before,' I said, reaching for a cigarette too. 'She completely overreacted.'

TJ wandered into the kitchen and came back with two cans of beer, more composed.

'Now where were we?' he asked, sitting down beside me and stroking my hair.

But Jacintha had frozen any desire that was left, and I edged away from him, uneasy now.

He got up and paced the room. 'Jesus, this place gets me down at times!' he said moodily, gathering his things together.

'Where are you going?' I asked, not wanting him to leave, yet not wanting to continue where we had left off.

'For a walk,' he replied shortly.

'It's still raining,' I pointed out.

But he didn't answer, just went silently out of the cottage.

Chapter Forty

TJ didn't return to the cottage that afternoon. I guessed he was either in O'Brien's or out flying, and didn't try to track him down, unsure again about the direction things were going. But I longed for his company all the same. Once it had stopped raining, I went down to the beach to watch the fishing trawlers setting out across the bay. The business with Jacintha had made me uneasy. I couldn't stop dwelling on it.

That night I lay awake, my heart beating erratically, unable to pinpoint the root of my fear, knowing only it was tied up with the future.

If there was to be a future for us here, then I was going to have to contact Michel and embark on a legal battle for custody of Jean. But if I lost, what then? Would I have access to him in the summer holidays, like other divorced couples who lived in different countries? Or perhaps, I thought fearfully, I'd be forced to take up residence in Switzerland, and live like Jeanette had done, within a twenty-mile radius?

Each scenario passed through my mind, until I was wide awake and trembling. I got up and made a pot of tea, then tiptoed into the other room and sat on the edge of Jean's bed to drink it. I watched him sleep, his fist clutching a chewed blanket, his black eyelashes fanning his cheeks, until it grew light outside, and the chatter of birdsong began. I knew then I couldn't risk it – that all I could do was wait and pray that, with the passage of time, Michel would let go, and somehow I'd be able to make a new life for us here.

There was nobody I could talk to about it. I was unwilling to go to Heronlough and face Jacintha's accusing stare, but knew it would look odd if I stayed away much longer.

The following day, when there was still no sign of TJ, I drove over to Heronlough, hoping to make amends. I bought some things from the chemist in Wicklow for Jacintha, lavender soap and talc and a bunch of freesias for Aunt G, then set off with Jean for the house.

It was a warm day, with the almond smell of gorse in the air. I passed fields of rape, golden in the sun, and campion and cow parsley growing among the hedgerows. There was no sign of the Daimler in the driveway, and I wondered with a sinking heart if Aunt G was out and I'd have to face Jacintha alone. I pulled up in front of the house, unstrapped Jean, then went around the back and slipped into the kitchen.

I knew immediately something was wrong. Jacintha didn't hear me enter. She was sitting at the kitchen table, staring into space as if she'd seen a ghost. Beside her was an open bottle of brandy, which she made no effort to hide from me. There was something alarming about the vacant look in her eyes, and the way she sat so still.

'Jacintha?' I said, approachingly warily.

She turned and looked straight through me.

'Oh, 'tis you,' she said, without animosity – more like indifference.

Jean rushed forwards to greet her, brandishing his toy rabbit, but she didn't respond.

'Are you all right?' I ventured.

'*I'm* all right,' she replied in an odd, echoey voice. ''Tis Geraldine . . .'

'Aunt G . . . Why, what's happened?' I asked with a stab of fear.

'She collapsed this morning – they took her into the hospital – 'twas my fault for telling her . . .'

'Oh, Christ,' I said, forgetting she loathed blasphemy in others. 'Telling her what exactly?'

But Jacintha was rambling on. 'Seamus is standing by in case anything happens . . . I caught the bus back . . . The telephone lines are down again . . .'

I watched, distressed, as a tear slid down her worn face. Aunt G was more like a sister to her than an employer, Heronlough like a home.

'Which hospital?' I asked.

''Tis on the Wexford Road,' she replied automatically, 'after Dunegan . . . Follow the coast road, then take one of them side roads, after the village.'

'I'll go there now.'

She nodded, still staring into the distance.

I paused at the door. 'How bad is she?' I inquired.

'Not good . . . 'Tis the emphysemia, robbing the breath from her body.'

The hospital was a large Victorian house overlooking the sea. I took a wrong turn, and ended up on a narrow lane that led down to the beach, but at last I was back on the coast road, and saw the sign reading *Ospidéal*.

The Daimler was parked outside in the car park, where Seamus paced up and down like a chauffeur, smoking a cigarette. Below us, the sea crashed against the shore.

'I was going to come down to you,' he said, as I pulled to a sharp halt.

'Is she bad?' I asked fearfully.

' 'Tis all under control now,' he replied, but I didn't believe him.

Jean had started howling, as he always did in the midst of a crisis.

'Could I leave him with you for a minute?' I asked. 'I don't want him disturbing everybody.'

'You could of course,' he said. 'Come here young fellow, we'll go for a walk on the beach.' But Jean was trying to climb into the Daimler.

'Don't let him play around in the car,' I warned, rushing towards the entrance of the hospital.

She was attached to some sort of breathing apparatus, two plastic leads up her nostrils. She could speak, but her voice was low and rasping. Her eyes were shadowed and puffy, filled with indignation at finding herself in such a situation.

'Dear girl,' she greeted me painfully, 'you got the message? Isn't this a nuisance? Don't look so alarmed, it's just to help regulate my breathing.'

I walked over and sat on the edge of her bed. 'What happened?' I asked, taking her stiff hand in mine. It looked blue with cold, as if the blood was no longer circulating there.

'I couldn't catch my breath . . . But it's all right now, this wretched machine is doing it for me.'

'You poor thing,' I said, shock and relief mingling.

There was a silence, the kind of silence that normally preceded one of her lectures.

'Now listen to me,' she began with difficulty. 'I want you to go back to that husband of yours, before it's too late. You still love one another . . . Forget about the silly things you said, and take the little boy back to his father.'

I stared at her in alarm, wondering what had brought this on. Was it some sort of last request, before she passed away?

'I know everything, child. You can't even shop in the village any more, now they know who you are . . . What in the name of God were you doing, writing articles about the Murphys?'

I flushed and looked away. 'I wanted to tell you, but knew it would infuriate you.'

'And now you're going about with the older boy?'

'Jacintha told you,' I stated, cringing at the memory of that awful scene.

'Half the village seems to know about it,' she replied, 'but yes, she told me.'

'He's been so good to me, Aunt G . . . I didn't see any harm in it.'

She tried to sit up, then fell back weakly against the pillows. 'What's been going on between the two of you?' she demanded in a strained voice.

'Not much,' I said, still unable to meet her eyes. 'He's a good friend, although I know he'd like to be more. Jacintha walked in at a rather inopportune moment, but nothing happened . . .'

I felt I had betrayed her trust in me.

'Thank God for that! You're in love with him, aren't you?' she demanded.

'It's not the same as it was with Michel,' I answered after a pause. 'He makes no demands. We're so alike in some ways – just really good friends,' I concluded.

'Emily, don't you understand . . . That's all you can ever be,' she said.

I stared at her with a terrible unease. 'What are you talking about?'

'Emily, you poor, poor child!' She reached across and took my hand. 'Thomas John Murphy is your half brother,' she said painfully. Then she took a deep breath and closed her eyes, as if the effort had proved too much for her.

317

Somewhere in the distance I heard the caw of a rook, and closer the sound of the lunch trolleys being wheeled in. There was a thumping sensation inside me, as if something were banging against my ribs, my heart pounding like the waves on the shore below.

'He can't possibly be,' I said in a dull whisper. 'It's not possible – TJ, my brother. . . ?'

Her eyes were fixed on me. 'I wish it wasn't true,' she answered. 'God, how I wish it wasn't.'

The room spun. I put my head in my hands and felt all sense of reality slip away. Now I was the one finding it difficult to catch my breath.

When Aunt G spoke her voice seemed to come from far away, echoing through the years.

'Tom Murphy was married when he met your mother,' she began, 'although he never told Peg that, of course. He married one of the O'Farrells – Jacintha knows Moira quite well. But one woman wasn't enough for Tom Murphy – he was no sooner wed than he started straying.'

She spoke as if he were a wild dog, roaming the countryside.

'Your mother was not the only one,' she added grimly. 'There was a young itinerant girl.'

'TJ told me his mother was a tinker,' I cut in. I was grasping at straws, anything.

But Aunt G had moved on. 'Peg was terribly naïve, she had no idea of the facts of life . . . My sister was never good at explaining things. She had a Victorian upbringing, where little girls should be seen and not heard. Murphy seduced Peg – and of course there was a baby.'

'Oh my God.'

'That's why she was thrown out of the house – it was a huge scandal for the family; Tom Murphy's child would never be accepted by the Flavells.'

Finally, everything was starting to fall into place.

'Is that why she stayed in the Railway Cottage for so long?' I asked.

'Yes, she lived there until her time came . . . she had nowhere else to go, the family cut her off without a penny. The nuns would have taken her in, but she didn't want that. I sold some of my paintings to make a bit of money, and we found a midwife, who came to deliver the baby . . .' She paused to gather breath. 'I'll never forget that day as long as I live. It was winter – I remember the Whooper swans had arrived. The cottage was as cold as the grave. Peg was in labour all night, she passed out at one stage – I thought we'd lost her, but she came round and battled on through the night. It took a terrible toll on her heart, leading to all those problems later on . . .' Aunt G's eyes were bright with tears. 'She was a brave woman, your mother,' she finished.

I had never thought of Mother as brave before. Now I felt a rush of admiration for her, and tears scalded my eyes.

'When it was all over, I brought the baby to the convent next door and asked the nuns to take care of him. I told them his mother had died and to approach Tom Murphy. The nuns informed Murphy they had reason to believe the boy was his, and that his mother was dead. Murphy asked no questions. Moira, his wife, had no say in the matter. They agreed to bring up the boy.'

Yet neither of them had accepted TJ as their own.

'What about the tinker woman who died giving birth?'

'That was the story they told – and nobody could contest it; the tinkers had moved on, as is their way. It was thirty-eight years ago, remember.'

I stared at her, feeling my hopes fade.

I remembered the way Tom Murphy had stared at me in the pub that night.

'He must have thought I was Mother back from the dead,' I said after a silence.

'If he remembers at all. According to Jacintha, he's become very confused from the drink. The true story has been buried over the years. Thomas, of course, believes he is the son of a dead tinker woman. I'm probably the only one who knows what really happened.'

I remembered the letter Aunt G had written years ago, saying 'she left a part of herself behind'. Mother had left TJ behind. Then I thought of the conversation between Aunt G and Mother on that first visit to Heronlough. Mother hadn't been asking for news of Tom Murphy at all, but of Thomas, who had taken himself off across the water to America, desperate to get away from his father.

319

TJ, the brother I'd always wanted, had almost become my lover. I shivered in the warm hospital room, my mind flashing back to that wet afternoon in the Railway Cottage . . .

'Charlotte will have to be told,' I said later, wishing suddenly Michel were here. He would know what to say; he always knew.

Aunt G was tiring now. She closed her eyes, and I feared that the burden of all this had exhausted her.

'Is this what brought it on?' I asked. 'TJ and me, making you collapse like that?'

'I was on my way over to tell you . . . Must have missed my footing on the stairs, knocked the breath out of my body . . . couldn't seem to get it back.'

I looked at her guiltily. She had tried so hard to keep me away, but I hadn't listened, and had almost killed her as a result.

'I'm so sorry,' I wept. 'It's all my fault you're not well.'

'Don't be worrying about me,' she said. 'I'll be fine. I'm going to see you right before I pass on.'

I remembered the dilemma in Mother's eyes before she died. 'Why didn't she tell me?' I said out loud.

'I think she would have, only she didn't live to tell the tale. Your father was very much against it. He didn't think there was any point upsetting everybody . . . and I promised to keep my mouth shut . . . Besides, there was no reason, until this happened. I never imagined you'd come and live over here.'

'Nor did I, ' I said, thinking it was more than a twist of fate.

'When you did, I wrongly imagined you'd lead a different kind of life. Still, things have changed now, there are no longer the social barriers – and of course you were curious about your mother, you always were a curious child!'

'I wonder if I should tell TJ,' I said.

Aunt G hesitated. 'That is something you're going to have to decide,' she said finally.

'God, Aunt G, do you realise it would have meant – incest?' I was testing the word for the first time.

'Shh, child. Don't be dwelling on what didn't happen . . . You weren't to know.'

She closed her eyes again and seemed to drift into sleep. I sat there watching her, afraid that, like Mother, she would never wake up again.

Chapter Forty-One

Aunt G came out of hospital the following week. Seamus moved her bed downstairs, and the drawing room was turned into a bedroom so she no longer had to use the stairs.

I brought my typewriter over to Heronlough and spent the afternoon with her, while Jean played in the garden under the steely gaze of Jacintha.

Jacintha now gave me a wide berth. I knew it would be some time before she would warm to me again.

Aunt G insisted one day she felt strong enough to walk down to the lough, so we set off together across the lawn, Jean trotting along beside us. She talked openly about Mother and Tom Murphy as we went – how they had met one another at the village fête, and he had seduced her with his love songs and his charm. It would be easy to succumb, I thought, thinking again of Damien who had inherited the gift. Only I had been searching for something deeper, to replace the hole left by Michel . . . and had found it in TJ.

I listened, spellbound, understanding finally why Mother had been the way she was. She had been carrying around the burden of TJ all those years. It had been this that had sapped her spirit, turned her into the ailing, nervy person she was, escaping into romantic novels to forget her own thwarted love affair. It must have taken every ounce of her courage to leave as she had – leaving her baby behind, and starting a new life in England. While in County Wicklow, a boy had grown up knowing only that he didn't belong.

I thought of all those wasted years – years when I might have known TJ. Yet there was still that feeling that I had known him all my life. In retrospect, our relationship had been almost fraternal from the start. Was it this that had caused me to hold back for so long? Jacintha had only known the half of it when she had walked in on us, I concluded unhappily. Adultery was one thing, what might have happened another . . .

Sick at heart, I returned to the cottage that night knowing I had to make a decision.

The following day I was up early, finishing an article for the *Wicklow Herald*, when there was a knock on the door and there was TJ. He seemed full of the joys of summer, tanned and smiling, his hair a tangle of wild curls. He looked, I thought, more like the 'rough diamond' than ever. He handed me a bunch of flowers and another carving he had made for Jean, a painted toy engine.

'Come in,' I said, with a pounding heart.

He said without preamble, 'I've had a bloody brilliant idea. I'm taking you and Jean away for a week, to the West. We'll drive over to the cliffs of Moher, and you can help launch me from there. I know a little place we can stay – belongs to a good friend of mine.'

I wasn't taking in the details. I was studying him, searching for a sign, a look, an expression, but there was nothing. Would I have seen anything if I had known all along, I wondered? Had anyone else noticed a resemblance between us? I thought of Kevin Ryan, who always seemed to be staring at us oddly. 'Is that really your name, Emily Summers?' he had said. He had seen something. Whereas I, through curiosity and a certain romanticism, had seen the 'rough diamond' as he must have once looked.

'Are you all right?' TJ inquired, noticing my expression.

'Yes, fine; I was in a daze.'

'You're not still dwelling on what happened last time, are you?'

'No.' I shifted my gaze away from him. 'It's just been a bit hectic recently. Aunt G collapsed.'

'Is she all right?' he asked.

'Yes, she came out of hospital yesterday, but she has to take it easy now. We moved her bed downstairs.'

'I'm sorry.' He lit a cigarette then said, 'Is there something else? You seem – different.'

I said nothing.

'It's Mr Perfect, isn't it? You're going back to him?'

'No,' I said, my mouth dry. For the first time in ages, I longed for a stiff drink. A whiskey, but there was nothing but beer in the fridge.

'I could do with a double whiskey,' I told him.

He didn't seem to find it an odd request, in spite of the time of day. 'I'll go to the pub and get us a bottle,' he said, getting up. 'Give me a couple of minutes. Are you sure you're all right?'

'Yes,' I lied.

'I'll take Jean with me, he'd enjoy the ride.'

'Don't forget to strap him in,' I called after him, but they had already gone.

I sat there staring out of the window, my mind in a turmoil. By the time he returned, with a bottle of Jamieson, I had made my decision.

He poured me a hefty measure, and one for himself, then handed me the glass. We both lit cigarettes.

'About that trip,' he was saying. 'We could leave on Friday evening – it'll take us a while to get up there . . .'

'TJ,' I interrupted.

He must have misinterpreted the look on my face. 'Single rooms, if you want.' he added.

I couldn't speak.

'Would you think about it, at least?' He knocked back his whiskey and poured himself another one.

'Yes – I mean, no . . .'

'What is it, Emily? Something's wrong, isn't it? What has that old biddy being saying about me now?'

'TJ, there's something I have to tell you,' I said.

'You're going back to Mr Perfect, aren't you?'

'No,' I replied.

'Then what? You're madly in love with me after all, but worried that I kick with the wrong foot?' he said with a wink.

'No,' I said. 'I mean, yes. I do care about you very much, but I can't . . .'

'I knew it,' he sighed. 'Another platonic Patricia, give me patience.'

'We can't fall in love with one another, TJ,' I said finally. 'We go back too far.'

He seemed uneasy now. He emptied his glass again. 'Now you're being pedantic.'

'TJ, your father and my mother . . .'

There was a dreadful silence. Neither of us moved.

He went completely rigid. 'No!' The denial sounded like the

crack of a pistol shot. There was something terrifying about the expression on his face.

'Yes,' I said hollowly.

'I don't believe you – you're making it up, imagining things, like one of your novels . . .'

'My aunt finally told me,' I said. My throat seemed to have closed up, so I could barely speak. 'My mother . . . *our* mother came here to this cottage thirty-eight years ago, and gave birth to you . . . Your Father knew nothing about it. He was married to your stepmother by then. The tinker woman was just a cover . . . nobody died giving birth to you,' I added, as if that might offer a shred of comfort.

He wasn't looking at me. His face had turned a deathly white, his expression closed, as if he wasn't taking any of it in.

'My aunt took you to the convent and handed you over to the nuns. They eventually brought you back to your father, saying your mother had died. But she hadn't died at all – she'd left Ireland on the mailboat. It was all hushed up by the Flavells, who considered it a huge scandal, and nobody in the village knew.'

He grabbed the bottle of whiskey, and for a moment I thought he was about to throw it across the room. Then he lifted it to his mouth, and took a deep draught. 'You're a liar,' he said, wiping his mouth on his sleeve. 'A fecking liar! That's the most twisted thing I ever heard.'

'TJ, listen to me, it's the truth . . . We've got to accept it! Why would I make up a thing like that?'

'Because you've lost touch with reality!'

'Not this time, TJ.'

I stared at him, realising that I had made a terrible mistake. He couldn't absorb it, would never accept it. He already hated his father, and this was the final straw.

He stood up, still clutching the bottle of whiskey and cursing, then turned around and smashed his fist against the wall. The pain must have been excruciating; I saw it cross his face. He snatched the van keys from the floor and, almost tripping over Jean, stumbled blindly towards the door.

'TJ, please, let's talk, don't leave like this!'

'You're deranged,' he said. 'A real nut case.'

'You told me yourself about your father straying – chasing the local gentry.' I remembered how he had said 'anybody can be a father'.

'You're off the wall, woman. You should see somebody about your condition, it's known as dementia!'

'TJ, wait!'

He paused at the door, swaying slightly. 'If you didn't want to get involved with me, Emily, you only had to say so,' he said, chilling me to the bone.

I knew then that not only was there no hope of him ever accepting it, but that I had destroyed our relationship completely.

'TJ!' I called after him, a desperate, futile last attempt that was drowned out by the noise of the van as he accelerated down the lane.

I stood there for a moment, then went back into the cottage and lay down shakily on the sofa.

An hour later I was still lying there, numb with shock. What now? I thought in despair. The silence in the room was becoming oppressive as the minutes ticked by. Unable to sit there a moment longer, I woke Jean and, without thinking what I was doing, bundled him into the back of the Fiat and set off after TJ.

Chapter Forty-Two

Outside, a strong wind had got up; the sky looked dark and bruised with rain clouds. I drove first to the garage, in case he had decided to go back to work, pulled into the forecourt and ran into the office. Kevin was there. He looked up as I entered and said, 'How's it going?'

'Fine,' I answered briefly. 'Have you seen TJ, by any chance?'

'He was here earlier – they've gone flying. Himself and Damien.'

'In this weather? Where?'

'Sugar Loaf, I presume – they wouldn't be able to fly from Devil Hill today.'

'Oh my God,' I said, knowing that TJ had been in no state to fly. I turned and ran back to the car, then drove in the direction of the Sugar Loaf, filled with foreboding. I felt the pull of the wind as I went. It bent the trees and blew the leaves across the road. I remembered that afternoon we had climbed up to the ridge together, lugging the equipment between us, and how he had said, 'I often come up here when I'm feeling bad, to forget my problems.' But today the wind seemed to be gusting from every direction.

The tinkers had moved on, leaving a burnt patch of grass and a pile of rubbish behind them. Some rags were laid out to dry on the bushes, and a couple of abandoned dogs sniffed at remnants of old food. I followed the road to the gravel car park, got out to open the iron gates, and drove up a short way, until I heard the thump of rocks beneath and, afraid to drive any further, pulled to a halt on the grassy verge. There was no sign of the van; I wondered if they had parked the other side. I unstrapped Jean and started up towards the ridge.

'Sheeps,' said Jean excitedly, running along beside me. The path grew steeper, and Jean held up his arms to be carried. He was a dead weight. I kept having to stop to rest and catch my breath, and all the time I had this dreadful feeling something had happened.

I looked up, hoping to catch sight of the kites circling, but there was nothing – just a few birds wheeling in the darkening sky. We reached the ridge and looked around, but there was no sign of the van. I thought I saw a tiny speck glinting far out to sea, too big for a bird, but it faded away, so I turned and made my way back to the car.

I stopped at the garage on the way back and spoke to Kevin again.

'They weren't up there. They couldn't have tried to fly from Devil Hill, could they?'

He shook his head. 'More likely they've gone to O'Brien's for a jar.'

'I'll try there,' I said.

But there was no van outside O'Brien's, so I set off for TJ's house, panicked now. The house was deserted. I sat there for a few minutes, not knowing where to look next, then drove despondently back to the cottage.

I tossed and turned most of that night, remembering the stunned look on TJ's face and wishing more than anything I could turn the clock back. Yet what other choice had there been? I thought, as the night wore on. I could have told him I never wanted to see him again, without any explanation . . . Said he was right, and I was going back to Michel. But I knew deep down that if it were to be done again, I would still tell him the truth.

When I finally slept, I dreamt we were making love on the sofa when suddenly there was a knock on the door. But instead of Jacintha it was Mother, back from the dead. She was saying, 'I wanted to tell you, Emily, but they were all against me . . .'

'It's too late, Mother,' I sobbed, then I woke up.

The following morning, I drove Jean over to Heronlough and left him with Jacintha, then went into Wicklow to drop off some work at the *Herald*. My eyes were burning from lack of sleep, and my head throbbed as if I had a hangover.

There was an unusual quietness about the place – the receptionist wasn't at her desk, and the phones were dead, as though everybody had decided to take the day off.

Michael was sitting in his office, staring out of the window, a half empty bottle of Paddy's Whiskey in front of him.

'Goodness, you're starting early today,' I said. 'What's the occasion?' Then I saw his face.

'TJ Murphy died last night,' he told me dully. 'Did you not know?'

I stood there immobile, shock waves running like rivers of ice down my spine. I had not known – only felt it in the stilly watches of the night.

I tried to speak, but no words came.

Then I watched in horror as Michael's face crumpled, and his body started to shake and wheeze like an old generator, tears running like rain water down his purple cheeks.

'How?' I said, when we had been sitting staring at one another across the cluttered room for what seemed like hours.

'Took off from Devil Hill alone, from what I can gather. The weather was bad – he landed in the sea.'

I remembered TJ talking about the cumulus nimbus, or storm clouds. 'They can suck you up and spit you out . . .' he'd said. I thought of the bottle of whiskey, and how he'd stormed out of the cottage still clutching it.

'I spoke to Kevin Ryan at the garage,' I was saying stupidly. 'Said he was with Damien . . . I can't believe he took off alone in those conditions.'

'You know TJ,' said Michael, wiping his streaming eyes. 'He always flew too close to the wind.'

He had known the risks involved, I thought, but had taken off anyway, to forget what I had told him.

Michael had moved on. He was talking about covering the story, but I hadn't taken any of it in.

'You're the only one who can do it, Emily, the only one who can do the piece . . . You and he were – ? Am I right?'

What was he trying to say? Lovers? Brother and sister?

I looked away. 'I can't do it, Michael,' I replied dully. 'I just can't. In fact I won't be doing anything more for the *Herald*. I've decided to move on,' I finished.

'Why, may I ask?'

'It's time I left,' I said, staring out of the grimy window over the harbour. A coal ship was sitting in the greasy water, waiting to sail.

Next port of call would be England . . . I would go, like Mother, leaving a part of myself behind.

'Where will you go?'

'I don't know yet, I haven't made up my mind. But whatever happens, I can't cover that story.'

'Not even in honour of TJ?'

I shook my head. 'No. You see . . .' I started to sob like a child. 'It was all my fault, it was because of me.'

He shot me a sideways glance. 'You need a rest,' he said kindly. 'Take a few days off – you look dreadful . . .'

I shook my head. 'No, I've made my decision. It's time I moved on anyway.'

He refilled his glass and took a large gulp. 'You're a good woman, Emily Summers, and a good writer. I don't know an awful lot about you, but I took to you straight away . . . In my view, running away never solved a damn thing!'

'I'm getting quite good at it,' I replied miserably.

'C'mon, have a drink,' he urged. 'It'll make you feel better.'

'No thanks,' I sobbed. 'It'll just make me feel worse.'

He stared at the amber-coloured liquid with a distant look. 'TJ was a real loner,' he was saying. 'He was looking for something – some identity, perhaps . . . He went to America to get away from the old man, escape his roots.'

Only to come back to Ireland and find them, I thought with irony.

'. . . met some woman there who broke his heart. Never really trusted women after that – but he trusted you, I know that.'

And I betrayed him, I thought, as I gathered my things together and left the office.

Chapter Forty-Three

'So you told him, and now you're blaming yourself,' Aunt G was saying. We were sitting in the kitchen at Heronlough and she had her arms around me, rocking me like a child. Behind us, Jacintha made tea and poured it into china cups. On the surface everything appeared normal, only I knew nothing could ever be the same again. I had dragged myself out of the ruins of an earthquake, and was now assessing the damage.

The day before, I had gone to the local doctor and for the first time in my life asked for some sleeping pills to get me through the night. Now my brain was fogged from lack of real sleep. I lit a cigarette in an effort to clear it.

'Why have you decided to carry the burden of this on your shoulders, on top of everything else?' Aunt G continued sternly.

'I don't know,' I wept.

'You know, child, we all have to make decisions in life, and then accept the consequences of our decisions . . . You didn't do anything wrong. He couldn't accept it – that's the dreadful part.'

'But if I hadn't told him?'

'It's no good thinking that. You did tell him, and you felt you were right to tell him.'

'Because he wanted us to be more than friends,' I told her.

I heard Jacintha's shocked intake of breath behind us, as she busied herself at the Aga. She'd hardly looked at me since learning the true story.

'You were a victim, Emily, along with everybody else. The course was already set when Peg fell in love with Tom Murphy – you were simply a catalyst. Now you can either spend the rest of your days blaming yourself, or you can get on with your life and make the best of it, like your mother had to. The choice is yours, Emily.'

I looked away, knowing she was right.

'Why don't you go and lie down for a while,' she suggested. 'We'll keep an eye on Jean for you. You look all in.'

'Maybe I will,' I said, getting up unsteadily.

'Guilt is a very self-indulgent emotion, child,' she said. 'Get rid of it. It'll only weigh you down.'

Jacintha suddenly turned around and faced me. 'I'll bring you up a nice cup of soup later,' she said. I looked at her gratefully, and saw forgiveness in her eyes.

'Thank you,' I said.

'Get along with you now,' she said, 'and try and get a bit of rest.'

I slept and dreamt TJ was soaring above me. The wind was lifting him higher and higher, then the kite seemed to take on the motion of a bird, flapping its wings frantically, before it was sucked upwards and disappeared into the billowing clouds.

TJ's funeral was held the following Saturday, in the Catholic church in the village. There were many mourners who came from Rathegan and further to pay their last respects, the men in their dark Sunday suits, the women wearing lace mantillas.

I crept into the back of the church and saw Sean, Damien, Ger, Sinead, and two smaller dark-haired Murphys in the first pew, whispering amongst themselves. There was a gap, then the bulky frame of Tom Murphy, his head bowed as the priest droned on. Next to him was a thin pinched woman, more brightly clad than the rest of the congregation – the 'wicked stepmother', who had not been able to love TJ as her own. It seemed to me, then, that we had all been affected by the illicit affair between Mother and Tom Murphy, the repercussions rippling through the years, like a pebble landing in a pond.

Somebody else had covered the story of TJ's accident, reporting that his body was found some two miles off the coast, bits of his hang-glider floating like driftwood in the sea. Only afterwards I remembered he never flew over the sea, since there were no thermals – no warm currents of air to lift the kite. This time, the lifeboat had been sent out on a genuine call.

'In the midst of life, we are in death,' the priest was saying, while I tried to blank out a vision of bodies, blanched and swollen, disintegrating into the sea.

This was a family for whom tragedy had struck over and over, I thought, as I watched them leave the church. None of the youth looked in my direction as they passed by, but I noticed Tom

331

Murphy glance at me out of the corner of his eye, then carry on walking painfully out of the church into the mild afternoon.

I slipped out behind the bulk of the congregation, and stood behind two dark-haired men who slapped each other cheerfully on the back – the worst was over; they would go to the pub now, and drink away their sorrows. The Irish were good at accepting death, it seemed, 'people dying who had never died before . . .' They lived life to the lees, then when their time was up slipped away into the sod, as part of the grand scheme of things.

I stood there, not knowing where to turn, and was brought up with a jolt. I must be dreaming I thought, wildly. Aunt G was walking up the narrow footpath towards the church, with Jacintha beside her. She wore a black felt hat with an ostrich feather, and the same tweed suit she had worn at Mother and Father's memorial service all those years ago.

I moved forwards, then stopped dead in my tracks. Tom Murphy was limping towards her, his face set like a piece of granite. The rest of the congregation were still huddled in front of the church, waiting for Tom to lead them around the back to the cemetery. I pushed my way through them and followed him, with a strange feeling.

As he reached her he stopped and swayed, as if his legs could no longer support him. Then I witnessed an extraordinary thing. He touched his cap and held out an arm.

I drew closer, so I could see both of them clearly. Aunt G's expression was hard to read. She had her no-nonsense look about her, which changed to one of incredulity as Tom Murphy said, 'Could I accompany you to the cemetery?'

There was a silence. Everything seemed suspended in time, like a photograph. Then she took his trembling arm in hers.

'It would be a bit like the blind leading the blind,' she replied.

The crowd parted as they approached, then turned to follow them.

It's over, I thought, the feud between the Murphys and the Flavells is over, as I watched the miracle of Tom Murphy and Aunt G make their way towards TJ's grave.

'So he knew all along,' I said to Aunt G as Seamus drove us away in the Daimler, 'that TJ was your niece's son.'

332

'He knew, he'd just chosen to forget. I used to think he seduced Peg as some sort of conquest . . . now I'm not so sure.'

I had told her about the evening in the pub, when he had sung that song of lost hopes and dreams and a girl called Maggie, or had it been Peggy?

'. . . so you see, not everything is lost. Out of a tragedy, something good has happened,' she finished.

We were approaching Heronlough now, the air sweet with summer sounds. I heard the twitter of birdsong in the hedges; soon the rowan tree would be bright with berries.

'I've decided to move up to Dublin,' I told her, as we reached the house. 'I'm not going to make the same mistake as Mother. I love this country, it's the only home I've got, and I intend to stay here. It'll be easier to find work, and a day school for Jean – and I'll be able to use the libraries . . .' My voice trailed away at the thought of having to start all over again.

'I always said the Railway Cottage was a hare-brained idea,' Aunt G replied, 'but I hate the thought of you moving away. I'd like to be able to keep an eye on you!'

I smiled. 'I'll drive out for Sunday lunch and a walk on the beach. It's funny, I'm no longer afraid of living alone. I think I've finally come to terms with the fact that the marriage is over – I'm actually thinking of trying to file for custody. Damien knows a solicitor who thinks I might have a chance now, since Michel has made no attempt to see Jean.'

'I'd hoped it would turn out differently,' Aunt G replied.

'Looking back, I don't see how it could have.'

'No,' she sighed.

Even she had finally acknowledged it was over.

Chapter Forty-Four

I found a flat in Sandymount, overlooking Dublin Strand. It was a small terraced house, with a decent-sized kitchen, two bedrooms, and a back yard that lay in the shadow of the houses on either side. It reminded me of the house where baby Declan had been stolen from his cot. The landlord owned the hardware store on the square, and had decided to live above it and rent out his house. From the sitting room I could see the waders searching for food along the silt stretch of the bay, and smell the sulphur smell when the tide was out. Jean would miss the shingled beach, but it was only temporary. As soon as I started to make some money, I would move on.

I drove into Wicklow to see Aidan Nugent and pay the rent for the last time.

'Now why would you want to go and live in the big smoke, for God's sake?' he inquired.

'I need a job,' I told him evasively. 'When I've made my fortune, I'll come back and buy the Railway Cottage. I've grown fond of the place.'

'I'll give you a dacent price,' he promised, making me laugh, because we both knew it would never sell. It would eventually become a derelict, like so many of the other cottages along that bleak stretch of coastline.

Driving back through the village, I stopped outside Murphy's Lounge Bar. Damien was behind the bar, his back turned as he measured whiskey from a bottle behind him. He didn't see me come in.

'Hello there,' I said, approaching warily. He turned around and stared at me.

'How's it going?' he replied, shifting from one foot to the other.

The memory of TJ lay between us. Neither of us knew what to say.

'Could I buy you a drink, for a change?' I said, perching on one of the bar stools.

'I'll have a pint,' he replied, and took down a glass from the shelf behind him. Sean came in through the side door from the public bar, and greeted me more easily.

'I hear you're moving up to Dublin?' he said.

I nodded. 'News travels fast!' I thought of that extraordinary moment when Aunt G and Tom Murphy had walked arm in arm to the cemetery, and wondered if they had finally pieced it together.

It was Sean who finally broached the subject of TJ.

'You and he were pretty close, seemingly,' Sean was saying.

'Yes, he was . . .' I paused. 'He was a really good friend.'

'He liked you a lot,' said Damien. He looked away, adding, 'He had a thing about foreign women.'

'I'm hardly a foreigner,' I replied.

'No, but you're not local either.'

I smiled, remembering how he'd called me a 'polishtin' all those years ago on the lough.

'They used to call us 'blow-ins' when we lived on the Isle of Wight,' I said reminiscently, wondering if I'd ever belong anywhere.

Damien put three pints of Guinness on the table. 'To TJ,' he said, raising his glass. 'He would have appreciated the toast.'

'To TJ,' I echoed.

Damien wiped away a tear angrily, while Sean started polishing glasses with great concentration.

Later, Damien asked, 'When are you leaving, then?'

'This week,' I told him. 'I need to hire a van to take my things up to Dublin.'

'I'll give you a hand, if you like,' Sean offered. 'I have the van, I could come up in the morning and shift some of it for you.'

'That would be really good of you. I was going to ask Seamus, my Aunt's odd job man, but he doesn't have transport.'

'It's no problem. I'll be up some time in the morning,' he promised.

'Thanks,' I said, moving to go.

'Will you come and visit us when you're a famous novelist?' Damien inquired.

I smiled. 'I'll come every weekend, I promised my aunt.'

'Good luck, then.' He smiled one of his beautiful smiles. I leant forward on the spur of the moment and kissed him on the cheek.

335

He smelt like TJ, of oiled wool and cigarettes, and for a moment seemed oddly vulnerable, with the sweet innocence of a choirboy. Then he smiled wickedly and said, 'There's always a bed at my place.'

'I'll bear that in mind,' I laughed.

I waved goodbye to Sean, saying, 'See you tomorrow,' and turned to go.

As I was coming out of the pub, I bumped into Ger on her way in. Her face hardened, and I felt sure suddenly that she knew. She had been close to TJ, almost possessively so. 'Off up to Dublin then, are you?' she inquired, blocking my exit.

'Yes,' I replied.

'Going to spy for one of them newspapers, then?'

'I'm not a spy,' I told her patiently. 'I'm a journalist, it's quite different.'

'Doesn't seem different to me,' she said.

'You know,' I said, looking at her closely, 'I miss him terribly too. He was . . .' I took a deep breath and said, 'like a brother to me.'

Her expression didn't alter. She opened her mouth as if to say something, and I saw the dark space of her missing tooth. Then she turned away.

For her at least the feud would continue, through habit and from a twisted sense of loyalty to TJ. I had sprung from the other side of the fence, from a family she'd been taught to hate. Whether she knew the full story or not, I knew she'd never forgive me.

That evening I packed away some of our things, then sat up until midnight working on the novel. It was still only a shell of a story, but I wrote the ending, my fingers flying over the keys of the small typewriter, until my eyes began to droop.

'We have found a home in Ireland,' I wrote. 'Jean has only a vague recollection of another life, a place of icy beauty, where the sun sparkles like diamonds on the Alps, and the lake shimmers below . . .

'. . . the day will come when Michel will want to tidy up the loose end of his life that I have become, and no doubt he will do it cleanly and painlessly, through some efficient Swiss lawyer. Then, when Jean is older, he'll be invited to go sailing on Lake Geneva, or skiing down the slopes of Mont Joly.

'Maybe one day Jean will want to return to that other life for good. . . . having a child is having a hostage to fortune,' I concluded.

Then I went to bed, and for the first time in ages, fell into a deep dreamless sleep.

I drove Jean over to Heronlough in the morning; Jacintha had promised to look after him while I packed up our things and waited for Sean to arrive with the van. I stayed for a while, drinking tea with Aunt G. She looked frail still, I noticed with a pang; the business with TJ had taken its toll on her. I promised I would be back the following Sunday, and returned to the Railway Cottage for what would be the last time, to gather the remaining bits and pieces together.

Our few possessions had doubled since we'd left Switzerland. I piled the kitchen equipment into a couple of cardboard boxes, and filled the bag with our clothes. I wrapped TJ's wooden hang-glider, sailing boat and toy engine carefully in newspaper, blinking back tears as I did so, then rolled up the rugs Aunt G had given me, and put them by the front door.

It was a dull overcast day, with a sheet of rain over the headland. I decided to go for a last walk on the beach before it reached us. A mournful voice on the radio sang, 'I'll take you home again, Kathleen, across the ocean wide and deep . . .'

I switched it off and went out of the cottage, across the railway track to the beach. I stood by the water's edge for a while, watching the waves breaking, thinking back to the first time I had stumbled upon the Railway Cottage with Aunt G. Only six months had passed since then, yet it seemed like a lifetime. Then I felt the first drops of rain on my face, and turned back towards the cottage, to wait for Sean.

The knock came at around one o'clock, and I called out, 'Come on in, Sean, the door's open.'

He couldn't have heard me, for he kept on knocking.

'Coming,' I called, moving towards the door. I pulled it open, then took a step back.

Michel was standing there, in a light cashmere jacket, the rain splashing down around him.

337

We stared at one another without speaking.

'I don't suppose I could come in?' he said finally, and his voice brought back myriad memories. 'It's rather wet out here, and I've been travelling all night.'

He looked as impeccable as usual, but I noticed the edge of exhaustion in his face. Behind him, some distance away from the cottage as if it did not want to intrude, the green Merc was parked. I wondered, with a feeling of dread, if he intended to drive away with Jean.

It's too late, Michel, I thought dazedly. You're going to have to fight me fair and square this time.

He followed my gaze and said, 'I came on the boat. No particular reason.'

I seemed to be rooted to the spot, pinned there by shock, then manners prevailed and I stepped back to let him in.

'I'm actually leaving,' I said stiffly. 'I'm waiting for a friend to arrive with his van and help me with all the stuff – he should be here any moment.'

'I know,' he said, surprising me.

'How do you know?'

'Your Great-Aunt told me. I went there first, to get directions to here.'

'And she told you where we were?' I inquired incredulously, unable to believe Aunt G would have done such a thing.

'Yes,' he replied.

'You must have seen Jean, then?' I said.

'No, the woman – I forget her name?'

'Jacintha,' I said, rather sharply.

'Yes, Jacintha. You know me and names! She'd taken him for a walk.' He looked around, and said, 'It must have been quite cosy?'

'Yes, I . . . we've been very happy here,' I told him defensively.

'You look thinner – it suits you,' he added.

'You look . . .' Older, I wanted to say, but said, 'different too.' The sight of him had set my pulse racing.

'Old age creeping up,' he said with a wry grin.

'Well . . .' I wished my heart would slow down. 'What now?' I felt trapped, hypnotised by those pale green eyes.

338

'I haven't come to take Jean away, if that's what you're thinking,' he said, reading my mind.

He took off his jacket, glancing around for somewhere to hang it, then draped it neatly over a rickety chair. Underneath he wore a pale blue Lacoste shirt, and khaki trousers that were hardly creased. He smelt of aftershave and toothpaste.

'Would you like a coffee or something?' I said.

'That would be nice,' he replied, following me into the kitchen. I plugged in the kettle with a shaking hand.

'I've only instant, I'm afraid. It's hardly what you're accustomed to.'

'Does it matter?' he anwered disarmingly.

'I suppose not.' I remembered he had never cared about things like that.

We sat down on the original lumpy chairs and stared at one another.

'How are you?' he asked, studying me closely.

'OK, under the circumstances . . .' I didn't know where to begin. I had lived another lifetime since I'd left him, a lifetime he knew nothing about.

But he was saying, 'I heard what happened. I'm sorry.'

'Aunt G told you about TJ, then?' I inquired incredulously.

'Perhaps I'd better start at the beginning.' He drew out two letters from his pocket, and handed them to me. 'Your Aunt sent me these way back, soon after you left. I only received the second one a couple of days ago.'

I took them from him, then opened the first one.

'My dear Michel,' some other hand had written, 'I am writing to you without Emily's knowledge and against her wishes. By now you will have learnt that the two of them are safe and well, but to put your mind to rest, I have taken the liberty of writing you a letter.

'I have thought long and hard about doing this, and even as I write the doubts are crowding in, but I can only lay my hopes at your feet, and pray to God that you will tread softly, and act wisely.

'It is hard to sit back and let events take their course again. I did so in the past with Emily's mother, and it is a burden I have carried ever since. I cannot allow tragedy to strike again. Now there is the boy to consider, so before you do anything, I urge you to act with thought and compassion, not hastily, or irrationally.

'I know you've had your ups and downs – what marriage hasn't? But I believe deep down that it is nothing that cannot be put right with a little compromise on both sides. Emily has always been a spirited, impulsive girl. She suffered deeply when she lost her mother and father. I don't believe she wants to lose you.

'Forgive me once again for being an interfering old busybody, but perhaps some good will come of it, and I will be able to go peacefully, knowing that Emily found the happiness that eluded her poor mother.

'Time now is the essence. She needs to know that she can survive alone, and come to terms with things herself. She has this daft notion that Jean will be taken away from her, as her parents and her dear friend were . . . I don't believe this is the case. I urge you to grant her the time she needs, six months at least, and I will keep you informed as to how they are coping. Yours faithfully, Geraldine Flavell.'

I re-read the letter, then looked at him in amazement. 'She didn't say where we were,' I said finally.

'She didn't have to – I assumed you were somewhere close by.' He rubbed his forehead distractedly. 'Bertrand did a quick check for me.'

'The robot!' I exclaimed. So I had been right. 'You mean to say you sent him to spy on us?'

Michel smiled. 'I'd forgotten you called him that . . . No – in actual fact, he was here on some other business. I asked him to have a look, but told him to be discreet. I just wanted to know you were both all right.'

'He's not much of a detective,' I said. 'He left an empty packet of Barclay cigarettes on the beach; Jean found it!'

I thought back to that awful night when I thought I'd heard somebody prowling around the cottage. I reached for a Major, and Michel took the box of matches from my trembling hand and lit it for me.

'So why now . . . why did you come? Is our time up?'

He handed me the second letter. 'There were other letters in between – just saying all was well,' he explained. 'Then this came a fortnight ago, only I was away on a business trip, hence the delay.'

I pulled it out of the envelope and read it quickly. It was short, only three or four lines.

'Dear Michel,

   I beg you to come to Ireland, before it's too late . . . please ring me on the above number at Heronlough and inform me of your travelling arrangements and time of arrival. Geraldine Flavell.'

I saw it was dated the day she had collapsed and been taken into hospital. The day Jacintha had finally told her about TJ and me.

'Did she tell you the details?' I inquired.

'Yes.' He looked faintly embarrassed, 'You couldn't have known.'

'Just as well we didn't finish what we were doing,' I said, losing control. 'It would have been incest – Anyway, there's no chance of that now.' My voice broke and I looked away.

He leaned forward and covered my hand in his, but I snatched it away as if it were red hot.

'I sometimes think it would have been better if I'd never found out,' I said.

'Not necessarily.'

'TJ would still be alive.'

'Em-i-ly, it was an accident – Don't do what your Father did when he lost his best friend; don't blame yourself.'

'Anyway, the feud's over,' I said.

'She told me about it. We talked for over an hour – it's an incredible story.'

'So what now?' I moved on. 'What do you plan to do?'

'I don't have a plan, beyond finishing this cup of coffee,' he replied.

I looked through the window. It had stopped raining, and a faint gleam of sunshine shone through the clouds. Jacintha would be coming over with Jean any moment, then what?

'What have you come for, Michel?' I asked him. 'To

341

make a deal? Ask for a divorce? Or to tidy up the mess? I won't try and stop you seeing Jean, if that's what you want – he could spend the summer holidays with you . . . As far as the divorce is concerned, you'll have to do it from your end, as it doesn't exist here!'

'Have you finished?' he inquired, tapping his blunt fingers against the chair. He was nervous too. 'I haven't come to make a deal, or take Jean away, or just because you were heading into trouble . . .' He hesitated.

'You came because of Aunt G's letter,' I filled in.

'That was part of it. I had planned to come anyway, when you'd had time to sort yourself out.'

'So?' I urged him on, my voice still defensive.

'I came because I still love you,' he said simply, 'and don't particularly like living without you both.'

I heard the screech of a gull above us, and then his words echoing in my head. I looked away, feeling my defences crumble like a pack of cards, and slip away from me.

'What about all those things you said – about getting a lawyer and telling him about the criminal record?' I asked finally. 'And what about Marguerite?'

'I don't love Marguerite,' he said, 'in spite of everything you think. I asked her to decorate my office, nothing more. She's a friend – although we're hardly even friends any more.'

'Why? What happened?'

'Nothing specific. I blamed her, perhaps, for what happened. I blame myself too,' he added, 'and oddly enough we haven't seen one another since. As for the things I said, I don't remember exactly what they were. All I know is that we both said a lot of things in the heat of the moment. You were threatening me with divorce, remember?'

'It was as if something else had taken over, and we weren't controlling events any more.'

'A lot of it was my fault,' he said, startling me. 'For pushing you too hard, and for trying to make you part of my old life.'

'Well it's too late now,' I said.

He stared at the bare stone floor with great concentration.

'Is it?'

I took a deep breath. 'I couldn't go back to all that.' I thought of

342

the woman with the scraped-back hair, of Séverine and Gregoire, momentarily forgetting they had split up. 'Not to the way it was.'

'I'm not asking you to,' he said. 'I'm asking you to come back to me.'

There was a silence, then he added, 'Things are going well – I finally sold my mother's apartment in Lausanne. I was thinking of buying a house on the lake – for us. You could feed the birds on the veranda! Of course, you can feed the birds here,' he added, 'but . . . Well, what I'm trying to say is, I miss my partner, and my son . . .'

I looked away.

'We don't have to decide anything now,' he continued. 'If the answer is no, I'll go – and as you said, we can make an arrangement so I get to see Jean.' He rubbed his forehead, and added awkwardly, 'If you do decide to come back, we could have a holiday here and drive back slowly through France. I've taken some time off – trying to ease up a bit.'

I stared at him, at a loss. It seemed he had finally managed to let go of the past – Marguerite, his mother's apartment, his old life – and there was a future for us after all . . .

It all sounded so simple. But then, Michel was never one for complications.

'I don't know what to say,' I said at last.

'Don't say anything,' he replied. 'You have time.'

But I didn't need any more time to make my decision.

Forty-Five

We finished our coffee in silence, then I said, 'Where will you stay tonight?'

'I'd planned to stay in a hotel, but now you're moving, I'm not sure.'

'I'm staying here tonight,' I told him. 'The flat won't be ready for another couple of days, they're putting in some new cupboards. Things take a while in this country,' I added.

'Then I'll stick to Plan A. Maybe I could take you out to dinner? I'd like to see a bit of the countryside.'

I didn't answer.

'It's very beautiful.'

I nodded.

'So many shades of green.'

'For me, it's more beautiful then anywhere else,' I said, thinking of the picture-book scenery of Switzerland that had somehow left me vaguely unsatisfied.

'Yes – I wish I'd taken the trouble to come sooner. Gregoire raved about it, too. He came here twice to play golf.'

'I feel free here,' I said.

He got up and walked over to the window. 'I can imagine. You used to remind me of a bird in a cage.'

'It was just so orderly . . .'

He smiled. 'You were never very good at abiding by the rules, as our poor neighbour found out that day.'

'I wonder if she reported me to the police in the end?'

'Probably! She hasn't spoken to me since, not even to complain!'

'I had the feeling somebody was watching me all the time.'

'I know, I feel it too, but that's the way it is there.'

There was a silence.

'I realise, now, that we come from different worlds,' I said finally.

'So? Cheese and chocolate, as they say. Switzerland is famous for both!'

I smiled. 'They just don't taste very good together,' I replied.

He shrugged. 'You and I were very good together,' he stated, making my heart lurch. He got up and went into the kitchen to make more coffee, then brought in two mugs, saying, 'By the way some mail arrived for you – I've brought it with me.' He took a pile of letters from his coat pocket and handed them to me. There were three invitations to fashion shows, one to view a private collection of jewellery, another to attend the yacht club ball, and two letters, one postmarked Paris. Charlotte, I thought, opening it first.

It was another invitation.

Dear Emily,' she had written almost six months ago, 'I'm writing to invite you to the opening of our new restaurant next month. Now we are living so close – only four hours by train – we should take advantage of it. You could bring the baby if you like. I have moved in with François, but there is plenty of space for you both. You have more time than me, so I leave the ball in your court. All the best, Charlotte.'

I turned to Michel. 'Charlotte wanted me to go to the opening of the new restaurant . . . way back in January.'

What a breakthrough, I thought. Perhaps we could salvage something after all.

'She must be wondering why you never replied.'

'Yes,' I said. How would I ever explain to her? She would never know TJ now, I thought sadly.

I opened the second letter.

It had a sticker on the back, reading *Jonathan Hill, Literary Agent* . . . I stared at it curiously, then ripped it open and read it quickly.

'Dear Emily Gautier,' he had handwritten; the rest was neatly typed.

'We have finally had an offer on *The Love Trap* from a publisher, but they are asking for a two-book deal, which is still under negotiation. Please ring me immediately.'

The letter had arrived two weeks ago.

'I don't believe it!' I exclaimed, then saw Michel's startled face. 'They're going to publish *The Love Trap*. Look!'

Michel took the letter, his face breaking into a grin.

'That really is good news,' he said.

'I can't believe it . . . I never expected it.'

'I never doubted it,' he said. 'You'd better phone him, in case he thinks you're not interested.'

'I've no phone – I'll have to go to Heronlough.'

'I'm really pleased for you,' he said. 'You deserve it.'

'I've started another one,' I told him. 'It's sort of our story. I wrote the ending last night . . .' I looked away. 'I wish life was like writing books, and you could edit the bad bits – just cut out the past as if it had never happened.'

'Why would you want to do that?' he said. 'The past is what makes you what you are.'

'I'm not sure whether that's good or bad,' I replied diffidently.

'It's part of the magic,' he stated.

'You didn't think that before!'

I remembered how he had reacted over Amanda's revelation; how he had joked about it coming back at me. 'You were horrified!'

'It was a shock,' he admitted, 'but it didn't change anything.'

'I felt it did.'

'You've always been far too sensitive.'

I lit another cigarette, and stared out of the window.

He was right. I'd always been plagued by dark thoughts, due to an over-active imagination. I thought back to our honeymoon, how I'd imagined Gregoire and Séverine hated me and that it was all some kind of test – a test which I'd then convinced myself I'd failed . . . And how I'd always believed that Michel was still besotted with Marguerite . . .

We'd both made mistakes along the way, I concluded.

Michel put his mug down and got up. 'Congratulations about the novel,' he said formally, then let himself out of the cottage, and crossed the railway track to the beach. There was a yacht race on, a line of white sails racing towards Wicklow Head. He stood there watching it, a solitary figure on the strand.

It all seemed unreal, I thought – the moment I had subconsciously longed for all the last six months had come at last. Michel had arrived, like in my dreams, to take us home again.

A knock at the door jolted me out of my reverie. It was Sean Murphy with the van, come to help move my things.

''Tis myself,' he greeted me. 'Sorry I'm late, who owns the Merc?' He looked tired, I thought, dark circles under his eyes.

'Oh, that's my husband's,' I replied dazedly, the words sounding odd to my own ears.

'Ah! He came for you then?'

'Yes,' I replied.

'So you won't be needing the van, I suppose?'

'No – there's been a change of plan.'

He nodded.

'But thanks so much for offering . . .'

'Don't mention it,' he said dismissively, but made no move to go.

What must he think of me, I wondered suddenly. That now TJ was gone, Michel had returned to take over? I had a sudden urge to explain.

'Sean,' I said hollowly, 'you know . . . TJ – He was my half brother.'

His face didn't change. 'I know,' he replied.

'How?'

'I guessed at the church that day . . .'

I looked away in confusion.

He shook his head, muttering, 'Nothing surprises me about the boss man any more.'

'If only I hadn't told him,' I said, my voice catching.

'C'mon now, stop torturing yourself, 'tis done . . .'

But I had started sobbing, all the tension of the last few weeks spilling over.

He pushed back his hair distractedly, in a gesture so like TJ's that my heart shifted. I heard him say, 'You know, TJ would never have accepted it – and that's a fact. He'd been burnt too many times. He loved you, Emily, but not as his sister . . .'

I looked away, at a loss. He had the same generous spirit as TJ and Damien, I thought; it seemed to be a Murphy trait. The hatred between the Murphys and the Flavells was such a waste, I concluded, its cause forgotten over the years, fuelled now only by ignorance and habit.

347

There was a silence, then Sean said, as Aunt G had said: 'It was fate, that's what it was. You weren't to know.'

I nodded. My throat seemed to have closed up. There was nothing more to be said, only the futile, silent agonising of regret, the 'if only's' that brought no comfort.

He turned away then, as if he too sensed the hopelessness of wishing it had been otherwise, and made his way to where he had left the van.

He lifted his hand in farewell as he drove away, reminding me of that foggy afternoon in the village, when he and Damien had passed by, and Mother had hurried us away, as if from the dark shadows of the past.

Aunt G was right, I concluded, as I watched the van disappear down the lane; guilt was a selfish emotion. I was so consumed with it, I'd almost forgotten how much Sean and the others must have been suffering.

I made my way around the cottage then, and crossed the railway track down to the beach, to where Michel was still standing by the sea.

Michel was standing in exactly the same position, but I saw now he wasn't watching the yacht race, but the progress of two distant figures walking along the water's edge. One was an old woman bent against the wind, the other a small boy: Jacintha, bringing Jean home. Her hair was covered with a yellow headscarf. I watched her pause to wait for Jean, who picked up a stone and flung it into the sea.

Michel took a few steps forward at the same time as Jean spotted him. And then they both broke into a run.

Jean was calling out as he ran, the sunlight glinting on his dark hair, while Jacintha quickened her pace to keep up with him.

As they reached each other, Michel scooped him up and spun him around in the air. I watched Jean fling back his head with abandon, laughing delightedly, then Michel was hugging and kissing him, carrying him across the beach to where I stood.

'Papa,' I heard Jean saying incredulously, as if Michel were a trophy he'd discovered lying on the beach. It struck me then that Jean, who had caused the rift between us, had now brought us together again.

'*Ma maison,*' Jean was saying, pointing at the cottage.

'He doesn't seem to have forgotten his French after all,' I said.

'No,' replied Michel, his eyes wet with tears.

Jacintha stood a few yards away, watching the three of us. Michel must have sensed her reserve, for he turned and politely introduced himself.

'Well, I'll be leaving yous,' she said, glancing meaningfully at me as she went.

Do the right thing, she seemed to be saying, as the three of us turned and crossed the railway track towards the cottage.

That evening we drove over to Heronlough for dinner, at Aunt G's bidding. Jacintha had prepared a feast of smoked salmon and soda bread, followed by a leg of lamb and an assortment of vegetables; for pudding, one of her famous sherry trifles. I helped her lay the table, while Michel and Aunt G chatted to one another in the drawing room like long-lost friends.

Aunt G kept calling him Michael by mistake, making me smile. Michel had already managed to charm her with his impeccable manners, I noticed.

We sat up until midnight talking to Aunt G – then, because it was so late, and Jean was already asleep, decided to stay the night at Heronlough.

'Marvellous dinner,' Michel said, kissing Aunt G goodnight – then forgetting his flawless English for once, 'It was so nice for you to have me.'

We all burst out laughing.

'You're very welcome, Michael,' she said, squeezing his hand. She lowered her voice, adding, 'And you'll always be welcome. We're a lot better with foreigners nowadays!'

We slept in the guest room that night – although I hardly slept at all.

At around four, I was awoken from a light doze by a thumping noise above. Alarmed, I sat up, wondering where I was for a moment. Then I felt Michel's arms around me.

'It's OK, *cherie,*' he said sleepily. 'It's probably a seagull or something . . .' he pulled me back into the circle of his arms, and I felt his warm breath on my neck.

As the early dawn broke across the sea, I was still wide awake,

349

in the same position, memories rushing through my mind, scrambled and disjointed, sometimes flashes of colour or bits of dialogue. 'Anybody can be a father,' TJ had said, that first time in the Railway Cottage . . . Now he was smiling at me and saying, 'I love you Emily, you know that? . . . You're going back to Mr Perfect, aren't you? . . . You're off the wall woman, imagining things, like one of your novels . . .' My mind raced on like a freight train, until I thought I was going mad. Then Michel was saying soothingly, 'Sleep, *cherie* . . . Sleep, everything's going to be all right.'

I must have drifted off then, for when I opened my eyes it was light, and Michel and Jean were playing together on the bed beside me.

Epilogue

It is summer again. Almost a year has passed since Jean and I watched the ferry slip away from Dunlaoghaire pier, Michel a dark speck on the deck. Then we walked along the pier and watched it sail, cutting a passage across the Irish Sea until it disappeared on the horizon.

Aunt G didn't survive another winter. She died peacefully in her sleep, from old age rather than emphysema. She left Heronlough House to Charlotte and me, although she knew Charlotte would probably never live in it.

'I don't like to think of you rattling around in this huge house,' she wrote in her will. 'I'd always hoped it would be a family home again, like the old days.'

Charlotte came over in the spring and sold me her deeds on the house, just as Mother had all those years ago. The story of TJ shocked her profoundly. She could not reconcile her memory of Mother – nervous, obsessive, and so often ill – with this other woman who had become caught up in an illicit love affair and given birth to a son. She asked few questions, and I only told her parts of the story. We moved on to the present, and her plans to marry François and live in France for the rest of her days.

They published The Love Trap *last month, and I've almost finished the second novel, which I've called* Hostage to Fortune *and dedicated to Jean. I've turned the attic into a writing room, my desk close to the fanlight window, so I can look out over the lough as I write. The walls are covered with Aunt G's paintings – 'The Sugar Loaf' being one of my favourites now, for it reminds me of TJ, who found some peace up there. 'The Three Old Biddies' hangs beside it, and I've framed the series of sketches of the Whooper swans Aunt G called 'Swan Season'. Michel brought the painting of the Railway Cottage and Mother's unfinished portrait back from Geneva, the last time he visited us. Wherever I go, I look out for the others – the ones she sold to finance Mother when she lived in the Railway Cottage. I would love to have them back, to complete the collection.*

I moved into Heronlough the day after Michel left for France on the boat, so I was able to take care of Aunt G in those last few months before she died. One evening in October, the day after the Whooper swans arrived, she fell asleep in her rocking chair and didn't wake up again. I miss her dreadfully – it is, as she once said herself, as if somebody has cut me in half and stolen the pieces. The pain has eased, slightly, but I know I'll never recover from losing her.

Poor Jacintha started to deteriorate after Aunt G died. She took to the drink, and was admitted into a home in the spring. She suffers from dementia, believing that she was somehow responsible for Aunt G's death. I know now how terrible the burden of guilt can be, and make a conscious effort not to dwell too much on the past.

The Railway Cottage is empty now. The windows are broken and there are holes in the roof where the tiles are missing. The tinkers use it when they are passing through, leaving their broken bottles and beer cans all over the place. Soon Aunt G's painting will be the only reminder of it.

I drove over to Howth on June 16th of this year – Bloomsday – and threw a bunch of wild flowers into the sea for Jeanette, with the promise that I would come back in three years' time to fulfil the Howth Oath. Then I walked along the pier and stood at the end, looking across to Ireland's Eye, and it's tear, remembering how she had stood there with her mother that last time.

At this time of year it's lovely here, with the gorse aflame and linnets singing in the privet bushes. Jean spends the afternoons paddling in the lough and building mud pies on the banks, while I sit beneath the rowan tree, writing. Damien often drops by, and they go searching for bait together, or fish from the jetty for sprats.

I do most of my shopping – or 'messages', as they call them here – in Wicklow (Fernando the Fiat is still going strong), but I often go to Murphy's Lounge Bar in the evenings. Sean and Damien run the place completely now, and it has come alive again. There is a music session once a week: Kevin sometimes plays the tin whistle, and local bands sing wild rebel songs.

Traces of the feud still linger on, however. Ger hasn't spoken to me again – Sinead, too, keeps away, and sometimes I hear whispered warnings in doorways when I walk through the village.

I believe Tom Murphy still suffers terribly from TJ's death. I see

352

him hobbling through the village from time to time – once he raised his cap, and I waved back, like an old acquaintance.

Michel comes over once a month to see us. He loves Heronlough House, and longs to turn it into the grand old place it used to be. He bought a small rowing boat for Jean, and on sunny days takes him rowing across the lough. He is far less of a fish out of water in Ireland than I was in Switzerland. But then he always was a very gregarious person, who had no trouble integrating. I remember how happy he was in London, in spite of the fact he couldn't go skiing and sailing every season.

He's planned a trip to the Fastnet Rock this August, in honour of Father. We will sail into Dunmore East, a small harbour on the south coast of Ireland, where some of the boats were washed up after the race.

A week ago, he called me from the Isle of Wight.

'I have some extraordinary news,' he said.

He had arrived on the island that morning to finalise the details, he explained. Running Tide *was ours now – a final souvenir. So we will be able to do the trip in her that Father was unable to do, that last time . . .*

The last time Michel was here, I took him to Murphy's Lounge Bar, and he met somebody in the property business. They sat there talking until closing time, then swapped business cards and slapped each other on the back like long-lost friends. They are meeting again next month, to talk some more.

Michel has finally sold the penthouse apartment in Geneva, and is still talking about buying one of those beautiful lakeside apartments, with mossy steps leading down to the water's edge. It would be my summer residence, he joked . . . Then, in the harsh winter months, we would return to Ireland and Heronlough – like the Whooper swans.